Geac
A Guide for Librarians and Systems Managers

Geac

A Guide for Librarians and Systems Managers

Second Edition

Duncan R. Westlake MA, ALA

With contributions by
Alison M. Hunter ALA
and
Margaret Sheridan BA, ALA

© Duncan R. Westlake, 1992

All rights reserved. No part of this publication may be reproduced, stored in a retrieval system, or transmitted in any form or by any means, electronic, mechanical, photocopying, recording or otherwise without the prior permission of the publisher.

Published by
Ashgate Publishing Limited
Gower House
Croft Road
Aldershot
Hants GU11 3HR
England

Ashgate Publishing Co
Old Post Road
Brookfield
Vermont 05036
USA

British Library Cataloguing in Publication Data is available

ISBN 1 85742 000 4

Printed and bound in Great Britain by
Billing and Sons Limited, Worcester.

Contents

Illustrations vii
Preface xi
Acknowledgements xiii

Section 1: Setting the scene

1. History of the company 3
2. Introduction to the systems 10

Section 2: The Hardware and its operation

3. Central configuration 19
4. Terminals and other peripherals 34
5. Telecommunications and networking 48

Section 3: The Software

6. Introduction to the Software 65
7. The Circulation package – core features 79
   - Patron Query 83
   - Bibliographical Query 89
   - The Public Query module 96
   - Loan transactions (issue, discharge and renewal) 101
   - Fines subsystem 106
   - Overdue recovery subsystem 109
   - Holds subsystem 113
   - Message transmission 123
   - Reserve room operations 127
   - Materials booking 131
   - Archival issue records 133
   - Inter-library loans 134
   - Bindery management subsystem 135
   - Cash management subsystem 137
   - Help subsystem 142
   - Library maintenance routines 144
8. Back-up systems and portable terminal operations 147

9	The Cataloguing module	155
10	The Acquisitions module	183
11	Community Information module and news services	211
12	Other Geac products	226
13	Management information	231
14	External communications	240

Section 4: Support services

15	Customer support	249
16	Response times	258

Section 5: Conclusion

17	Concluding remarks	265

Section 6: Appendices

Appendix A	Geac users – worldwide	269
Appendix B	Glossary	284
Appendix C	Annotated bibliography	292

Index 297

Illustrations

4.1	Diagram of a date stamp arm attached to a light pen	45
5.1	Diagram of a point-to-point communications network	50
5.2	Diagram of a multi-drop communications network	51
5.3	Diagram of a multi-node communications network	52
5.4	Diagram of a typical X.25 network	54
5.5	Connection to TCP/IP LAN via Geogate	56
5.6	Connection to SNA host via TRAX and Geogate	57
5.7	Possible uses for a Terminal Control Server	58
6.1	Terminal Control Program main menu (staff terminal version)	77
7.1	Circulation package main menu	81
7.2	Name index from a patron search	85
7.3	Full display of a patron record	86
7.4	Brief bibliographic records within a patron record	87
7.5	Full bibliographic record within a patron record	88
7.6	Partial display of a bibliographic record in Circulation	93
7.7	Brief copy display of a bibliographic record in Circulation	94
7.8	Initial patron display within Public Query	100
7.9	Example of a data-mailer	112
7.10	Received message	125
7.11	Display of income accounts within Cash Management System	141
7.12	Help screen for the Hold System	142
7.13	Help screen for available help commands	143
7.14	Help screen for part of the system rules	143
8.1	Diagram of the wiring sequence of terminals + back-up micro	148
9.1	Screen header from BPS system	161
9.2	Terminal Control Program main menu (Hillingdon public version)	169
9.3	OPAC initial help screen	170

9.4	OPAC main menu	171
9.5	OPAC screen for an author search	172
9.6	OPAC title index display	172
9.7	OPAC brief entry	173
9.8	OPAC full entry	174
9.9	OPAC author index display	175
9.10	OPAC author citation entry	175
9.11	OPAC combined author/title display	176
9.12	OPAC subject index display	177
9.13	OPAC brief display showing mixed classifications	178
9.14	OPAC Boolean search citation list	181
9.15	OPAC search limit choices	181
10.1	Acquisitions main menu	185
10.2	Acquisitions search query	186
10.3	Bibliographic screen in Acquisitions request query	187
10.4	Acquisitions miscellaneous screen	188
10.5	Acquisitions location screen	189
10.6	Acquisitions vendor screen	189
10.7	Acquisitions fund screen	190
10.8	Acquisitions miscellaneous full screen	190
10.9	Brief screen in Acquisitions request query	191
10.10	Order display in Acquisitions purchase order maintenance	192
10.11	Acquisitions purchase order receiving	193
10.12	Adding Acquisitions vendor reports	193
10.13	Acquisitions purchase order information	194
10.14	Acquisitions serials subsystem levels screen	195
10.15	Acquisitions frequency screen	196
10.16	Acquisitions vendor record	197
10.17	Acquisitions account transaction information	199
10.18	Acquisitions account display	200
10.19	Acquisitions invoice record	201
10.20	Acquisitions cheque request display	204
10.21	Acquisitions currency record	204
10.22	Acquisitions staff record	205
11.1	Community Information System Information entry	214
11.2	Community Information System status details	214
11.3	Community Information System main menu	216
11.4	Community Information System name index	218
11.5	Community Information System keyword index	219
11.6	Community Information System list of available subjects	220
11.7	Community Information System added entries	221

11.8	Community Information System contact index	222
11.9	Community Information System news screen	224
14.1	Diagram of 8212 controller and associated terminals	242

Preface

As the task of writing the first edition of this book proceeded in 1987 John Clarke and I found that there was much about the Geac system that we did not know, and that changes were happening to the things we did know. Since that time changes have accelerated, both within Geac itself, and the world of Information Technology.

As before, it has to be stressed that in a rapidly changing field such as this, a book is not the very best medium for passing on the latest information, although it has value as an in-depth assessment of the systems as they are at this moment. I hope that it will be of use to people responsible for managing Geac systems already, and I also hope that people evaluating systems for purchase will find something of value here, particularly as it will provide pointers for pertinent questions to Geac, and more importantly, Geac users.

When the publisher approached us asking if we would revise the book for a second edition, John Clarke backed out, largely because his career had taken him away from close involvement with the subject, but also remembering no doubt the millstone such a task can be around the busy librarian's neck. I however, could think of no excuse quickly enough, so agreed to revise the bulk of the book more or less on my own!

Last time we were writing about a system we were using, this time I was updating that information to cover the capabilities of a system that we did not yet have. The work needed to try to come to grips with the 9000 family of machines accounted for a considerable amount of the year I have spent on the book.

In 1987 we said that there was much about Geac systems we had not anticipated. The situation today is that Geac has grown and diversified considerably, so that it would seem difficult for any outsider to know the full facts. I have tried to describe the main changes brought about by the development of the 9000 series, and the software that has been evolved to exploit the potential of these powerful machines. Even more than last time, my knowledge of actual working systems has been confined to the UK, and my apologies for the seeming parochialism of this approach are extended to Geac users in the rest of the world.

One of the significant developments in the past few years has been the acquisition by Geac of another system, called ADVANCE. This is aimed at present at the smaller end of the market-place, as Geac are not yet happy to sell UNIX-based relational database systems to large sites requiring high performance. It is my impression that this product will grow in importance to Geac as more institutions insist on systems they buy running under UNIX. I believe that in the cut-throat world Geac inhabit conditions will soon be such that a high performance UNIX-based system will be essential, and I submit that if there is a third edition of this book, it will be to describe that transition. As it is, this book is not able to address the ADVANCE system in anything but the sketchiest outline, but it is to be hoped that it will be the subject of another book in the series.

As with the first edition, I have tried to be fair to Geac and only express criticism where it seems to be generally relevant, rather than rehearsing site-specific complaints. There are inevitably some criticisms, but it remains my conviction that the Geac 9000 (and still the 8000) systems remain at the top of the list of turnkey library automation systems, and many of the new developments make them more exciting than ever.

Acknowledgements

Although the bulk of the text has been my responsibility, I have been able to draw heavily on the work done by John Clarke for the first edition, and for that relief I am most thankful. I must also record my particular gratitude to Margaret Sheridan of Lancashire County Libraries for writing the chapter on Acquisitions, and my Hillingdon colleague Alison Hunter for rewriting the chapter on the Community Information system.

Clearly a book of this kind cannot be written purely as a result of knowledge gleaned by a few users, and once again I received considerable information from staff at Geac. In particular I would like to thank Graham Morris for general information and channelling my requests for further detail to the right person, Hans Kruiniger for his helpful comments on networking, and Larry Stock for his comments on the Acquisitions chapter.

Although Hillingdon Libraries have tried to use their Geac system to the full, there are many aspects of the various modules unknown to me, and I am very grateful for the help extended to me by colleagues I have visited and corresponded with. In particular, David Easton of Edinburgh University and Jim Craig of Glasgow University provided much needed comments drawn from working experience of the BPS system. Similarly, my knowledge of the 9000 machines is still as yet at secondhand, so the visits I made to Essex County Libraries and Suffolk County Libraries were invaluable. Many thanks to Diane Whittaker at Essex, and Doug Reed and Keith Riley at Suffolk. David Hayes at the London Borough of Camden remains a mine of information about Geac software, and I am grateful to him for all his guidance over the years, as well as for the information about Camden's numerous enhancements. Catherine Cooke at Westminster City Libraries also kindly provided details of the working of the Home Library Service software, and the link between Westminster's Acquisitions system and T.C. Farries. In addition to the help extended to me specifically for this book, I am conscious that a large part of what little I know about Geac systems I have picked up from colleagues at the very sociable gatherings known as User Group and PLUG meetings, and to them I extend my thanks.

Many colleagues at Hillingdon have also provided me with considerable help and knowledge over the years, especially Pam Pollicott, Chris Bamford, Judith Chennels and Roger Kimber. Cathy Perry no longer works for Hillingdon, but when she did she provided a constant flow of good ideas and sound judgement. Particular mention should be made of John Appleby, who has worked with me for several years and kept the system running far better in my absence than it does when I am at work. As if this were not enough punishment for him, he voluntarily proofread the text for me! Grateful thanks are also due to Harry Boote for his support, and for continuing to employ me.

Warmest thanks of all must be reserved for my dear wife Sarah, who has now been abandoned twice for the same book. What little knowledge repeated here is due to her forebearance during all those evenings when I should have been home from work on time but wasn't, as 'that machine' was doing something I didn't understand. I can only hope that some information in this book will once in a while prevent a hard-pressed system manager somewhere from getting home late to a partner less understanding than mine.

Section 1　Setting the scene

1 History of the company

Early development

Geac was founded in May 1971 by R. Angus German and Robert K. Isserstedt in Ontario, Canada. At its inception the emergent company had no involvement with the library profession, the first product being an inventory control system for municipal school boards. That was followed in 1974 by a significant move into the banking world with the development of a retail banking system, which was installed at Vancouver City Savings Credit Union, Canada's largest credit union. There appears to be no solid evidence for the derivation of the company name but one plausible suggestion is that it derives from General Accounting and Computing, a reasonable title in view of the early activities.

In these early years, Geac relied on hardware manufactured by other companies; in particular, mini-computers were supplied by Hewlett-Packard. Analysts within Geac examined a customer's needs and selected the most suitable equipment. Though Hewlett-Packard supplied the mini-computers, peripherals such as disc drives, printers and terminals were generally purchased from other suppliers. Geac restricted itself to providing a packaged solution and writing the applications software. However, Geac staff found themselves increasingly restricted by the operating systems of the equipment; to remove this limiting factor, a range of proprietary products was developed which has continued to be the backbone of all Geac systems.

Within a few years of the company's foundation, another Canadian, Ted Gruneau, joined as a third partner. The two original founders continued as directors with a very strong role within the organization. They have both subsequently spent a period as Chairman of the Board.

Geac's involvement with libraries commenced in 1976 with the development of an online circulation system for the University of Guelph in Canada, in conjunction with Guelph librarians and library systems analysts. This early collaboration very much affected the ultimate system. Though the banking and library applications may seem very different, they have similarities from the computing viewpoint in that they share the need for large databases and high transaction processing levels.

In examining its two major markets, Geac recognized that ever larger databases and the need to support increasing transaction workloads would eventually lead to the erosion of the response times which are so important in these fields. At this time, the development of Large Scale Integration technology had reached a point where Geac felt that it had the expertise to design and build its own digital computer with a system architecture appropriate to online processing.

Geac thus committed itself to move into the hardware manufacturing business in 1976, with its System 8000. When it was launched on the market the following year, System 8000 was claimed to be the first commercially available multi-processor. It was designed specifically to operate in an online environment where high transaction processing rates were the major factor. The 8000 was an immediate success within the banking industry; as many as 56 being installed for one customer's applications within the US alone. Although the 8000 was conceived on the basis of its anticipated niche within financial institutions, it was simultaneously seen as being very well suited to the library world.

In the mid-1980s the 9000 series was introduced, initially into financial installations, but soon following into larger libraries. Continuing the trend of high transaction throughput, the 9000 series provides considerably more processing power, enabling many more terminals to be connected to the system. It has now become the norm for new library sites, although smaller installations now have the option of using the ADVANCE system.

ADVANCE is a system supplied by Alii, based in Hawaii, which Geac bought in 1989. Running on a variety of hardware platforms, it operates in the PICK and PICK/UNIX environments (unlike the systems running on the Geac machines, using Geac's proprietary operating systems). ADVANCE is selling primarily to small and medium-sized academic and public institutions, such as The South Bank Polytechnic in the UK, Seton Hall University, New Jersey, USA, and the Yvelines Bibliotheque Centrale de Pret in France. France seems to be a particularly keenly contested market; at the time of writing there were 38 ADVANCE customers there. It is anticipated that ADVANCE will be the subject of another book in this series; this volume concentrates on the 8000 and 9000 based systems, which are known as GLIS (Geac Library Information System).

Though growth was confined initially to North America, a wholly-owned subsidiary, Geac Computers Ltd, was formed in the UK as early as 1975; following the introduction of a Geac system into a major leasing company. Since then there have been other subsidiaries in Ireland, the Netherlands, France, West Germany, Australia and the United States. Growth has been consistently spectacular in both Europe and North America during recent years with regular annual increases of over 50 per cent.

Following a decade of continuous expansion, shares in Geac were offered to the public in 1983, thereby generating over $17m Canadian for future growth. Shortly afterwards the company was listed on the Toronto Stock Exchange. The 1984/5 financial year showed the company's worldwide turnover to have reached $71m Canadian by which time the workforce had expanded to over 900 (an increase of 104 in that year alone). Up to this point the company had been growing at a rate of 30–40 per cent each year. Such rapid growth had allowed the company to support the intensive development costs in attempting to stay at the forefront of technology in library and financial applications, but when that growth pattern suddenly slowed, the effects of maintaining those development costs produced cash flow problems for the Corporation in Canada.

Reasons for this included the first banking failures in Canadian history, which involved some of Geac's major customers in Canada. The two major bankers supporting Geac in Canada asked Geac for a business plan to reduce its indebtedness, which sparked off concern in the Canadian Stock market, and trading in Geac shares was suspended for a short time. In December 1986 the Corporation announced that it had reached agreement with its bankers concerning a plan to deal with the financial situation and seek strategic partners for investment. At this time the banks also appointed an independent trustee to ensure that the creditors' interests were safeguarded whilst Geac was afforded protection from their claims until the business plan was put into operation. This trustee was referred to as an interim receiver, a phrase which caused much concern amongst Geac's customers, although in Canada the role of the receiver is very different to the UK concept of receivership, and the company continued to be run by its Board and senior executives.

Reduction of costs, by shedding staff, closing some facilities and selling some assets had the desired effect, and Geac became attractive again to potential investors. Rather than selling any business units, Geac chose to enter into an equity investment partnership, and in June 1987 Helix Investments Limited invested $20 million. Helix is a large Canadian venture capital firm with investments in a wide variety of industries, including a significant high technology component. This major investment permitted the payment of debts to creditors, and the ceasing of the interim receivership.

During all of this unsettling period it was constantly stressed that the Canadian companies were the only parts of the organization directly affected. Geac UK remained a viable company with significant balances in their bank account, and whilst potential new customers were understandably cautious, several existing customers demonstrated their confidence by upgrading their systems. In recognition of its success in selling systems worldwide, the company was awarded the 1988 Canada Export award.

A period of consolidation has followed the upsets of 1986, with growth increasing. Within the UK and Northern Europe library division the acquisition of several large new sites prompted the employment of many new staff, both for support of those new, and existing customers, and in anticipation of further sales. These expected new contracts were however not forthcoming, and in line with the newer, more strictly controlled régime necessitated by the earlier fright, cutbacks were made in early 1990. This involved the reduction of staffing levels to a point prior to the expansion, and the withdrawal of software support from Edinburgh and Leeds. This caused some dismay amongst the customers who had been accustomed to support from these offices, and Geac had to work out new procedures to ensure adequate levels of support. On the positive side, it has meant greater control over the creation and amendment of software, and has brought levels of expertise previously hidden away within the company into direct contact with its customers, with advantages on both sides.

The year ending April 30th 1990 saw record earnings for the corporation of $8,150,000, compared to $4,520,000 for the previous year. The cash balance was $13,474,000 with no bank debt, an increase of $7,658,000 over the previous fiscal year.

During 1990 Geac grew quite considerably by buying two companies. Fact International, a New Zealand-based software company develops and markets a manufacturing/business software application. With over 300 accounts in Australasia it accounts for an annual revenue of approximately $9.0 million Canadian. The other acquisition in 1990 was Jones and Erickson Software Technology Inc's software programs, which are used in several vertical markets, including the construction, property management, apparel distribution and hospitality markets. There are over 200 users of this software in North America.

Library customer base

As mentioned earlier, Geac entered the library world with the installation at the University of Guelph, closely followed by the University of Waterloo; the circulation systems in these two sites being fully operational by 1977. There followed other prestigious North American contracts such as those at Princeton and Yale Universities and Geac's clients on that continent now number over 125 (including ADVANCE customers).

In the UK, the first library to take the plunge was, understandably, also academic. The University of Hull chose Geac to provide a circulation system in 1980, followed by public query of the online files in 1981. Several other British universities and polytechnics followed suit in the early 1980s (Sussex, Durham, South Bank and London) but it was not until 1982 that a British public library authority made the decision. Somerset County Library Service was followed in rapid succession by several London boroughs – Redbridge, Camden, Bexley and Hillingdon. This last authority was a significant departure in that it was the first UK public library to agree to take all the major software modules then available; cataloguing and acquisitions as well as circulation, with Local Information an added part of the contract. With the advent of the 9000 series machines, several of the larger counties signed up, including Suffolk, Norfolk and Essex.

Suffolk County Library has a 4 FFP 9000 system, running multi-threaded Circulation, Acquisitions, GEM (Electronic Mail), TRAX (accessing outside databases), and the Report Generator and Statistical Tabulator packages. There are currently around 265 terminals and 23 polled printers attached to the system. All Suffolk branch libraries are connected to the system, which is capable of handling very high loads, one measure of which is the number of times terminals send to the cpu (known as GODOs). The London Borough of Hillingdon's 8000 machine is considered to be very hard-working, and at peak times on a

Saturday has been seen to handle 21,000 GODOs to the Circulation system in an hour. By contrast, Suffolk have recorded 60,000 GODOs in a single hour, with no deterioration in performance. As an illustration of the system's fault tolerance, one Saturday at Suffolk they noticed that the system was running unusually slowly. Engineers discovered that one of the processors had failed, yet the system had been able to compensate for this. Replacing the processor was a simple job carried out with the system remaining available to all users.

Essex County Library is a very large installation, and much development has been done to meet its requirements, with consequent ongoing benefits for other customers. At the time of writing, 22 of Essex's libraries are already automated, accounting for 5.8 million issues annually, with some 315 terminals attached. By the end of Essex's first phase of implementation 43 libraries will be automated, accounting for 13 million issues per year, with some 400 terminals attached. The entire County Library service will then be added to the system, consisting of 92 libraries and some 600 to 700 terminals, which will make it the biggest British public library site in terms of number of attached terminals. At the commencement of 1990, Geac were supporting 29 library installations in the UK (12 academic and 16 public plus the British Library Lending Division – see Appendix A). (It is worth noting that several of the early 8000 sites, such as the Universities of Hull, Sussex and Durham, and Somerset County, have since upgraded to 9000 systems.)

Having taken a significant portion of the North American and UK markets during the years since 1982, the company has not been slow to expand elsewhere. Using the British offices as a base, inroads have been made into continental Europe. Several large and prestigious institutions, both national bodies and universities, have signed contracts – as have several public libraries. Most ambitious of the installations is that at the Bibliothèque Nationale, for which the entire library software was rewritten for the 9000 system. Other major customers are the Universities of Utrecht, in the Netherlands, and Stockholm, in Sweden; the Vatican Library; the National Library of Portugal; and the Library of Academic Sciences of the USSR in Leningrad. Holding a stock of 18 million items, a major part of this project involves a full language conversion. In May 1990 Geac announced that their products had been approved by the US Military to operate over its worldwide X.25 network – DDN/ARPANET, which allows each networked Army and Air

Force installation in Europe to search the resources of each other's libraries and to facilitate inter-library loans. They already had a well-established installation in Germany running all library applications over 240 networked terminals; this extra contract will connect 135 joint US Army and Air Force libraries, serving all forces stationed in Europe.

In North America Geac has again captured some of the bigger and more prestigious contracts such as the Smithsonian Institution, New York University and Toronto Public Library. Each of these sites now has in excess of 100 terminals in their network. Princeton University has been a Geac site for 12 years, and recently upgraded to a 9000 system.

There has also been a limited excursion into the Far East, leading to agreements to supply systems in Singapore and Australia. The first Australian site, the College Library Activity Network in New South Wales (CLANN) is a dual c.p.u. installation with over 600 terminals serving, in the main, higher education institutions but also including the City of Grantstown public library service. Recently Griffith University in Queensland, Australia upgraded their 9000 system to enable them to incorporate the Mount Gravatt campus, which is converting to Geac from an AWA/URICA system. The database will be in AUSMARC standard, and be loaded onto the Geac system via magnetic tape early in 1991. Library system suppliers have to be able to demonstrate their ability to convert data held on a customer's previous system to a format suitable for their own systems. Recently Geac have also converted the London Borough of Bromley's database, which was previously held on an ALS system, achieving the transfer from one system to the other in a remarkably short period of time (Harrison, 1989).

Reference

Harrison, D. (1989) 'London Borough of Bromley: from ALS to Geac in six months,' *VINE 75*, October, pp. 4–7.

2 Introduction to the systems

There is now a whole family of Geac mini-computers, ranging from the desk-top System 2000 to the large and powerful System 9000. The family is totally compatible at the lower end of the range, making it relatively simple to upgrade from one system to the other, or to run more than one machine in a multiple configuration. However, the Concept 9000 is an entirely different system, for which new software has been developed, and certain features designed for that system will never be available on alternative machines. It is, however, completely upward compatible from the other systems.

To make use of the mini-computers, there is a growing range of terminals and other peripherals – though many of these are derived, in part if not in whole, from the products of other companies. It is the expressed policy of Geac to provide a whole solution to a client's requirements and the use of other kit has always been recognized as a sensible way of achieving this. There are, of course, occasions when Geac leave it to the customer to decide whether to take the total solution from them or to use, for example, modems supplied from another source. The author has cause to be glad that in the London Borough of Hillingdon Geac carried out a complete installation (modems included) and would recommend other librarians to do the same. There is considerable virtue in dealing only with one supplier should anything go wrong.

The System 8000

Geac entered the computer manufacturing business with the System 8000. It is probably still the most commonly used of Geac's growing family of c.p.u.s although UK library applications now generally employ either the 9000 or the ADVANCE system, depending on size of application. It is built around a number of high-speed processors, the Model 250, developed by Geac.

The basic System 8000 has four processing subsystems which communicate with each other through a shared memory. The four subsystems are:

Communications processor
Disc processor
Program processor
Tape processor

The operating languages are ZOPL and HUGO, Geac's own high-level programming languages, developed to provide the maximum operating power needed in high transaction processing, online systems. The 8000 also contains a C compiler.

Although the 8000 was usually provided as the only c.p.u. for the majority of library operations, it is frequently installed in banking and other financial institutions in a dual or multiple configuration, where all files and tasks are duplicated to avoid downtime completely. There are a number of library installations which have dual 8000s, though in these cases the tendency is for one unit to control circulation functions and the other the catalogue or acquisitions functions.

The Series 150

For the sake of completeness, mention here should be made of the Series 150 machine. This is a kind of hybrid 8000, with its board power increased from the normal 8000 range. Running on a different operating system, the 150 is only marketed in the financial sector.

The System 6000

Following the success of the 8000, Geac developed a smaller version – the System 6000 – in 1980, working on the same principles of multi-processing as its larger relation. In this case, however, there are only two processing subsystems:

Communications processor
Program processor/Disc controller

It uses the same language, ZOPL, but will support standard languages such as BASIC and PASCAL.

The 6000 enables Geac to market their products to smaller companies and libraries which have neither the need nor the finance available for the larger machine. Geac claim that the 6000 needs no special environmental arrangements and can be powered by a standard 13 amp domestic electricity supply. It has been used by some libraries as a start-up unit during data preparation operations, the site subsequently being upgraded to the 8000.

Being totally compatible with its larger stablemate, it offers a mechanism for smaller sites to upgrade or for larger sites, already possessing an 8000, to expand to a dual processor system. In library terms, the 6000 has found greatest favour in polytechnics and colleges which have neither the large catalogues of universities nor the high circulation volumes of public libraries. It has also found a use in libraries supporting Geac's office automation system, GOAST, for which it is in use in New York University's Elmer Holmes Bobst Library and several other US sites. More recently it is to be found supporting Boolean search facilities on the Online Public Catalogue module, thereby keeping the heavy processing loads needed by Boolean searching separate from the other activities.

The 9000 family

The third member of the family to have an impact on libraries is the latest, largest and most sophisticated of all the Geac hardware products. Having moved downwards in scale to develop the 6000 the next logical move was to develop in the opposite direction, and this is perhaps the most important step taken by the company in recent years. The development of the Concept 9000 not only provided a very powerful machine within Geac's family of computers, but also introduced something more significant. When it was unveiled in 1983 the 9000 was claimed to be the fastest and most powerful, fault-tolerant, online, transaction processing system in the world. As with its predecessors, it gained an immediate foothold within the financial market-place; three 9000 systems were contracted within the first three months of its life. It is capable of supporting thousands of terminals and extremely high transaction processing levels. A 9000 installation can be viable with a basic network of 100 terminals; growth can then be accommodated to 500 terminals without any significant change of the c.p.u.. Company documentation states that there is 'almost no practical upper limit'. With the move to greater integration of library routines and the need to support additional functions, the 9000 family will become increasingly familiar to librarians.

The significant difference between the 9000 and its predecessors is the use of Full Function Processors (FFPs), which are capable of handling any task thrown at them. This is the opposite of the other systems, which had dedicated processors, which could often mean one processor being totally underemployed whilst another was struggling to cope. A typical medium-sized library installation will have three FFPs, whilst at the top of the range, a very large county library system such as Essex will use seven FFPs.

One of its most attractive features is its ability to route data by more than one pathway, so that if individual elements within the processor fail the system can continue to deliver the same high quality of service whilst repairs are effected. Naturally, within the banking community this facility is regarded as vital, but to a lesser degree it applies to a library's need to keep services such as online catalogues available to users.

A new processor has recently been incorporated into the 9000 series, allowing for a differentiation between medium, large and very large systems. The new processor gives a further improvement of 25 per cent power per processor. The 9300 machine has been brought into the range, aimed at 8000 machine upgrades not requiring more than four FFPs. The footprint of this machine will be similar to the 8000, a further attraction, as the original 9000 was considerably larger, a source of difficulty for sites with cramped computer rooms. The 9500 makes use of the same processor, but will be able to extend to the maximum eight FFPs, as did the original 9000.

Other systems

Besides the three large systems which can support the Geac Library Information System there are three other, smaller ones: the 2000, 4000 and 5000.

The System 2000 is a desk-top computer designed around a single processor. Its primary use is in the smaller pharmacy and leasing applications which Geac support, and it is used in the UK by Rank Xerox for this latter purpose. It is claimed in the company literature that libraries utilize this hardware; presumably in North America but as yet the author cannot discover where. The somewhat larger System 4000 has also not yet been identified in a library environment.

The System 5000 is operational in the publishing industry; Realtime Publications have installed it in the offices of *Adweek* magazine in New York. In the UK it has been used by Highland Leasing plc in remote regional offices linked by dedicated telecommunications lines to their headquarters. They are, however, being phased out with the introduction of the Concept 9000 installation which allows salesmen to download information from home using a cheap teletext terminal connected to British Leyland's Istel network. Again, no library applications have yet been discovered, but there is the potential for them to be used as part of a distributed library network. The author sees a potential for their use in large secondary schools or small further education establishments which would wish to have library links to a county or state library authority, without adding to the processing burden of that authority's own equipment.

Some financial customers have also made use of 'hybrids' of 8000 and 6000 systems.

ADVANCE system

A full description of Geac's PICK-based system is beyond the scope of this book. However, a brief description may be appropriate here.

ADVANCE is capable of running on any industry-standard UNIX platform. The number of platforms supported will, for obvious reasons, be limited. One of the supported platforms will be badged as the Geac 3000.

ADVANCE is aimed at the small to medium-sized system, typically a college or polytechnic. It is proving to be a popular choice in this market, particularly in France. It incorporates all the advantages of a relational database, providing excellent access to the database, but Geac have always been wary of the ability of systems running such databases to cope with high levels of transaction processing, and currently show no inclination to move this product up into the larger application market. Developments are being made in the computer industry in general in the area of operating systems and relational database products, and no doubt Geac will in time be able to offer the benefits of relational databases and a standard operating system combined with the ability to process very high transaction throughput.

This system, like others employing relational databases, is fully integrated. In general, data is stored once only, and only needs to be updated once. All modules access common files for bibliographic, authority, holdings, etc., data. As each transaction occurs, data and files are updated in real time. Software routines called phantom processors perform specified system activities in a background mode so as to minimize impact on real-time activities, e.g., online searching. Phantom processors such as the batch and calendar processors allow jobs to be run in background mode instead of setting aside dedicated systems time for notice printing, etc. This is a significant difference to the GLIS products, which typically use overnight time, when the systems are down, to produce notices, remove redundant transactions, etc.

One of the major benefits of the PICK operating system is the ease with which information for reports can be retrieved from the system. The system is provided with over 100 standard reports, but by using the English-like report writing language users are able to perform *ad hoc* queries with ease.

The programming language used is PICK extended BASIC, and by using the PICK programming tools users are able to develop their own complementary programs

Current modules available are Online Catalogue, Bibliographic control, Circulation and Acquisitions, with Serial control expected early in 1991. ADVANCE is still a very young member of the Geac stable, and no doubt in the coming years further developments will be made.

Section 2 The hardware and its operation

3 Central configuration

Within this chapter, the author has tried to give an insight into the rather complicated workings of the c.p.u. For the librarian who wishes to know what the equipment is capable of delivering, and is unconcerned as to how that is achieved, the later chapters are more relevant and they would be equally understandable without reading this chapter.

Memory

Geac systems are multi-processor systems: in the case of the 8000, four processors are used. These are the Communications Processor (also known as the ASTRO), the disc processor, the Program Processor (also known as Fast Fred) and the Tape Processor. There are two distinct areas of memory within the c.p.u., local memory and shared memory, and there is an area of local memory associated with each of the different processors, with the exception of the Tape Processor. Each of these areas is used only by that processor and it is within them that the operating system for the various processors is stored. Their sizes are limited, with only the Program Processor's local memory being capable of expansion.

The processors communicate with each other through the much larger shared memory. Within an 8000 System this shared memory can be up to a maximum of one Mbyte, contained on 8x128k MOS memory boards.

Jobs are divided into data and program code. The (re-entrant) program code is stored in the Program Processor's local memory, whereas a job's data is stored in the shared memory. Thus many separate jobs can use the same set of program instructions in the Program Processor's local memory, but each job has its own set of data in the shared memory. Each job stores its data in a data partition in shared memory; each partition being a multiple of 256 word blocks (16 bits = 1 word = ¼k), with the minimum amount being five words and the maximum being 256 words (64k). (The convention within Geac, for referring to memory, is to use the digit after the decimal point to signify quarters; thus 1.1k = 1¼k.) When more space is required in shared memory to carry out a job, it is attached to the relevant port by attaching more blocks of words, thus increasing the size of the data partition.

At the beginning of each data partition is a header, through which the job communicates with the operating system. To do this it makes a system call to another processor, and the Program Operating System moves certain parameters into the header of the data partition and puts a message into the partition's 'mailbox'. The mailbox is the memory location where the transmitting operating system can read it.

Each operating system constantly scans through the mailboxes of all the partitions for system requests addressed to itself and when it finds one, proceeds to deal with it. Having no local memory of its own, the Tape Processor works in a slightly different way. It scans only one mailbox in shared memory, into which the Communications Operating System posts messages which it has collected from scanning all the partitions. Having received a message in its mailbox, the Tape Processor executes it and returns a message to that effect to its mailbox. The Communications Operating System then collects that message and posts it back to the partition originating the system call. Bearing in mind the nature of the Communications Operating System, British readers would recognize it by its appropriate nickname, 'Postman Pat'.

Only one program can execute in a partition at any one time. The online terminals can get round this obvious handicap because they are under the control of a Terminal Control Program. The online terminals therefore have an indirect relationship with a partition or a program. The partition is referenced by a 'dummy port', which acts as a queue number for real ports. (For an explanation of ports see below.) The Terminal Control Program therefore allocates space to the online terminals on a time-sharing basis.

Program operating system

The Program Operating System is responsible for executing user jobs. Depending on the size of the programs and the size of its local memory, it contains the code for many of the programs which are in use. 'Least recently used' logic is employed to overwrite programs that have not been used for a long time or which are in little demand. To this end the Program Operating System maintains a usage table for all resident programs.

Its second major function is to maintain a time-slice and priority control over programs it is executing. It does this by assigning a job identification to each job execution, allocating a time slot for each partition in memory, and sets a clock to tick down to zero. Should the clock reach zero before the job has made a system call to another processor, the job is timed-out and must wait for another time slot. If, however, the job does make a system call before it is timed-out another job is given a time slot.

Jobs can have either foreground or background priority; jobs with foreground priority always take precedence over those with background priority. Foreground jobs interrupt background jobs, even if they have already been given a time slot. The time-slice can be increased by up to a factor of seven, effectively giving seven times the length of time before a job is timed-out. Thus, a job having foreground priority and a time-slice of seven (indicated in the system as 7F) will execute considerably quicker than a background job having a time-slice of only one (1B). Priority and time-slice can be assigned by the operator, which means that the highest rating can be determined locally. Typically, circulation transactions are given highest priority in order to achieve quickest response times whereas the Acquisitions package or OPAC are given lower priorities.

Communications operating system and ports

This operating system, known within Geac circles as the ASTRO, has the task of moving data between user jobs in the shared memory and peripheral terminals. The means of entry to and exit from the computer is called a 'port', of which there can be 64 on an 8000. This interface with the machine can be divided into two distinct types: 'real' and 'dummy' ports. Real ports have a physical plug, an RS232 interface, through which connections can be made to the outside world. Dummy ports exist to form a means of reference for the system. The Geac system insists on an association between a partition in shared memory and a port, which is achieved by the use of dummy ports in certain circumstances. Dummy ports are usually employed to run individual software packages.

Of the real ports, there are again two types, each controlled by different chips. The most common type is called an ASTRO port (Asynchronous-Synchronous Transmitter-Receiver). The second type is an ADLC (Advanced Data Link Control), which is needed for connection to external data networks such as the British Telecom PSS network. Ports of this type conform with the X.25 international standard and have thus come to be known colloquially as X.25 ports.

Two different types of terminals can be attached to an ASTRO port:

1. Control consoles, used to control the system. These are interactive devices, which is to say that each character is sent direct to the computer as the key is depressed. They are also known as 'KQ' terminals since the program to which they default when not otherwise occupied is !KQ. (In Geac's own peculiar parlance '!' is referred to as 'Bang'.) !KQ interprets whatever is keyed in and attempts to run it.
2. Online terminals, otherwise referred to as 'TCP'. These terminals are run by the Terminal Control Program, hence their name. They are completely different from control consoles in that they only interact with the computer indirectly. Data is sent to the computer in polled block mode, a chunk at a time, when the SEND key is hit.

There is more than one real port associated with a dummy port. The terminals on the real ports share the data partition for the dummy port on a time-sharing basis under the control of the Terminal Control Program. Terminals on a TCP port each have a table in the Communications Operating System's local memory, called a CRT table. The CRT table holds information peculiar to the terminal, such as the program it is currently running and job data. The job of a TCP terminal must share a data partition with other jobs, since it has no dedicated data partition of its own. The terminal therefore has to wait its turn in the job queue used by the data partition. When it is time for the terminal to execute its job, the data from its CRT table is loaded into the data partition and the Program Operating System starts executing its program. More than one data partition is able to use the same job queue, so that a job from a terminal can possibly be executed in more than one data partition.

The ASTRO also handles all the protocol processing required for a port to communicate with one or more terminals on the same telecommunications line. In order to achieve this, the TCP needs a unique address for the terminal. This is the poll-code, which quickly assumes a near mystical significance to library staff faced with the installation of terminals. The TCP is constantly polling the terminals, in contrast to some other systems which are only in communication with a terminal when there is actually some data to send or receive. Very often (especially in the early days of a site's life) it will transpire that two or more terminals on the same line have inadvertently been given the same poll-code, resulting in that line 'hanging'.

In order to be able to address a terminal, the ASTRO requires the port and poll-code. It follows that, although a poll-code has to be unique for a port, the same code can be repeated on each TCP port without problem.

The ASTRO also handles all the different protocols for communicating with different devices. In addition it plays a large part in internal communications, carrying out the internal memory management in shared memory when attaching or re-attaching ports. Memory partitions are allocated by the ASTRO.

Disc Operating System and discs

A short description of how disc storage is structured may prove useful. The basic unit of measurement of data is the bit, of which eight add up to a byte. Although not necessarily the case, in library operations one byte tends to represent one character of text. Two bytes equal one word. A word is the smallest addressable unit in the disc storage system. The most relevant statistic is that Geac use 16-bit words.

Discs and memory are addressed in sectors. Each sector has a capacity of 128 words (or 256 bytes). Sectors are arranged in segments, each containing six sectors. Data is transferred to and from the disc by segments. Finally, four segments constitute a track which therefore contains 3072 words or 6144 bytes. When referring to the size of large files the unit of measurement used is the track.

A logical file is a collection of logical sectors from the disc area containing data recorded in a specified format. Logical files can be either temporary or permanent. Temporary files have no file name or entry in a directory, whilst permanent files have both. A directory entry contains the name of the file and a pointer to its index sector. Without such an entry in a directory a file cannot be accessed.

The data stored in the disc storage system is managed by the Disc Operating System as a single logical disc structure, regardless of the number of individual disc drives.

Geac's philosophy is that they provide online systems; a central part of that philosophy is the insistence that the entire database must be available online at all times, rather than requiring an operator to load tapes of relevant files when they are needed. Since, in a library context, there is no way of knowing which files will be needed at any time, this is just as well!

Disc accesses are time consuming, so unnecessary accesses are eliminated by the use of the cache memory maintained by the Disc Operating System. Data is read from the disc in 768 word blocks known as segments, and the cache memory keeps current segments immediately available for use by various jobs. The operating system delays writing a segment until it is either not busy or the cache memory space is required. Writing to disc is expensive in terms of processing time because a written segment must be compared to its buffer in local memory before the cache memory is released. To achieve this, the disc platter has to make a complete revolution before the comparison can be made.

The disc operating system supports two types of logical files, one known as dynamic files and the other known as large files. The dynamic area is always contained on the first disc drive in the system, Drive 0, and is always 2720 tracks in capacity. This capacity cannot be increased. The Geac name for this area is DYNA.

Dynamic files are, as their name suggests, susceptible to constant change in size. They do not exist as one logical whole. The segments of disc that make up a dynamic file are widely scattered, so the file itself maintains a list (contained in its first sector) of which segments constitute its various parts. This is called the index sector. The availability of free sectors for use by a dynamic file is determined by reference to a system-maintained bit map.

In addition to the DYNA area, each of the user areas (which comprise most of the remainder of the disc space) has its own dynamic file area, so that dynamic files can exist within user areas, and frequently do. Permanent dynamic files are used primarily for programs and batches, whose sizes are generally not particularly costly in space, but which are subject to change. DYNA also contains the first sector of each large file in its large file map, so it is easy to see that its role is crucial. Some dynamic files are temporary: spool files, of which there can be a maximum of 255 each supporting up to 32,000 characters, are completely impermanent.

Large files fundamentally differ from dynamic files in that they are made up of contiguous tracks of disc, rather than being spread in several separated areas. A large file can span several disc drives and can theoretically occupy the whole of the large file area, except for the system module areas. Large file spaces are allocated by the programmer. Done skilfully this allocation can minimize the number of disc head movements during operations, which in turn will have a beneficial effect on response times. This assumes considerable significance as systems develop, since it becomes necessary to redistribute the files on occasion to improve response times by optimizing head movements.

When creating a large file, its size must be set. This cannot be changed except by creating a new file, and then copying the contents of the old file into the new area. In systems which grow rapidly this becomes a fairly familiar routine.

A user area is a special large file format. It is, in essence, a mini logical disc area containing a dynamic area of its own, plus a large file area. A good knowledge of the various user areas in a system is essential for its management. In a large system running several packages there will be numerous user areas, and amendments can only be made to files, or special batches run, if one is 'signed up' to the correct user area. In the past this has caused problems as Geac allowed a high degree of variation in the use of these areas, so that it became difficult for software support staff to find their way around systems with which they were not in regular contact. These problems have been largely overcome by an insistence on greater standardization of nomenclature of user areas and batches. The latest release of Circulation software (10.3 for 8000 systems, 21 for 9000) represents a considerable effort to standardize.

User areas can be, and indeed usually are, linked together. When attempting to run a program, the system first scans the directory beginning with the user area currently in use. It then proceeds to the next area up the chain, and so on, until it reaches DYNA. Finally it scans the system module areas. Using this technique, programs may access files in the current directory or further up the chain, but not in other directories on the same level or levels further down the chain.

User areas can be protected by passwords to prevent access by unauthorized personnel. This is covered in the section on security in Chapter 6.

In common with many bibliographic databases, Geac's databases are hierarchical. Although this gives less flexibility in terms of the possible data structures in comparison with relational databases, it allows for designs which emphasize the need for speed of use.

System 9000

Much of the above description, which was written about the 8000 architecture, can be applied to the 9000, except that in the 9000 all processors can function as program, communications, disc, or tape processors as the need arises. These processors are known as FFPs. The minimum recommended configuration to allow the benefits of their ability to act as any processor is three FFPs. The original 9000 has an upper limit of eight FFPs, but recently a smaller machine, the 9300 series has been announced, with an upper limit of four. The new machines employ a redesigned processor, called the 950, giving approximately 25 per cent more power per processor than the earlier version, so allowing smaller installations to upgrade to the 9000 more cheaply. With the advent of the new processor, the larger systems are now known as 9500 machines. As before, these machines can be expanded to contain eight FFPs, but with the processors' 25 per cent improvement in speed, these equate to ten FFPs on an original 9000. The original 9000 design ceased production in October 1990.

Sharing the computer industry's fascination with giving model numbers to every combination possible, the 9300 series actually consists of the 9302 (two FFPs), 9303 (three FFPs) and the 9304 with not unsurprisingly, four FFPs. Upgrading from a 9302 to a 9303 or from a 9303 to a 9304 will be possible. Similarly, the 9500 series ranges from the three processor 9503 to the eight processor 9508, with smooth migration up the range possible.

Memory is shared by a group of FFPs. The configuration

of two or more FFPs sharing a common memory is termed a cluster. The system architecture allows a cluster to contain up to eight FFPs accessing a shared memory of up to four memory chassis with a combined memory capacity of 64 MB or 32 megawords. With the present memory boards using 64K-bit RAMS, the current maximum memory capacity of a fully configured cluster is 64 MB (48 MB on a 9300).

The FFPs within a cluster are connected via an interprocessor bus which consists of various status signals. These signals provide for the following actions:

(a) Enable a job executing on one FFP to interrupt another FFP when access to one of its peripherals is required;
(b) Route reset and power fail status between FFPs within a cluster to facilitate coordinated operations during power fail recovery;
(c) Allow the addition of diagnostic and monitoring equipment.

One FFP in the cluster is assigned control of operations during power fail and recovery sequences. This FFP is referred to as the 'Boss', with the other FFPs in the cluster called 'slaves'. The Boss is normally FFP number 0 and is connected to cluster disk drive 0. This drive contains the operating system and is also used to store the contents of memory during a power failure.

Increasing the processing power or number of peripherals from the minimum configuration is achieved by adding cabinets, FFPs, interfaces, and memory chassis and boards as required, to the limits of the cluster architecture.

To facilitate further enhancement of processing power or the addition of fault tolerance features, 9000 architecture allows the use of multiple clusters. In these configurations the clusters combine with each other via one or more high speed buses (H-bus) between one or more FFPs in each cluster. For this use the H-bus is called an Inter-Cluster Communicator. To provide for ease of expansion and maintenance the processor and memory chassis in different clusters are housed in separate system cabinets.

Each processor cabinet can accommodate up to four FFPs that are mounted in individual chassis and powered by separate power supplies. All of the power supplies are normally connected to a power distribution panel in the cabinet that provides fused AC outlets. However, if one of the FFPs is the Boss, it is powered by an uninterruptible power supply (UPS) so that it can control power fail and recovery operations. If the cabinet is loaded with four FFPs the UPS is located in an adjacent cabinet.

Each FFP chassis contains 11 circuit board slots interconnected by a printed circuit backplane. These slots contain circuit assemblies for a 16-bit processor, a memory interface to perform accesses to shared memory, and interrupt I/O board to control communications between the processor and the peripheral interfaces and to provide connections to the interprocessor bus and a port for the control console, and eight slots that can accommodate various combinations of peripheral interface boards, such as serial interface, disk interface (four drives), tape interface (one drive) and real-time clock, and H-bus interface (one port). The serial interface has 12 ports, which can be either all ASTRO ports, or eight ASTRO and four ADLC (required for X.25 communication).

Each memory cabinet can house one or two memory chassis. A memory chassis accommodates circuitry to provide up to 16 MB of memory. Each memory chassis has eight slots for pairs of memory boards, as required, with each board pair containing two MB of RAM.

To avoid the loss of memory data due to loss or fluctuation of the main power source, the AC power source for each supply is a separate UPS mounted in the base of each cabinet. Each UPS is in turn connected to the AC line via the power distribution panel. In the UK, a fully charged UPS at full capacity will typically be able to keep a memory chassis functioning for $9\frac{1}{2}$ minutes, a processor chassis for $15\frac{1}{2}$ minutes, and a disk drive for 20 minutes.

Whereas on the 8000 each port is only capable of handling one job at a time, the Operating System for the 9000 family allows up to nine jobs to run concurrently through a single !KQ port. The operator simply toggles between jobs to keep track of the progress of each job, as required.

Keyman

Keyman is a menu-driven, user-friendly interface with the 9000 family machines, running on its own PC, which also acts as a control console for the system. It is used to boost the system, and constantly monitors and logs the processors, regardless of what other work the console may be engaged in. Keyman is a very powerful aspect of the 9000 system, and Geac warn that it must be used with caution. Most of the more sophisticated functions exist for use by Geac engineers, who are able to benefit from greatly improved diagnostic facilities.

Environmental controls

The System 6000 is marketed on the basis that it requires no special environmental conditions other than that found within a 'clean office'. It can also be operated on a single 15 amp domestic electricity supply.

The larger systems, in common with most minis, do require special environmental protection; regulation of temperature and humidity and dust-free air. Geac require that the c.p.u. is operated within a temperature range of 15°C to 28°C (60°F to 80°F). Humidity should not exceed a maximum of 65 per cent, nor fall below 35 per cent, non-condensing (60 per cent and 40 per cent for the 9300 series). In practical terms this means that the c.p.u. must be housed in an enclosed room fitted with an air-conditioning unit powerful enough to maintain these conditions within the dimensions of the room in use. Back-up air-conditioning will help to obviate the need to shut down the c.p.u. in the event of failure of the main unit.

Since an enclosed room is usually necessary for the purposes of air-conditioning, it is a relatively easy matter to have the room made reasonably air-tight, thus excluding dust from the atmosphere. The disc packs themselves are based on Winchester technology and are thus sealed from the external environment. If the filters become clogged with dust particles this can lead to overheating of the drive motor, and in these circumstances the drive will shut down automatically to prevent damage. This may result in the system being down for some time for recovery of the database. For these reasons, any work carried out in the computer room, which could lead to the generation of dust, must either be carried out with the c.p.u. powered off or with the work adequately screened and some form of dust extraction system in operation.

As well as clean air, computers also require 'clean' electricity; that is a mains power supply that is protected from sudden peaks or drops of the current. The consequences of a 'dirty' power supply are potentially disastrous corruption of data. Geac insist on clean electricity and to achieve the correct conditions invariably requires a supply dedicated solely to the c.p.u. and not shared with any other equipment. Fitting of constant voltage transformers is also recommended. A back-up battery power supply retains data in memory in the event of a power failure, and users generally have high praise for how well this works in avoiding problems when mains power is interrupted. It is one of the most impressive features of an already very robust system.

Where there is a concentration of electrical equipment, such as in a mini-computer installation with its attendant modems, printers and terminals, there is also a risk of fire. In the event of fire it is important that it be extinguished at a very early stage, before thick smoke develops. Protection of the c.p.u. from direct damage by flames or heat is not sufficient, as smoke is just as detrimental in that it comprises minute particles which will have the same effects on the disc drives as dust. Heat and smoke detectors are therefore highly recommended; they should be placed in positions where they can detect smoke quickly and the author would recommend following the guidelines given by Gibbs, Jenner and Rolf (1985). At least one Geac client has cause to rue the siting of the c.p.u. in an unprotected room within a library without overnight staff. The damage caused by smoke from a faulty air-conditioning unit which caught fire over a weekend led to the writing off of the c.p.u. There is no substitute for detectors monitored on a 24-hour basis by security staff. Some sites also have humidity and smoke monitoring equipment linked to the c.p.u., which is automatically powered off if in danger.

Fire-fighting equipment can be either in the form of suitable extinguishers or halogen gas systems, which operate by denying oxygen to the fire. The balance must be drawn between the need to protect the equipment and databases from damage and the safety of staff who may find themselves engaged in putting out a fire. The equipment is replaceable and the database, if properly secured onto tape and stored elsewhere, is largely, if not 100 per cent, recoverable. The non-renewable resource is staff, so what is required is a fire-fighting system that is both reasonably efficient and safe to use. Further exploration of this subject is beyond the remit of this book.

A further point has to be borne in mind when considering housing the c.p.u.; the weight. Before installation, the load-bearing capacity of the floor must be established. To wheel a machine into a room without such a check could prove embarrassing. A weight-distributing plinth of ½" (13mm) blockboard is often all that is required to prevent wheels from puncturing the floor.

Another sensible precaution, at comparatively low cost, is the installation of an anti-static mat, earthed through the computer. Static electricity is dangerous to both staff and the equipment, so a mat makes for good insurance.

Finally, being electrically driven, computers have a low tolerance to flooding, and Geac's are no better at working underwater than anybody else's. A basement in an old library may have its advantages as a site for a c.p.u. but before siting one there precautions should be taken!

It is worth stating that, although air-conditioning and clean electrical supplies are needed to run a System 8000, Geac machines are able to tolerate otherwise very basic conditions. The London Borough of Redbridge now have their machine housed in an excellent computer room in their new central library, but it was previously housed in a room in an old house which served as the Library Department's Headquarters. This room was simply an ordinary small room, such as could be found in any house, except for the addition of two air-conditioning units; but Geac were able to supply and maintain a sophisticated computer in less than ideal surroundings without any qualms.

The terminals are also very tolerant of environmental conditions and will operate perfectly well in a wide range of library buildings, most of which were never designed for the computer age (see Chapter 4).

Central configuration reliability

Central processing units are immensely complicated pieces of equipment. If one works on the principle that the more bits there are to go wrong the more a machine will go wrong, it seems to the author little short of a miracle that they go wrong so rarely. It is a common experience of Geac users that the c.p.u. itself is generally extremely reliable.

Broadly speaking, the purely electronic components in the c.p.u. are particularly robust, and all sites spoken to in the preparation of this book were happy with its reliability. Sussex University, which is one of Geac's longest established British customers, are extremely happy with the c.p.u.'s reliability and its ability to cope with the workload. Several years ago, they published figures for the availability of the system which show an average of 98.3 per cent over four years of operation (Young 1986). Sussex staff also had high praise for the engineering support they received.

The components containing mechanical parts are, understandably, more prone to failure. These are the disc drives, tape drives and line printers. Since the publication of the first edition of this book, these have all been replaced as older equipment has become obsolete. There is now a considerable range available, including Keystone tape drives, Fujitsu disk drives, and a variety of printers. A recent development has been the introduction of helical scan technology to enable the entire database to be backed up onto videotape. This represents a very considerable advantage for sites without night operators, as the entire system can be backed up overnight, without any operator intervention. Previously, such sites have had to do their backing up during the day from duplicate disk files. It would theoretically be possible to dispense with the normal ½" tape drive, but this is not recommended as transfer of data on tape is still required, and also a tape drive acts as a back up to the video drive in the event of the latter failing.

The Helix tape drive is supplied by Digital Interfaces Ltd, and is built around an Exabyte 8mm cartridge drive, video 8 cassette tapes and Helical Scan technology. The tape capacity is about 2.2 Gigabytes per tape, and 4-5 Gigabyte Video 8 drives are expected soon. The product as supplied by Geac does have a drawback in that it takes as long to read the contents of a file back into the system as it did to write it; a problem when the wanted file is at the end of the tape. A company called APAK supplies a similar product, called 'BAKPAK', using VHS tape and claim that their system can find any file within five minutes. Nonetheless, the London Borough of Islington, who were the UK library Alpha site for the Geac version, were very happy with it, particularly in terms of staff savings and increased security.

The modern types of Winchester technology disc drive are fortunately reliable, especially when one considers the extremely fine limits of engineering involved and the fact that they are spinning constantly. A disc 'crash', where the head actually comes into contact with the surface of the disc, is virtually unheard of. Other failures are often described, though inaccurately, as crashes, and these, although still infrequent, are more common. They are usually associated with the magnetic material of the disc, or the efficiency of the read/write heads. Overheating motors cause a drive to power down; this is often caused by clogged filters which prevent a sufficient supply of cool air being taken in. Severe disc drive problems are, fortunately, unusual occurrences.

There is a wide variety of different disc drives in use in Geac installations, and experience around the world appears to differ. The author would recommend that any potential new sites ask that the model to be supplied is identified so that technical staff can satisfy themselves as to its reliability.

Several line printers are supplied by Geac for use in conjunction with the 8000 and 9000 family machines. These are known as the 325, 625, 925 and 1515 models, the numbers standing for the number of lines printed per minute by each. Geac will also provide high quality laser printers for those sites which require a higher quality of print output.

References

Gibbs, L., Jenner, R. and Rolf, R. (1985), 'Recognizing air flows in computer suites when siting fire detectors', *Fire*, September, p. 31.

Young, R.C., Stone, P.T., Pickles, J.S., Lee, S.R. and Lamber, P.J. (1986), 'Geac with local enhancements: the real-time system at the University of Sussex Library', *Program*, 20 (1), January, pp. 1-25.

4 Terminals and other peripherals

Geac's early history as a non-manufacturing supplier of computer systems has made possible a relaxed attitude about the peripheral devices which it uses. Though the company now manufactures its own terminals, even the latest models rely heavily on other suppliers' kit. Since the first edition of this book was published in 1987, there have been numerous inevitable changes in the Geac peripheral product line. At that time it was said that keeping track of UK developments was possible for the authors, but that inevitably there would be many developments worldwide about which the authors would be ignorant. In the intervening years all that has changed is that the present author no longer is able to say confidently that all UK hardware applications are now covered! The single biggest development is that whereas previously users were forced to buy proprietary equipment, usually from Geac, there is now a much greater opportunity to purchase standard equipment, often with considerable cost savings.

Systems now sold by Geac are licensed to run a certain number of terminals (actually polled devices, so this figure may include polled printers). Within the licensed limit the customer is free to add as many terminals as desired, but wishing to go beyond that limit is done on a terminal by terminal basis, with suitable amendments to the contractual commitment if necessary.

A varied range of terminals is marketed for library systems. Although they differ in appearance, and to some extent technology, they all have in common the fact that they are multifunctional units, consisting of a keyboard and a visual display screen. Provided a terminal is fitted with a light pen, it can perform the full range of library functions; although some functions can be carried out more efficiently on one terminal as opposed to another (e.g. a terminal intended for public use has a simpler keyboard, lacking several function keys useful to staff).

With the exception of terminals using VT220 protocols, all terminals have RS-232-C daisy-chain capability using ANSI X3.28 poll-select protocol (see next chapter on communications and networking) and are all compatible provided they have been fitted with the appropriate firmware. Though this firmware did give rise to compatibility problems in the early days, when the newer models were first released on to the market, this is no longer the case.

The terminals are all robust pieces of equipment and will operate in temperatures ranging from 10°C to 30°C (50°F to 95°F) and humidities from 20 per cent to 80 per cent, non-condensing. They can operate with power supplies at both 120 volts or 240 volts and have a consumption of around 70 watts.

Screens have a display format of 80 characters × 24 lines though in some modes the display uses double height characters of which there are 12 lines each with a maximum of 40 characters. All terminals have brightness controls and support highlighting to some degree.

The earliest terminals were the Informer models. These are no longer marketed, though many older sites still use them. There are two versions: one with a 12"(30 cm) screen, which is typically used for staff enquiry purposes; the other with a 9"(23 cm) screen, intended primarily for issue transaction work. They differ in that the 9" model has the screen mounted on a stalk extending above the keyboard, whereas the 12" model has a separately mounted screen.

These terminals were not particularly stylish though they were robust and workmanlike. By comparison, the next generation was a significant step forward both in terms of appearance and operation. There are two library terminals in this, the 8300, series: the 8370 has 16 function keys and full diacriticals and has greatest use within cataloguing departments; the 8360 is much simpler, having only eight function keys and does not even possess insert and delete keys. This latter terminal is specifically designed as a simple public enquiry terminal and is marketed under that description. It is a matter of great regret to this author that Geac have ceased supplying these models, quoting the high unit cost of specialized keyboards.

The latest range of terminals is marketed under the name 'Elite' (a condensation of European Library Terminal) and is again a step forward in terms of appearance and operational sophistication. It was originally based on an Apricot screen (now Phillips) and supports a keyboard with 16 function keys.

The models in this range replace the older Informer range, one possessing a 12" screen, the other a 9" screen (which, unlike that of its predecessor, is a separate unit). The latest Phillips models have 14" screens.

The Elite series

These are certainly more attractive in appearance than the Informer terminals they replaced, with latest technology 14" monitors manufactured by Phillips. Unlike the Informer series, the 9" Elite has a separate screen rather than an integral one mounted on a stalk. The separate keyboard, though multi-functional like the Informers, is somehow less cluttered and more inviting in appearance, being significantly less bulky. The keys have an easy but positive feel. As a significant improvement over earlier models, it is now possible to plug a light pen or CCD scanner into either side of the keyboard.

Whereas the Informer terminals were set up for use by the manipulation of switches, the more modern terminals' parameters are retained in software, and can be amended with the terminal in local mode. These parameters include the poll-code (required by the X3.28 protocol), the baud rate, parity, whether the cursor blinks or is stable, etc. These parameters can be easily accessed, or protected.

All terminals suffer from the lack of a solidly attached light pen holder.

It should be remembered that all terminals can be used for all operations, providing they have been given appropriate permissions within the software tables. The variation in keyboard or screen merely makes them more suitable for some operations than others. In terms of cost there are minor differences between them; as a basic rule the more complex the keyboard the higher the price. Optional extras such as cardholders and light pens also add to cost.

VT220 terminals

The latest development in Geac's library terminal strategy is to allow for the use of industry standard DEC VT220 compatible technology. This is a significant departure from the previous position, which was that only terminals using the proprietary Informer protocol, or later the ANSI standard X3.28 protocol, could be used as library terminals. The introduction of VT220 protocol seems to be recognition that users wish to have more freedom of choice in the terminals they use, and in particular they want to be able to take advantage of the likely price advantages of being part of a bulk purchasing scheme within an organization. Users, particularly in academic institutions but also increasingly in local authorities, often want to be able to use any terminals on their corporate networks as library terminals, and also wish to use their library terminals for applications elsewhere on the network. This is best achieved by the use of industry standard protocols such as VT220. Naturally, Geac sell VT220 terminals themselves, the WYSE-185 and the Wyse 30.

Geac have not abandoned the X3.28 protocol however, and indeed it is still the method by which terminals communicate with the c.p.u. With VT220 terminals this is achieved by the use of an extra piece of kit, the terminal controller, known as the 8212, which converts the VT220 signals from the terminal into X3.28, or X.25, signals for communication with the host. All features of the library system are then available to the VT220 terminals, although if a bar code reader is required the addition of a small bar code decoder is also needed. The 8212 converter has some limitations, and Geac see this as an interim step before using a more intelligent unit, a microcomputer which they will call a Terminal Communications server in the same role. This will allow VT220 terminals to run in back-up mode, which is not possible with the 8212. A further explanation of Geac's strategy regarding terminal protocols is included in the following chapter on networking.

PCs and back-up terminals

There are two kinds of back-up terminal marketed by Geac: the first is a powerful microcomputer unit which is permanently wired within a library to several terminals which it protects; the other is a highly portable unit which is more commonly seen providing a service on mobile libraries.

The equipment originally used in the UK for the former was provided by Commodore in a whole range of models. If computing generally changes very quickly, the world of microcomputers changes even more rapidly, and Commodore micros are no longer sold by Geac. Difficulties with obtaining spares for now obsolete equipment has left Geac with a problem in supporting those Commodore units still in service, and wherever possible they are being replaced. Amongst the many disadvantages of the earlier approach was the fact that it relied upon floppy discs, which were limited in their capacity, fragile in the hands of stressed library staff not always sympathetic to the need for treating them with kid gloves (messages stapled to discs are not uncommon!) and dependent on floppy disc drives whose reliability was often suspect. They were dedicated back-up units, with little practical use when not in use for that purpose, which one hopes is nearly all the time, although some sites did experiment with using them for word processing and other applications.

The new approach to back-up units is to make the sensible choice of employing an IBM AT^{TM} compatible micro, with all the resulting advantages of hard discs, standard software and operating system that follow.

The micros currently used for what Geac call the Professional Services Terminal include WYSEpc and Compaq models. If bought with all the appropriate software and hardware they can be used as a back-up unit, driving normal library terminals further down the daisy-chain when required, as a library terminal itself, thanks to library terminal emulation software, or as a normal PC workstation running most commercially available software written for the IBM AT environment. As such it represents a considerable step forward, opening up the door to much more sophisticated computing than is possible on a standard terminal, and allowing for colour and graphic displays from viewdata or CD-Rom systems. Although it is called the Professional Services Terminal, this author believes that it is likely to have wide-ranging effects, and could equally become the terminal used by the public, allowing for switching between Geac databases and others, such as Prestel, and perhaps having an offline, windowed help facility. A new project, called Screen Manager, will enable the library to determine screen appearance to a greater extent than at present, and will have its greatest use in the micro environment, so radical changes in the way the system is presented to all users are to be expected.

This is an area of considerable fluidity but the Wyse PCs currently being sold by Geac are the 286 processor-based Wyse 2012I, and the 386 processor Wyse 3116 SX, or the 3225 if for use on a LAN.

A recent improvement with Release 21 of the Circulation software allows the same terminal attach on the system to be used for a micro, regardless of whether it is used as a terminal running LTE or LTS terminal emulation software, or as a micro back-up unit. It was previously necessary to have two attaches on the system; one poll-code for the terminal, and another for the back-up unit, which was rather wasteful. A menu on the PC's screen will allow the operator to choose which use the machine is to be put to.

An upgrade kit for PCs already in use can be purchased. The London Borough of Islington use ICL PCs adapted with daisy-chain boards, whilst in Suffolk County ICL PCs running Office Power and Library Terminal Emulation software are linked directly into their NIMs (see Chapter 5) without needing a daisy-chain board.

Geac also market a small portable data capture unit for use on mobile libraries, in outreach and stock-taking duties. This can equally well act as a single terminal back-up system. The unit originally was an Epson HX-20 (with a memory expansion unit) and was fitted with a built-in printer and visual display screen and had a detachable light pen.

As with the history of the main back-up unit, times have changed, and the unit now employed is a Psion organizer. This uses interchangeable datapacks having a minimum storage capacity of 320K bytes, (upgradable by 64k or 120k blocks) onto which transactions are recorded. When out on a busy mobile library, changing to a new datapack is accomplished very quickly. Once back at base, the data is transferred to the Micro Backup unit (new style), and then transferred on to the Geac host. As would be expected, the unit is supplied with a bar code reading wand (light pen), and can work off battery power or mains electricity.

Health and safety considerations

Geac maintain that all of their terminals conform to the current Health and Safety requirements, including those concerning radiation. In the only independent survey known to the author, the Informer and Cifer equipment installed by the London Borough of Camden was given a clean bill of health by the National Radiological Protection Board.

The 8300 series terminals were provided with their own

mesh anti-glare screens, which were moderately successful. They did have the drawback of being difficult to clean, and in time the image behind the anti-glare mesh became obscured. Elite terminals have a glass screen which is claimed to have anti-glare properties, but in areas with high levels of reflected light users may still need to employ specialized add-on anti-glare screens.

In terms of ergonomics the terminals are generally excellent. However, Geac do not attempt to advise sites on the arrangements they make for the location and operation of equipment from the ergonomic point of view: this is left to library staff. Engineers will always leave wiring as tidy as possible but if terminals are installed in locations that result in trailing cable Geac consider that to be the customer's responsibility. Likewise, screen glare and counter heights are deemed the customer's concern. This whole topic would require a book of its own; the author recommends the British Library research report on the ergonomics of library issue desks by Grey and Wilson (1983).

Printers

Geac supply printers which will print receipts or messages and can be used as an internal 'telex' system in multi-site libraries. Few British clients actually use them, though they are found more frequently in North America and Continental Europe.

The printer can output fines receipts, messages to indicate that a recently discharged item should be placed in transit for another library, and search slips when a hold is placed. It is unusual for there to be more than one printer associated with a cluster of terminals, but this gives rise to a further complication. At busy times, there can often be a queue of messages for the printer, and staff have to be alert in order to put the correct routing slip in the correct book, or give receipts to the correct reader. Response times may be excellent for the circulation terminals, but this benefit is soon lost if the patron has to queue for a receipt, or the staff cannot discharge the next item until the slip for the current one has been produced.

The first model of printer was criticized for being both slow and noisy; later models are an improvement on both counts, but the queuing problem remains to some extent, and paper handling was not ideal. This criticism is overcome by Geac's model 8113 mini-printer, which has been designed specifically as a self-contained printer for due date slips, fines receipts and routing slips. It has a print speed of 1.25 lines per second, each line being able to take 32 characters at 12 to the inch. It can be used with paper up to a maximum of 3⅞" (10 cm) width, and can accommodate two-part stationery if required.

Also available is a letter quality printer, the 8123, various models from the Epson range, and Laser printers.

Printers are also set up as attached terminals to allow for the remote printing of reports, overdue notices, etc. The Community Information module allows for screens to be printed, not only as a straightforward screen dump to a printer attached to the terminal, but also in a somewhat 'cleaned up' version to a designated printer elsewhere in the library. A similar feature in the OPC module allows for the user to create reading lists by marking selected records for later printing during a catalogue search.

Screen image printers

Unlike the mini-printers, screen image printers do not need to be attached to the c.p.u. and have no effect on response times. Their task is simply to print out the contents of the screen currently displayed on the terminal to which they are attached.

Following criticism of the original screen image printers, Geac have adapted their system and terminals to take standard printers working in series with a terminal. Geac supply Hewlett-Packard ThinkJet printers, but it is possible to use other manufacturers' products with equal success.

The printer is connected to the serial outlet of the terminal, using an RS232 interface. The terminal parameters need to be set to accommodate such a printer but once this is done, a simple task with the screen display mechanism of these models, the use of a function key on the terminal will activate the printer. The terminal ouputs a message at the foot of the screen ('Printing screen') and the printer is activated.

Some Inkjet printers, including the Hewlett-Packard ThinkJet, give best results when specially-treated paper is used, which is inevitably more expensive than standard computer listing paper. The ThinkJet uses the relatively recent technology of spraying a precisely controlled and directed jet of ink on to the paper, thus avoiding the need for a concussive action by a key or other device. It is therefore almost totally silent, the only noise being that of a very quiet motor as the paper drive is activated. Not only is this perfect for a library situation but it makes an office environment, especially an open plan office, more amenable to concentration. The actual print quality achieved is beyond anything that a conventional screen printer achieves and is better than equivalent dot matrix types. ThinkJet printers appear to be agreeably reliable, with the main cause of poor copies due to blockages on the ink cartridge, which are easily resolved by wiping.

Many sites now attach printers bought from suppliers other than Geac to their library terminals; the London Boroughs of Hillingdon and Bexley have both had success with very competitively priced matrix printers supplied by Citizen. Although somewhat noisy in comparison to an inkjet or Laser printer, if only used infrequently they are not very intrusive in the average branch library, which suffers from many other noises than used to be the case.

Firmware

Those who are dismayed at having to grapple with the terms 'hardware' and 'software' for the first time will be further alarmed to learn about the existence of firmware. This is best described as a piece of hardware (a microchip) containing some software which is non-volatile; that is to say, memory chips which cannot be amended. These are typically programmable read-only memory chips, or PROMs.

PROMs are easily mass-produced once a master has been created. They are programmed as they are made, and this programming cannot then be altered. If a change is necessary, a new PROM has to be manufactured and fitted. Firmware is fitted to the c.p.u., the terminals and the modems. It is the experience of the author that a great many problems which can be experienced in the operation of a complex installation can be laid at the door of the firmware. These problems have generally come to light when new equipment has been produced which appears to undertake many of the same routines as performed by earlier models, but which will suddenly develop some inexplicable aberration. In operating a site with virtually every piece of software and most variations of terminal hardware, the author believes that he has seen the full extent of the power of firmware to disrupt smooth operations.

The subject is a complex one and a proper explanation is beyond the competence of the present book. Suffice it to say that there are numerous PROMs, each having their own functions. There are PROMs to determine how many terminals can work on a single telecommunications line (separate ones for modems and terminals); PROMs to allow a mix of the various terminals on the same line; PROMs to give a public enquiry terminal a tab key; and countless others.

The important point to be made is that it is the firmware which gives the Geac system its flexibility. When a new idea emerges, it may only require a different PROM for it to be made to work, and this can often be fabricated. Whilst problems have occurred in the past over control of firmware, Geac engineering are making efforts to ensure that all sites will in future have standard releases of firmware in their equipment, which will prevent confusion when equipment is moved around.

Bar codes and label printers

The Geac system supports a range of bar code label formats, though for sites which are converting to automated circulation for the first time the codabar format is recommended and this format is the one around which the system was developed. As Geac have gained experience in dealing with sites which were previously automated with other suppliers' systems, they have adapted the software for a variety of label formats. On occasions this has presented difficulties since some other suppliers, notably Plessey, supported a number of formats over the years. Problems have arisen mainly with the ancillary software of the back-up systems and the Epson portable units, but the author believes that these units are now capable of use with all versions of Plessey bar codes, so relabelling of stock is not necessary.

Codabar format bar code labels can be printed in-house using a variety of label printers or they can be purchased from specialist printers. Size of label and detail printed can also vary.

For sites which wish to build into their labels some form of additional identification, a label printer is the best approach. In these circumstances the label can be printed under operator control or under computer control, via a standard communication line at speeds of either 1200 or 2400 baud. The model used, Geac reference 8121, outputs onto adhesive label stock and can add optional text. Print speeds are approximately 30 characters per second, depending on label size which can vary between 0.6 × 2.0 inches and 1.0 × 3.5 inches (1.5 × 5.0 to 2.5 × 9.0 cm). In the author's opinion, any labels produced by a printer need to be protected from wear by the light pen by the addition of an acetate cover. The printer also has the disadvantage of being a noisy piece of equipment, and Geac recommend that it is not housed in a working office. At the Massachusetts Institute of Technology an IBM PC has been attached to an Epson FX-80 printer to provide bar code labels using an inexpensive program which is being tailored locally to provide their own precise requirements.

The alternative of purchasing pre-printed labels from a specialist supplier has several advantages. Labels can be produced on A4 sheets for easy handling and storage, and they can be supplied with an acetate protective film so that the task of affixing them to items is a single process. They can be produced in a range of sizes and styles for different purposes, quality control is the supplier's problem and cost is highly competitive. Readers will gather that the author would recommend this course of action, not least because he believes that purchase price can be negotiated at a level close to that for blank label stock and acetate cover. Equipment costs are nil and there are no labour costs. North American sites seem to prefer to generate 'smart' bar codes by sending tapes to commercial suppliers.

Specialist printers also have an edge when it comes to printing bar codes for membership cards in that they can produce the card with the bar code printed as an integral part, rather than added afterwards. Despite this, the author would recommend the alternative of sealing the bar code within a plastic credit card style of membership card which will have a very long lifespan in comparison with a paper or card based version. Though these are expensive to purchase, their extended life makes them cheaper in the long term.

Date stamping systems

There are a variety of ways of providing borrowers with information on the due date of the items which they borrow. For those sites with a very complicated set of loan periods, the use of mini-printers associated with the issue terminals is the best option. These produce a printed slip giving a record of the transaction including the due date and time. However, such highly complex approaches are likely to be in the minority and in most sites it is more likely that the majority of items would be loaned for a standard period. In these circumstances the author would recommend the use of pre-inked date slugs attached to light pens by a simple plastic holder.

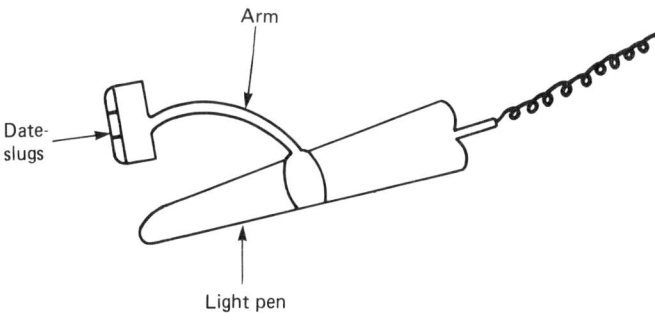

Figure 4.1 Diagram of a date stamp arm attached to a light pen

These slugs are expensive but they present a very neat and efficient way of date stamping a traditional library date label. The action of stamping takes very little time as the operator does not have to put down the light pen, and it can often be accomplished in the short time it takes the system to respond to the transaction.

Another system in use in some sites is to provide the borrowers with pre-dated transaction cards for insertion in a pocket attached to the item. This again takes very little staff time.

Bar code readers

The standard method for reading bar codes in libraries is still the light-pen, or wand, but other methods are now available for libraries which have particularly heavy throughputs.

Over the years Geac users have seen many models of light pen come and go, and different sites seem to have their own favourites and their own villains. It is a complicated matter, with some wands working better on some terminals than others, and always as an added complication is the quality and format of the bar code to be read. It is possible to reduce the amount of error checking done to increase the frequency of first-time reads, but this would be self-defeating.

Geac also supply laser readers. They have the advantage over light pens that the speed of operation is greater than with the hand-held pen, and the need to repeat the operation due to misreads caused by operator error is much reduced. They work on the principle of a scanning laser which detects the bar code and reads it automatically. They present the possibility of membership cards being read automatically as soon as they are inserted into a card holder. Another option would be to fix the bar code label to the exterior of the item so that the operator need only pass it over the laser reader without the need to open the book. Laser scanners were devised for supermarket checkout operations which need high speeds of throughput and they would seem to be most suited to those libraries where similar conditions occur.

An intermediate stage between the wand and the laser sceanner is the CCD scanner, which can be either hand-held or mounted. Unlike the wand, which has to be passed across the bar code, and which only reads a very thin segment of it, the CCD scanner reads the whole bar code. The advantage is that minor blemishes on the bar code will not cause a misread. Reading bar codes with the CCD scanner is at least as speedy as using a wand, and the number of misreads is impressively low. The scanner plugs into the terminal in the same way as a wand, so there is no need for any extra equipment.

Other peripherals

Geac is an international company with a fast developing range of alternative solutions to the problems of different libraries. It has not been possible to correspond with sites overseas but the author has been able to identify some of these other applications and can only note them here.

Colour is something which would greatly enhance displays, particularly within the OPAC and Local Information package. It is understood that the installation at the Massachusetts Institute of Technology uses colour monitors in some way, but the precise nature of the application is unknown. The use of colour on PCs is promised soon, as the Screen Manager project comes into operation, whereby users will be able to define their own screen layouts, and, where appropriate, colours.

In France there are several interesting new developments, particularly at La Villette. At this site it is now possible to use printers attached to banks of public terminals to produce a coded card detailing the entry being displayed. This card not only carries shelf location details but when placed in readers attached to other terminals the coded data can be used to instruct the terminal to automatically load a CDRom or Gigadisc and display the full text of the document required. La Villette will also shortly make its catalogue available through Minitel, the French Government's Prestel-style information system. Since Minitel has a very wide distribution throughout France, where it is used to carry the telephone directory, the catalogue will probably have the widest general public availability of any automated catalogue in the world.

In similar vein, in Limburg in the Netherlands the library catalogue is being made available in viewdata format over a local cable TV service.

Another new development in the Netherlands is to link the circulation terminals, using laser scanners, to a book security system, provided by the Dutch company ID Systems. Incorporated within the bar code, which is attached to the outside of the book, is the security system's magnetized tag. At the same time as the bar code is passed across the scanner, the security tag is also activated or deactivated, thereby accomplishing two operations in one movement. A drawback of the current system is that one station has to be dedicated to issuing/deactivating items, whilst another handles returns/reactivating. The ability to switch from one function to the other is obviously needed for smaller libraries, and it is understood that a switchable version is planned.

A possible further development which will be of interest to smaller, infrequently staffed libraries, is the adaptation of the ID Systems approach described above to the idea of self-service. In this mode, the borrower would only be able to remove a book from the library if it had been properly issued, the security system otherwise preventing its removal. Before this dream can become a reality, much would need to be done to make the circulation system 'friendlier' for use by untrained library users, but with the Screen Manager project's ability to hand over control of screen appearances to system administrators, that should not be an insurmountable difficulty.

Reference

Grey, S.M. and Wilson, J.R. (1983), *'The ergonomics of library issue desks'* (Final report), British Library Research and Development Department, 214 pp.

5 Telecommunications and networking

Library terminals use synchronous/asynchronous ANSI X3.28 poll select protocol to communicate with the mini-computer. Also supported are X.25 protocol, DEC VT220, IBM 3720 BSC host and CRT emulations, and IBM 2780/3780 host and RJE emulations.

X3.28 protocol conforms to ANSI standards, but is relatively little known. It was originally developed by NCR and used in their point of sale terminals. As might be expected from its original use for moving money around, it is a very reliable and secure protocol.

Since it is a somewhat unusual protocol, a brief explanation of the history of why it came to be used might be appropriate here. As outlined earlier, Geac started out running on Hewlett-Packard equipment, which was incorporated into a machine called the Geac 800. This had 64K of core memory, and four communications ports. The terminal chosen to use the first library system was the Informer, largely because it communicated with the host using the Informer Polling Protocol, enabling the connection of several terminals to one host port; a most important consideration when the available ports were limited to four!

When Geac then developed their own 8000 machine, the number of possible ports grew to 64, but Informer terminals, and their protocol, continued in use for the following five years. By this time Geac had come to realize the limitations of the Informer Protocol, which was not robust or reliable, and the Informer terminals, which were themselves unreliable, could not support the full ALA character set.

Geac therefore decided to build their own library terminals, the 8300 series described in the previous chapter. They continued to use polling so that daisy-chains of terminals could be connected, and switched to ANSI X3.28 protocol. Using this system, each terminal is given a unique identity on the line (its poll-code). The CPU sends down a stream of poll-codes to the libraries. As the poll-codes are sent down each terminal examines them to see if its own unique code is present. If it recognizes its code, it sends a character back to the c.p.u. to say that it is there and ready to do business and the transaction then occurs.

Although X.25 fulfils the same requirements as X3.28 it is not yet possible to connect it directly to the terminals. For longer distance links X3.28 is used in conjunction with a Network Interface Machine (NIM), with X3.28 running between terminals and NIM, whilst communication between NIM and CPU is achieved using X.25.

This was seen as a good solution for the kind of closed, stand-alone library system which traditionally existed, but this kind of configuration has become increasingly restricted in light of moves towards open systems and the integration of data across university or corporate networks. Polling, although technically possible across a Local Area Network, is wasteful of the LAN's bandwidth and its capabilities, as you cannot use the terminal to connect to any other host because of its special protocol, at least not so that all the functionality of a direct connection can be achieved. As shall be described later, communication across LANs is achieved by other means.

Where it is required to operate terminals within a reasonably short distance of the c.p.u., they can be wired directly to their respective ports, several being daisy-chained together and using the same port. Geac recommend that the distance to the first terminal be no more than 250 metres and that the distance between all others be no more than 75 metres, though the author has exceeded these distances without problems.

Communication over wide areas

For remote sites there is a need to provide a telecommunications link, at either end of which must be a device to transmit and receive the data (modems or line drivers). There are four basic possible types of network currently used to support remote sites, but there are many possible variations on those described here.

1. Star or Radial systems. This is the network design most commonly employed by Geac users with remote sites. It is a point-to-point network with analogue B circuits connecting

the system centre to each remote site. Geac recommend that no more than four to five devices should be operational per line, although users have been able to exceed this number when local data traffic conditions have been low enough to permit it. In other words, lines which are not too busy may find that there is spare capacity which can be taken up by increasing the number of terminals in a site. The author has consistently been able to operate seven terminals and one back-up terminal on a single line.

Geac regard the star network as a high quality arrangement as each remote site has its own line. A line failure will only affect one location, and even then, if the library concerned is large enough to require two lines, a restricted service may continue.

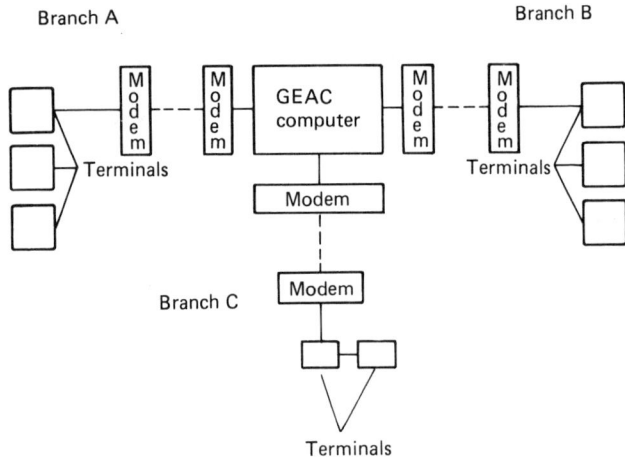

Figure 5.1 Diagram of a point-to-point communications network

2. Multi-drop network. A multi-drop network involves the sharing of one line by a number of small remote sites. This will often be less expensive than the point-to-point network, though in networks which are in limited urban areas they can be more expensive since the saving in line charges are offset by the cost of equipment. It is also limited in two important respects. Firstly, if a line develops a fault, more than one library will be affected. Secondly, the line will usually have the maximum number of terminals connected to it from the start, leaving little

or no room for expansion in the future. Another area of consideration is how to protect the line with back-up equipment.

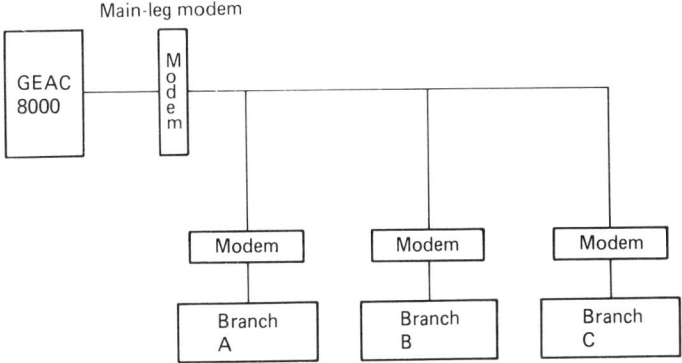

Figure 5.2   Diagram of a multi-drop communications network

3. Multi-node network. This type of network design consists of a high speed line between the c.p.u. and one library which serves as a node. A network interface machine (NIM) is located at the node, which can then serve a number of lines forming a point-to-point network from the node to several other sites. In a geographically dispersed network, there would be several nodes serving a number of libraries clustered around each one.

4. X.25

Recent years have seen library systems with wide geographical spreads opting to use CCITT X.25 packet switching protocol for the bulk of their communications, with X3.28 or VT220 used for communication within the branch library. As more UK local authorities invest in their own private X.25 networks, this method will become increasingly common, with significant cost savings over several years. Essex County Library Service runs entirely over a council-wide private X.25 network, supplied by Case Communications Ltd. Because they remain open longer than most other local authority establishments, the

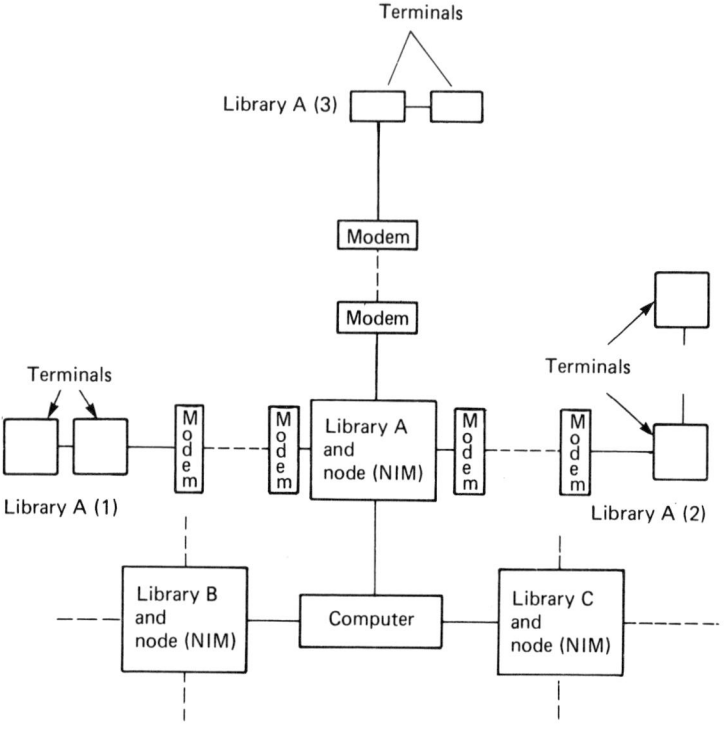

Figure 5.3 Diagram of a multi-node communications network

main nodes for the network are situated in libraries. Each library has a NIM, with up to 12 terminals attached.

To operate in the X.25 environment the Geac 8000 or 9000 requires X.25 software and HDLC ports. At the branch end the connection is made into the NIM, (Geac number 8215), which drives up to 12 X3.28 terminals. The multi-node network described above is likely to be part of an X.25 network, with the connection to the node library made by X.25, and then short leased lines running X3.28 terminals in smaller branches plugging into the NIM via modems. X.25 connections may be made over a dedicated line, as well as routed via a public or private packet switched network. This is the case in Suffolk County Library Service.

A significant advantage in using NIMs is that the host is relieved of the need to perform polling, as poll-codes are downloaded to the NIM which then polls terminals itself. It also reduces the total number of host communications ports required, since the network may be used to concentrate the connections into a smaller number of high speed ports. The usual configuration for a NIM is to use six of its ports, with a total of 15 devices attached. This can be achieved either by having three ports with three devices each attached and three ports with two devices attached, or one port with four devices, three ports with three devices, and two ports with only one device attached. The configuration will vary according to circumstances.

If VT220 compatible terminals are used, they are connected to a Geac 8212 controller, which comprises the same hardware as the NIM, but with downloaded software that performs the emulation of the X3.28 terminals. In this mode the 8212 can support up to eight terminals simultaneously, although daisy-chaining is not possible.

The 8212/8215 controller has been successfully integrated into many different X.25 networks. Public networks include Datex-P (Germany), Datapac (Canada), Datapac (Portugal), DDN (US Department of Defense, who have applied strict conformance tests), Transpac (France) and in the UK on private networks using Master Systems switching equipment. Using as it does a completely standard implementation of CCITT X.25 (1980), it has not proved problematic to interface to any form of standard X.25 switch.

The 8212/8215 controller is likely to be superseded in the near future by the Terminal Communications Server, which will in effect be a PC capable of handling the conversion between VT220 and X3.28 and X.25 protocols more elegantly. It will also be able to act as a micro back-up unit, driving the VT220 terminals in back-up mode, which is not currently possible with the NIM.

Communication across local areas

In addition to the networks used to support remote sites, Geac have also installed local area networks within single compact libraries, or institutions of which the library forms a part.

Hitherto, the problem has been that the use of the X3.28

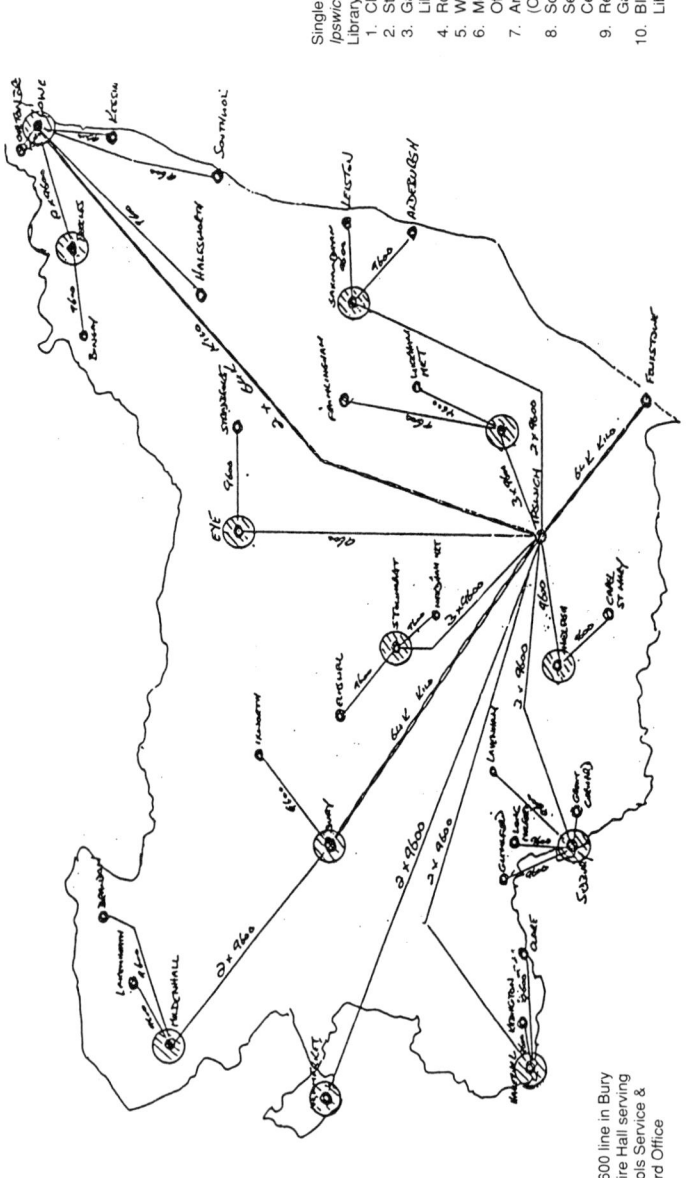

Figure 5.4 Diagram of a typical X.25 network (Reproduced with permission of Arts and Libraries Department, Suffolk County Council)

protocol caused many difficulties for terminals using more common communication environments. A new development is the introduction of the Geogate 8240 Series of communications processors to provide gateway functionality between the Geac 8000 or 9000 and the LAN or WAN. The Geogate series currently enables Geac systems to interwork with TCP/IP and IBM SNA networks, which can be linking resources within a building, or right across a country.

Geogate is a front end communications processor which interfaces VMEbus hardware and UNIX communications software to Geac applications. As it currently stands, the link to a TCP/IP network allows for access *to* all other systems on the network from Geac terminals, and *from* all terminals on the network to the Geac system. The link to IBM SNA networks only allows Geac to terminals out; the Geac system remains isolated from terminals attached to other systems.

A document issued by Geac describing this product says that the library functions accessible to users from other systems are: On-Line Public Access Catalogue; Acquisitions; Circulation; Cataloguing; and Geac 9000/8000 system administration via KQ access. There is no mention of Community Information, but since in reality the connection is made to the Geac system main menu, and the system administrator decides which packages to make available on the menu for each terminal, it is clear that Community Information will also be accessible. Its oversight from the document is one example amongst many of the woefully low profile the Community Information module has within the company, which in view of its value, particularly across networks linking many different users, is perplexing in the extreme.

Geogate communicates with the Geac host via one or more high-speed X.25 lines, and to the network via hardware and software appropriate to the network technology. For TCP/IP connectivity, Geogate is attached directly to an Ethernet LAN. For IBM SNA connectivity, Geogate is attached to a 3270 link. All the performance and functionality provided to users of X3.28 terminals directly connected to the Geac is provided to users on the TCP/IP network, although these applications and functions are controlled via access privileges in the normal way.

The new replacement for the NIM 8212 and 8215 controllers, called the Terminal Control Server, will have as one of its applications a LAN controller. The TCS, running on a PC, will be capable of running terminals using X3.28, X.25, or VT220

55

as well as controlling a LAN. At present, the VT220 option will not be possible across a network.

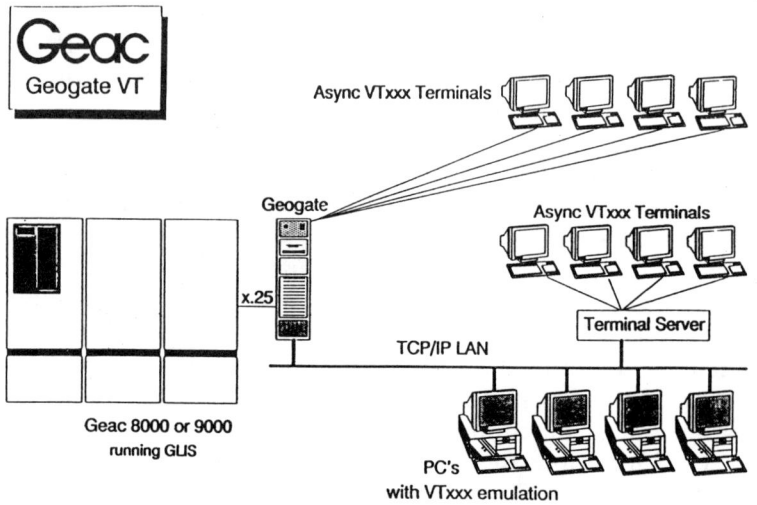

Figure 5.5   Connection to TCP/IP LAN via Geogate (Reproduced with permission of Geac Computers Ltd)

Geac have recently converted the network at Linkoping University in Sweden to run using the Novell network operating system software. The library previously had a Geac 8000 connected to a diversity of university computers and PCs using Ethernet cabling. The introduction of the Novell LAN resulted in fewer physical connections being required to link the hundreds of PCs on the campus. The PCs run Geac terminal emulation software and are split between cataloguing and public enquiry functions, with the Novell network running a dynamic allocation of sessions. This connects the terminal to the host at the first available point, when a session becomes free.

Geac also adapted the system to enable the PCs to support full Swedish character sets and bar code readers. PCs on the network are used in all library functions, as well as for word processing, electronic mail and desk-top publishing.

In Essex County, a Token-Ring LAN in the headquarters building allows PCs to link into the Geac host.

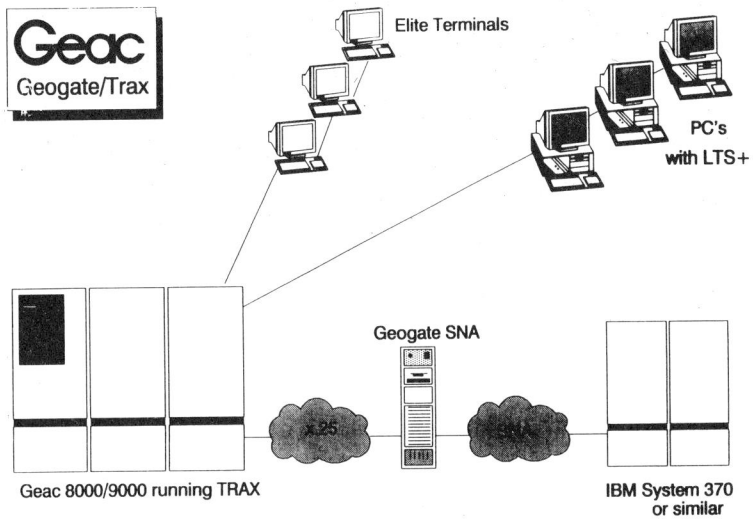

Figure 5.6 Connection to SNA hosts via TRAX and Geogate (Reproduced with permission of Geac Computers Ltd)

Open systems interconnection

It is impossible to discuss modern day telecommunications and networking considerations without referring to the extremely complicated, but equally exciting, area of OSI. Considerable work is being done by the International Standards Organisation (ISO) and the International Telegraph and Telephone Consultative Committee (CCITT), to develop standards for Open Systems Interconnection. The objectives of OSI standards are to provide solutions to the problems associated with the interconnection of information processing systems from different manufacturers, under different managements, of different levels of complexity, and of different technologies. Geac have long made claims to be committed to OSI, but recently, as standards in the upper layers of the OSI model have begun to emerge, significant progress appears to be under way towards making some of the dreams reality.

Geac has its own OSI group, which has done a considerable amount of work, and written a development strategy. OSI is an extremely complex area, well beyond the scope of this

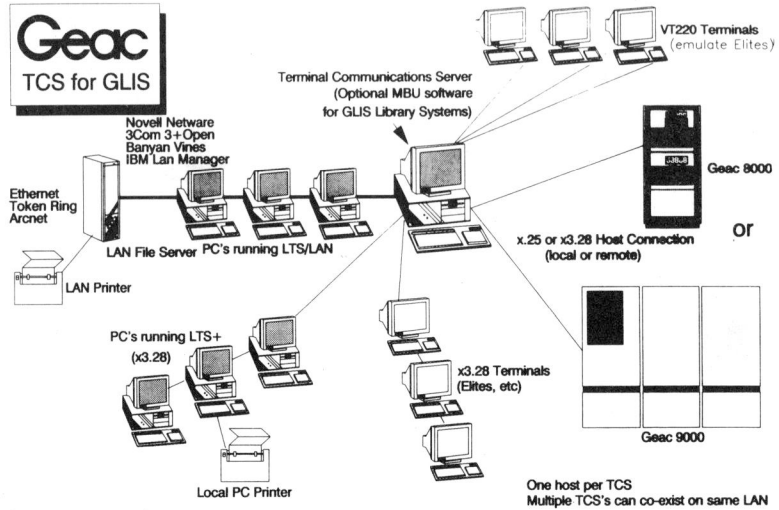

Figure 5.7   Possible uses for a Terminal Control Server (Reproduced with permission of Geac Computers Ltd)

book, but a brief account of Geac's ambitions in this area may be appropriate here.

The Geac OSI Project has been established to develop OSI products for libraries, with the intention of getting closer to Geac's Visionary View of the Library Community. In this view, in a cooperative community of libraries, a library user at any particular site will be able to access the resources of all the libraries within the community, regardless of the location of the individual libraries, or the type of information processing system in use.

Geac's OSI products are intended to provide for the following requirements from the library community:

Remote bibliographic search and retrieval for cataloguing;
Remote searching of online catalogues;
Electronic Mail;
Inter Library Loan;
Support of Acquisitions;
Support of distributed circulation,
e.g. reciprocal borrowing:

- *authenticate borrower,*
- *determine borrower status,*
- *determine borrower privileges.*

In order to satisfy these requirements, Geac have selected the following set of protocol standards from the very large number of 'standard' OSI protocols available:

- The OSI Directory standards.
- *CCITT X.500 series of Recommendations/ISO International Standard 9594; parts 1 through 7;*
- The OSI Message Handling System standards *CCITT X.400 series of Recommendations/ISO International Standard 10021; parts 1 through 8;*
- The OSI Inter-Library Loan standards, *Currently at the ISO draft proposal stage: ISO DP 10060 and ISO DP 10061.*

It is also expected that other OSI standards will be included as required, such as:

- Remote Database Access (RDA);
- Bibliographic Search and Retrieval (SR);
- File Transfer, Access and Management (FTAM);
- OSI Network Management.

In order to provide products to suit the diverse environment of different types of system, network architecture, size, etc., Geac has developed its *OSI Platform*, which will provide a common operating platform for all Geac OSI products. This platform consists of Hardware (a Motorola Delta series model 3208 system), UNIX operating system, supporting communications modules (e.g. X.25, TCP/IP), the OSI Communications module, and the OSI Development module.

Geac have several OSI products under development:

Library Directory products will allow users to find and retrieve 'information of interest' (i.e. not necessarily restricted to bibliographic information) distributed among many individual libraries in a library community. The entire concept of Directories in the OSI context is a complicated one, but in essence the Directory will allow the user to perform a search (for instance) once, but actually searching many different systems, and being presented with the results of that search from all the systems at once, in a consistent manner. The Directory does not hold all the information, but through the use of addresses 'knows' where to find it. In many ways the development of the Directory is essential to the success of OSI.

OSI Electronic Mail products, which will be based on the OSI Message Handling System, offering services to allow users to exchange messages on a store and forward basis between different Electronic Mail systems, regardless of the type of equipment used.

Inter Library Loan (ILL) products, which will be based on the OSI ILL standards. The ILL module will provide the basic requester/responder communication defined in the draft proposals, allowing the automation of many ILL activities, such as requesting the loan of an item, renewing or recalling a loan, and tracking of outstanding loans. Complementary use of the ILL module and the Library Directory will allow for parallel searching of libraries, and determining whether the desired item is available at those libraries which have copies.

Much research has been done, and valuable knowledge gained at Geac, but as yet no commercial applications have resulted, largely due to the high cost involved, for Geac and their customers, in developing 'real-life' OSI projects.

Modems and line drivers

In the UK Geac use modems and line drivers supplied by Micom Borer, GPT and others depending on circumstances, though sites are at liberty to select and install their own (e.g. by purchase from British Telecom). The author would, however, recommend that libraries give careful consideration to obtaining the complete installation from the one supplier to avoid the possibility of being caught in an argument between the two should there be a telecommunications problem.

In earlier times these modems were a source of considerable trouble, but since new models have been brought into use complaints have become rare. (Geac did in fact arrange for the complete replacement of all the modems at several sites; it is this that leads the author to his recommendation.)

The modems are usually operated at line speeds varying from 2400 to 9600 baud. It is usual to house them in a cabinet, supplied as part of the system centre, each being contained within a plastic casing. It is possible to opt, instead, for 'nested' or 'racked' modems, which have their casing removed and the all-important internal board slotted into racks within the modem cabinet. This has the advantage of greatly increasing the capacity of the cabinet; an attractive configuration for those sites which require a large number of modems within a limited space as modem racks are fairly bulky pieces of equipment. There are also advantages in ease of maintenance.

At both the system centre and at the remote site, the modems are connected to the telecommunications line and should be no more than five metres from the end of the line. The first terminal must then be within 25 metres and other terminals on the line must then be within 75 metres of each other. Recommended wiring is copper sheathed and Geac generally only agree to provide sufficient for the initial installation, occasionally restricting the contract to only a limited length of cabling per terminal.

Line drivers can be substituted for modems in certain circumstances, when the distance to a remote site is limited to less than two miles and the telecommunications line passes through only one local exchange. They have the advantage of a lower price, but in all other respects can be considered as being the same as modems, transmitting at 9600 baud. They are equally reliable.

One final word on telecommunications should be said about the links to mobile libraries. In the UK the only mobile libraries operating as part of a Geac system are those using a portable unit which collects data for subsequent batch downloading to the c.p.u. In North America things are different, and several sites operate booktrailers using modems on multi-drop networks (as at Regina). More interesting is the investigation being undertaken by Mississauga into the use of short-wave radio transmission to provide not only circulation but the online catalogue to their bookmobile. The London Borough of Camden in the UK has experimented with linking a normal library terminal via a modem to a Cellular Telephone network, and has established the fact that it is technically feasible. Costs of such an online link are likely to be prohibitive, however.

Other methods of communication

Many methods of connecting terminals to c.p.u.s have become available in recent years, often doing away with the need for modems due to the increasing use of digital circuitry.

Many sites now use high speed links using Kilostream or Megastream telephone circuits. Depending on the speed required, several channels can use one line.

The London Borough of Enfield have linked their Geac terminals into the Local Authority's digital telephone exchange, and they are doubtless not unique. Doncaster Metropolitan Borough, also in the UK, have been able to take advantage of improvements in modem design to utilize two wire leased line circuits, which are considerably cheaper than the four wire circuits essential hitherto.

Section 3   The software

6 Introduction to the software

Geac's library system developed in a piecemeal way commencing with the creation of a Circulation system. Having created a system which, of necessity, had to hold a form of library catalogue it was a logical step to introduce public query facilities. In this way Geac entered the tortuous field of cataloguing with its considerable complications for data processing.

An examination of the market-place led to the conclusion that the company's background suited it to the task of developing a Cataloguing package which would meet the detailed requirements of the library world. In particular the package had to be to MARC standard. The resulting software, the online public access module (known by Geac as the OPC), can be considered in two parts: the data input software and the public access software. Input is via the Bibliographic Processing System (BPS) which can either take MARC standard data from other computer files or direct input from a terminal. The public access elements control the eventual availability of the data to public query terminals.

The third of the major packages was the Acquisitions module which was created in the early 1980s as a direct response to customer requirements for a totally integrated system. The module includes subsystems for the control of serials, receipting of consignments, invoicing and the generation of cheques.

The latest of the major packages is that for Community Information. Unlike its predecessors, this package has not been developed in Canada, but in the UK. This reflects the British library world's concern to move in to the field of community information and the desire for economy (the package does not require additional terminal hardware, unlike comparable viewdata systems). The first version was called Local Information, and was originally conceived for use by Somerset County Libraries. It was subsequently subject to modifications suggested by a working party comprising several British public library customers. It first appeared for public use in Hillingdon in November 1985 but has been superseded by Community Information, which first went live in the London Borough of Sutton. This new package is still subject to revisions to meet the requirements of the Community Information working party, a subgroup of the Users' Group.

In addition to the software designed specifically for libraries, Geac markets an office automation package called GOAST (Geac Office Automation Support Tool) which is increasingly being adopted by library networks in North America but has yet to be seen in libraries in the UK. GOAST incorporates many of the standard Geac facilities such as the inclusion of both menus and direct commands, help screens and password protection. Its main facilities are electronic mail and messaging, executive support such as a time planning subsystem, a spreadsheet, records processing, text processing and spelling verification. The package is bilingual (English and French).

Also available is Geac Electronic Mail (GEM), which is used by several UK sites, including the London Borough of Hillingdon, as a stand-alone electronic mail service. As outlined in the previous chapter, developments with OSI no doubt mean that GEM need not always be completely stand-alone, but could be interfaced with other electronic mail services.

A detailed description of the facilities of each of the four major library packages is given in Chapters 7 to 11; but before they can be considered, it is necessary to have an understanding of how they operate within the c.p.u.

Setting up the system

One of the most important stages in the development of a Geac library system is its initial setting up. Numerous decisions have to be made which will affect the future policy of the library and, although most are reversible, it is obvious that, as far as possible, they should be right the first time. It follows, therefore, that a most important task for the library manager is the correct setting up of the system. This is not work which can be done in a hurry; it requires a working environment that allows for careful thought, and the opportunity to consult with colleagues.

The work begins with the arrival of a large document from Geac. It is known as the 'Policy Parameters', and like so much else with the system, quickly assumes considerable significance. The document is, in effect, a large questionnaire, and it gives

Geac's software staff the information they need to tailor the packages to the individual needs of the client. It follows that it helps if the implications of the answers are clear to the systems manager at the time of making the decisions, but it is fair to say that, in the past at least, the accompanying documentation has not always made things crystal clear. Indeed, they have not always been clear to the programmers, which is a rather more serious problem. It will often transpire that the reason for an apparent failing in the system can be tracked down to the way the policy parameters were set up in the early days. This is not infrequently discovered by the systems manager in the light of experience.

What do these policy parameters do? In short, they determine the way the packages work – by assigning agencies, book locations, and terminal numbers. In addition they set the permitted functions for each terminal. In setting them up one is actually setting up the matrices from which the CRT tables used by the Communications Operating System are compiled.

As already mentioned, such factors as library closed days, fines rules and privileges for different categories are set. The stages at which patron privileges are suspended are determined, as are the default values for membership expiry periods. Loan periods, which may vary according to the patron type have to be selected as do the numbers of items which each category of patron may have on loan at any one time. This can vary for different material types for different patron privileges, and indeed can vary according to which agency the items are borrowed from.

It is in the process of setting up the policy parameters that an understanding of the way in which the system works is built up. It is possible, and in some sites it has been decided that it is sensible, for each location (e.g. branch library) to be a separate agency. It is equally possible to treat the entire network as a single agency. Within an agency one may have a number of terminal groups, but it is possible to designate each branch library as both a separate agency and a terminal group and to run each on its own port. Equally one can have more than one agency, or terminal group, associated with a single port.

A large library can have several terminal groups, for adult, junior, reference and music stock or some other such division. This has the effect of producing shipping messages should an item be returned to a terminal in another department, and giving extra details on the precise whereabouts of the item when it is in transit from one department to another, invaluable in a large departmentalized institution. After assigning an agency and a terminal group, one then assigns book locations. It is possible to have several locations per terminal group or to restrict it to one. Book locations are used to refine the location of items, such as adult fiction, junior fiction, paperback collection, etc., within a library, so making the retrieval of items from the shelves easier. Used in conjunction with the report program LPEXTR, precise figures about a library's stock can be obtained.

Having assigned agencies, terminal groups and book locations, the next task is to assign terminals to them. Each terminal is given a unique number, and then its 'terminal bit permissions' are set. This involves entering a 'Y' or an 'N' in response to certain questions relating to the various functions. This table is consulted by the system constantly, and through it one may achieve considerable flexibility. Should one wish, it is possible, for instance, to restrict access to the financial screens to terminals on an enquiry desk, or to allow some terminals to discharge but not to issue. Public terminals can be restricted to the Public Query module, if desired, so making it impossible for the public to obtain access to the staff functions.

On the 8000 system it was only possible to examine how each terminal had been set up by running the program for building the tables, and laboriously ploughing through a number of screens until the screen containing information about the relevant terminal was reached. (It was an unwritten law that terminals early in the list never needed attention; only those at the end!) The 9000 has a utility called USYS which shows the bit permissions for any nominated terminal, along with information about which terminal group and agency the terminal belongs to. The table builder program itself allows the system manager to go straight to the appropriate terminal to carry out amendments to its permissions, which, when one considers the large number of terminals supported by a 9000 family system, is just as well.

Another useful improvement with the 9000 family's table handling capabilities is that the table builder program (LPTABB) is now accessible as a choice from the TCP menu, rather than the system operators having to bring it up on a single terminal.

Incidentally, terminals are assigned to their port not through the policy parameters, but through a program run on the system called SPCNFG. Through this program, the terminal is linked to a port and the third vital ingredient, its poll-code. As explained earlier, each terminal attached to a particular port has to have its own poll-code, but these can be duplicated on other ports. The system addresses the terminal through the port by its poll-code. From this, it is able to establish the terminal number and, by reference to the tables, can establish the terminal groups, book location, agency, and permitted functions.

As with the tables, checking the configuration file, **CNFG, is a somewhat laborious process on the 8000. The 9000 operating system includes another utility, UTE, which displays the contents of the file in convenient form, showing for any port the terminal numbers, poll-codes, allowed onlines for each terminal, and the online package each terminal is currently using.

Although many matters of policy are controlled by the tables, there are also many other parameters that are set up by 'Conditional Compile Options' or CCPs. The Circulation system uses a great many programs but, to avoid duplication, a large number of these can be compiled in different ways. Thus one program can have several different variables and, depending on how various questions are answered, will behave in slightly different ways. The number of compile options is very large and varied, and often some subtle aberration in the working of the system can be traced to a compile option. Unlike the tables, these have to be looked upon as more or less fixed in that they should not be recompiled without the assistance of a programmer. Even then, a change is often inconvenient as it frequently requires the entire package to be taken out of operation for a short while. It is therefore especially important to think about these options before the damage is done. They are concerned both with the way the online system works and how the programs that run overnight perform.

New releases of software

Most Geac sites have entered into a software maintenance contract which entitles them, amongst other things, to new releases of software whenever they are produced. Some sites, notably Sussex University and the University of Hull have undertaken considerable local enhancements, taking little or no support from Geac. This is however an unusual situation, and requires the willingness to devote considerable in-house programming resources to develop and maintain such a system. It is undeniable that the work done at Sussex and Hull has been most impressive, and those sites have benefitted enormously from their ability to tailor the system much more closely to their specific needs than is possible for most sites. Many developments have found their way to other users as Geac products, particularly the report generators developed at Sussex University.

New releases always include bug fixes and major enhancements to the system, recommended by existing sites or potential new clients. These enhancements then become options available to all sites which take the new release. They usually take the form of new compile options, which have to be considered just as carefully as at the initial setting up of the system.

At this time too, existing compile options can be changed, although this has to be done with great care. Options which affect the appearance of the system require especial treatment: the author has found that changing the superficial appearance of the system can have a dramatic affect on staff morale unless great care is taken to explain the changes to as many staff as possible *in advance*. Of course, it is rarely possible to explain accurately the effect of changes before the event. To overcome this problem, Hillingdon has deliberately retained the Training Circulation Package. This is usually an exact copy of the Circulation software running against a small database, and is usually provided in the early days of an installation in order to make training possible without the risk of corrupting the working database. However, if it is retained for the purpose of installing and testing new releases of software prior to using it in earnest, it presents an opportunity of demonstrating changes and retraining operators. There is, of course, a disc and processing power implication in retaining such a package. At Sussex University, where software is subject to considerable local enhancement and is constantly being modified, a similar duplicate area is maintained for development work. This is taken one stage further by the use of duplicate security files for test running of new software against full-size 'real' databases.

A new release of software is usually tested on site by one of Geac's customers, designated as the 'alpha' site. This is followed by a reworking of the package and further testing at a 'beta' site, and further modifications, before the package is put on general release to the remainder of the sites. In most cases the two test sites are different in nature, to ensure proper testing of all facilities. In the early years of their involvement with UK libraries, Geac staff found themselves constantly providing individual variations for each site in a very confusing and unrelated way. The company has since adopted the sensible policy of writing this vast mass of requirements into the software in a more logical way prior to releasing them *en masse*.

Running the system centre

An important element in the selection of a computer system for library use is the extent to which such a system requires supervision. Some users house their c.p.u. in the local authority (or university) data processing department, whilst others house it in the library, using library staff to operate it. Handing a machine over to data processing experts has obvious attractions, but keeping it in-house and having complete control also has many advantages. Despite any computer supplier's claims that one need only 'turn a key' for the system to run itself, it is clearly helpful if the system manager has some expertise and experience in the task. Indeed, it could be argued that a complex library system 'off the peg' can hardly be tailored to one's own requirements.

The Geac system can be run with a fairly minimal level of attention; although, if this is the case, it is probably not being used to the limit of its potential. The more work which is put into the system, the more results can be obtained from it. However, there is a basic minimum of attention that *must* be devoted to the system centre, and allowance has to be made for this.

Geac set great store by the necessity of ensuring the security of the database; which, in practical terms, means copying data onto tape frequently – ideally daily. Sites that have the luxury of night-time supervision can leave this task to be accomplished in those hours, but this is far from commonplace and not always practical. Alternatively, the copying could be done before the circulation system is brought up in the morning, but this ties the site to a very strict timetable. Geac's solution is to copy live files to separate security disc areas automatically, as part of the overnight procedures. The result is that during the day the system can be run normally, with the live files constantly changing, whilst the security files, representing the situation at the end of the previous day, can be copied onto tape at the library's convenience. This solution is unavoidably expensive in disc storage, and this is reflected in the price of the system to those who take up the option. It is a price that those sites which have paid it would almost certainly be unanimous in saying is worth every penny. The latest method of securing the database, as outlined elsewhere in this book, is the automatic recording overnight of the entire database onto video tape, a solution which seems particularly attractive.

As a second stage of security, the day's transactions can be automatically copied, first to disc and then to a single tape (known as a TCP tape) when the circulation system closes down at the end of the day's operations. Should a disaster occur, involving corruption of the disc files, it is therefore possible to restore the database from tape, with the loss of few, if any, transactions.

The time taken to copy on to tape obviously depends on the size of the database; in the author's own library, the circulation database requires eight tapes and the operation lasts for about two hours. Unfortunately, it is common experience that use of the tape drive appears to adversely affect response times if the system is at all busy. It is therefore a common rule amongst sites that as much as possible the security copies are made before libraries are open to their patrons.

Another chore is the printing of reports generated overnight by the system, along with any notices. This procedure does not necessarily have to be done daily, as they are dumped on to a file from which they can be printed at relative leisure, at least until the file becomes full. The frequency of printing obviously depends on the frequency with which the system is required to generate notices and reports. Many sites, including the author's own, work on the principle of 'little but often' and produce notices on most nights: others, such as Camden, have adopted the opposite technique and generate large volumes once each week. Hillingdon has adopted the former practice since the security copies are taken daily and the printing of notices can be done at the same time by the same member of staff. Indeed, it helps to relieve the tedium: there are few more boring tasks than backing up files on to tape, with only the excitement of loading a new tape to break the monotony. The point is that the amount of time spent on printing is a quantifiable factor that the library is committed to spending; how that time is apportioned is a matter that is within the library's control.

A careful check must be kept on the extent to which the many files are filling up; unlike PICK-based systems which simply appropriate disk space as required, the Geac operating system works by file sizes being set at their creation. A program called LPFCHK provides the information required, and it is then the responsibility of the system manager to scan the resulting report so that action can be taken to expand files that are getting full (or arrange to garbage redundant data from them). Release 21 of the Circulation system for the 9000 provides additional help in this respect by checking the fullness of the database as the online system comes up, and putting a message in the system log when any file has reached a predetermined percentage full – Geac recommend 95 per cent as the point at which warning should be given.

Other lesser duties that add to the volume of staff time spent in attending to the c.p.u. include tasks such as cleaning the tape drive read/write heads and changing paper in the line printer. The author's own experience is that there needs to be a regular commitment of about two hours per day. Any time in excess of that is employed in work on system alterations/enhancements or problem solving, often carried out over the telephone with the assistance of a Geac programmer. The former is under the control of the library but the latter is far from quantifiable; when a problem arises, its solution may be quick or it may involve hours of work.

Time is also spent in the challenges involved in using the statistical extract programs, which use Boolean logic to search the database. This can result in many happy hours being spent in getting sophisticated and very precise data out of the system. Having worked out a search strategy, it is sometimes practical to write it into a batch program and run it as a matter of routine. Not only is this effort rewarded by a sense of achievement when some obscure figure is finally wrenched from the system's embrace but the fact that it produces valuable management information is no mean consideration. This topic is covered in fuller detail in Chapter 12, but it is important to recognize that time spent on the system in this way is valuable in developing an understanding and confidence. The amount of time involved can be considerable though it does decline as the user learns and the use of such refinements becomes more routine.

It bears repetition that the Geac system centre can be run quite adequately with a small degree of staff input; the value of additional input is in the extent to which peripheral functions of the system can be exploited.

The use of 'SBAUTO'

Geac are able to claim that, beyond the daily routine of security tapes, the system runs itself, because of a batch program called SBAUTO. This can be described as a daily diary for the system, containing instructions for the order in which various other batch programs are run. This includes such jobs as bringing the packages up in the morning, taking them down at night, and all the overnight work such as garbaging the transaction file, notice production and index building.

Clearly, the more complex the system, the more complex will be its diary. A site running only the Circulation package will have a small and relatively uncomplicated SBAUTO: running five packages increases the complexity and the room for error.

An essential part of SBAUTO, which allows batches to run at specified times, is a program called LPTIME. This simply reads the system's internal clock every few minutes, until the time for which it is waiting arrives. At that time the system executes the next command in SBAUTO, which will typically be to bring the packages up or down.

The need to amend SBAUTO can be frequent, especially in the more complex sites. This need invariably serves as the librarian's introduction to editing, the principles of which can be employed in other batches. This is not to imply that the librarian/operator is actually programming; that must still be the province of the software specialist. Editing batches is simply a matter of inserting or moving commands. It does not require any knowledge of ZOPL, Geac's programming language; just an appreciation of the meaning of the commands and their implications, and a knowledge of how to use the Editor. This comes partly from Geac's introductory course, partly from gradually learning when carrying out instructions given over the telephone by the software support staff of the company and, beyond that, bitter experience.

Many sites now use a program called LPAUTO instead of the batch. It does much the same job, but in a somewhat updated fashion. Having said that, this author has never been accused of being fashionable, and persists in the use of SBAUTO, which has the merit of being easily understood and therefore easily amended.

Security

There are two levels of security involved in the use of Geac: protection of the software, and protection of the database. Since the programs themselves can only be accessed through KQ ports (i.e. control consoles), it follows that those ports and the operators who use them can be fairly strictly controlled. Access to the database is controlled through the use of passwords or access levels assigned to operators, and individual terminals can be restricted in the functions that can be performed on them.

It is for each library to decide how much security they wish to build into their system. A site with a secure computer room, with strictly controlled access, may well feel that the use of passwords is an unneccessary inconvenience, whilst less fortunate sites, or those with KQ terminals in less restricted areas, may wish to make the system software very secure.

Where KQ terminals are password protected, the operator must first log on to the system. If the name entered is not present in the password file the terminal is automatically signed off to minimum memory and no privilege, thus preventing any action on the operator's part. If the name is present, the password is requested. If the password is incorrectly entered, once again the terminal is signed off.

Clearly it is highly undesirable to allow unrestricted access to all of a library's database – some data may require protection because of data protection legislation, while others will require protection from unauthorized amendment. There is the curious mentality of the hacker who delights in changing records, just to show how clever they are, and systems need to exclude these people. Some libraries may also wish to strictly control which of their staff has access to all of the database.

The Circulation database can be protected by password or, as explained in Chapter 7, by bar code controlled access levels, or a combination of both. Whilst the password method can be cumbersome, it is also very flexible. The access level method is equally flexible, although its capabilities are not always so easy to appreciate at the initial setting up of a system. Its great virtue is that only the holder of a valid bar code has access to sensitive data. Use of access levels, requiring the physical wanding of a bar code does restrict the full use of the system to those people with a terminal (or terminal emulating PC) with an attached bar code reader. Whilst to some sites this is a positive security advantage, to others it is too restrictive. Terminals themselves can be restricted in the access they are permitted, either by limiting the packages which they can access or, in the case of the Circulation package, through the functions permitted in the tables, as explained in the section on policy parameters.

In setting up security, it is as well not to get too carried away with the almost limitless possibilities, but to have regard to the practical needs of the library. It is usually an advantage for all terminals to have the capability of accessing all parts of the system, and in some sites it is policy to allow all staff to have similar freedom. However, for those who wish to be more sophisticated in the control they exercise over their systems, and limit quite specific routines within functions, the security system should go a long way towards satisfying their requirements.

Inter online communications

Before considering each of the major applications packages, a word must be said about the Inter Online Communications package (IOC). This package has the task of linking all the others together. Through it, it is possible for the OPAC to view part of the Circulation database and for an operator using the Acquisitions package to load data from Circulation files or the Bibliographic Processing System (BPS). It is essential to any site that wishes to integrate the separate packages, though it is not needed by those sites which operate only the Circulation package.

It is a sophisticated suite of software and its influence is all pervasive. It contains the terminal controller, which as its name implies controls the ability of terminals to switch from one package to another. This runs on a dummy port of its own.

The IOC software is housed within a separate area of its own, which the operator has to access before the package can be manipulated. The ability of the terminals to change from package to package is determined by a program called SPCNFG, which uses the configuration file for the particular 8000 or 9000 machine. SPCNFG is used to assign a terminal to its port and assign its poll-code, baud rate and parity. If a terminal is not listed in the configuration file it will not be polled by the system and so will be inoperative. In addition to assigning the parameters of the terminals, it is also necessary to determine which of the packages will be available to the terminal. This allows for great flexibility in the way terminals can be used: a terminal in a public area might be permitted access to only the catalogue, or Community Information, or both, whilst a staff terminal might be restricted to Circulation or Acquisitions. When used in conjunction with the terminal bit permissions in the Circulation tables, very considerable flexibility is possible.

The configuration file is also used to determine which package the terminal first uses when the packages are brought up at the start of the day. In Hillingdon nearly all terminals are configured to come up in the Terminal Control Program (see Figure 6.1), to which it is hoped that all packages will eventually time out. The benefits of this for public terminals are clear; the TCP screen serves as the first menu of the entire system, and it is only from here that the full choice of packages is visible. The author has found that it is also valuable to have the staff terminals start on this screen as it gives staff an opportunity to look at packages such as Electronic Mail, which they would not normally see as these terminals tend to be linked to the Circulation system for most of the day.

Figure 6.1 Terminal Control Program main menu (staff terminal version)

Amendments to the configuration file are very easily made, using SPCNFG, and take effect immediately the file is reloaded into memory. Thus, unlike changes to the tables, changes to the configuration are almost instant. It is possible to add terminals, delete them, add or delete them temporarily, or modify them without difficulty. The mnemonics by which the packages are known are also kept on the configuration file, and these too can be easily changed. Hillingdon's OPAC was at one time accessible only by typing the code 'CAT', but this was subsequently changed to '2', being the second choice on the TCP menu. Likewise, the packages' names can be altered, within a limit of 15 characters, so in Hillingdon the Circulation package is accessed under the name 'Your Details', this being what the public use it for, the staff being aware of the true nature. Although the change of names is easy, restraint has to be exercised to avoid confusing staff and public alike!

7 The Circulation package

Introduction

Circulation is the oldest and best developed of all the packages offered by Geac, having begun life in 1977 in the Universities of Guelph and Waterloo. Since that date it has been subject to continuous updates and has been revised to allow for working practices in a variety of libraries, both public and academic, on both sides of the Atlantic. The package is now highly complex and each new release of sofware requires recipients to indicate their policy through a multitude of compile options; the package thereby remaining exactly the same for each site but operating in remarkably different ways. In the first edition of this book a very full description of the software release 10.2, running on 8000 machines, was offered. Since then, the software has been amended to some degree with release 10.3 in the UK, and 11.5 in North America, but beyond that developments for circulation on the 8000 appear to have ceased. It should be the job of a work such as this to describe the latest software which is release 21, running only on 9000 series machines. Whilst due to the different architecture of the c.p.u. much has changed in the way the software works inside the machine, to the user much remains the same. Rather than attempt a full description of the many functions available in Circulation here, a somewhat briefer examination of the software follows. Those readers wishing to learn more about the detail of individual commands are referred to the first edition.

The description given below uses terminology and phraseology which follows Geac's own standard use. However, the package is multi-lingual in the sense that each user site can provide its own terminology if desired (in English or any other language). These terms then totally replace the base text which the system would normally display. This is usually achieved by the use of a program called LPLANG, and in the UK one of the main exponents of this technique is the London Borough of Camden. A large number of modifications to the wording on screens in the Circulation have been made in Camden, providing a much more locally attractive system. The drawback of this approach is that care has to be taken that new releases of software do not cause a reversion to 'standard Geac' wording. The Screen Manager facilty for the 9000 family will in time supersede this facility, and it is to be hoped make the local tailoring of the system's appearance much easier to achieve.

This chapter describes the 18 main functions and subsystems which the author considers to be of most general application or worthy of comment by virtue of their potential. It is not possible to include descriptions of all the features of the package, as it is now so vast. The systems and their command codes are:

Patron (or user) query	PAT
Bibliographical query	QRY
Public query	PUB
Issue function	ISS
Discharge function	DIS
Renewal function	REN
Fines subsystem	FIN
Overdue recovery subsystem	Not an online function
Holds subsystem	HLD
Message transmission	MSG
Reserve room operations	RES and RRP
Materials booking	MBK
Archival issue records	CHK
Inter-library loans subsystem	ILL
Bindery management subsystem	BND
Cash management subsystem	CSH
Help subsystem	HLP
Library maintenance routines	LIB

The more important functions are represented on the main circulation system menu (see Figure 7.1) and are usually accessed by their three character command code, either from this menu or from any of the other elements. Some functions cannot be accessed from certain others (e.g. the holds subsystem, which can only be accessed from either the bibliographical system or the Public Query module). Many of these commands are represented on standard terminals by a function key, the others can be allocated to function keys by the use of the program LPLANG, which will allow both commands and subcommands to be

```
109 ONLINE CIRCULATION SYSTEM 21-02-91
LOCATION: ADMIN/ADMIN  TIME: 17:26
FUNCTION: TERMINAL MODE SELECTION


ISS   ISSUE              DIS   DISCHARGE
REN   RENEWALS           FIN   FINE PAYMENT
QRY   BOOK QUERY         USR   USER QUERY
RES   RESERVE QUERY      LIB   LIBRARY MAINT
PUB   PUBLIC QUERY       MSG   MESSAGES



SELECT:
```

Figure 7.1   Circulation package main menu

assigned and permits the use of the shift key to double the effective number of function keys. A further standard function key, XXX, represents the abort command for certain operations and returns the display to the main circulation menu on completion of a transaction.

It is possible to give each individual terminal access to various elements of the module or to deny access. It is also possible to control the use of these elements by individual members of staff through bar code registration so that even where a terminal can access a function, the password level of the staff member will deny it. In some cases the system provides warnings which can be over-ridden by those with a high password level but which prevent action by those whose password level is below a set limit.

Release 21 of the Circulation module, for the 9000, set a number of landmarks in terms of the increased performance and functionality it achieved. Throughout this chapter those features of Release 21 most worthy of description will be mentioned, but a small summary of them would seem appropriate here.

The main feature of the Release is the optional use of multi-threaded operation, to achieve a greatly enhanced transaction processing rate. It is possible to have Release 21 operating in the conventional way with a single interpreter called ZQHUGC which handles all the activities of the online system in a perfectly satisfactory manner and gaining from some of the benefits of the more powerful 9000 architecture. The higher throughput requirements of some of the larger sites, such as Essex and Lancashire Counties have been addressed by having more than one copy of ZQHUGC running at the same time. Having multiple copies of the job means that the message queue can be serviced more quickly, rather as in a bank several cashiers deal with a queue.

In addition to fast online processing, multi-threaded mode allows for very fast recovery after failures, something that users of single-threaded circulation will appreciate the need for. In Suffolk County Library System a recovery that would have previously taken four or five hours to complete was recently performed in under an hour. A new file for the day's transactions, called **RCV1, is used for fast recovery, and as an added refinement a utility exists to allow the system manager to monitor how full that file is. Should it accumulate so many transactions that it is becoming critically full, a warning message will be broadcast to the system control console.

The system also carries out integrity checks on the database when the system is first started up, and if necessary wherever possible the system will endeavour to synchronize the database before permitting terminals to access and modify the database. This automatic recovery will typically take place when a hardware failure has caused the machine to be handed to the engineers, serviced and rebooted, and would previously have probably taken several hours of recovery before the online system was operational again. After some initial teething troubles, multi-threaded circulation has proved very successful.

Release 21 allows for an increased capacity in several respects. It is now possible for up to 999 terminals or devices to access the system; the limit was previously 255. Extra terminals inevitably mean extra workload, so at very high terminal levels the use of multi-threaded mode is likely. Two hundred and fifty-five was also the previous limit to the number of copies linked to a single title; this has now also been increased to 999.

One of the most welcome features of the latest software is the ability to place holds against titles for which there are as yet no copies; i.e. usually titles on order and attracting waiting lists, as happens all too often with bestsellers in British public libraries. This was a failing in the system about which users have complained long and hard, and its resolution should make life for library staff considerably easier.

Patron query

The Circulation package contains a database which holds details of patrons and which is linked to other files related to them (e.g. loan records, financial transactions). The database consists of fields for

- name (up to 39 characters)
- title (up to 8 characters)
- privilege status
- statistical class
- library, residency or departmental code
- agency where enrolment has taken place
- two separate addresses (each in two lines with a maximum length of 66 and 39 characters respectively)
- two postcodes (zip codes)
- mail code
- home telephone number (up to 15 characters)
- business telephone number (up to 12 characters) plus extension (4 characters)
- expiry date
- date of birth
- notes (maximum 1500 characters but only 147 are displayed in the normal display format).

There are three further fields for date of registration, date of last use of the system and status. These are set (and in the latter two cases constantly reset) by the system.

There are also up to a maximum of six optional fields available to the library, each of which can handle up to 999 classes of data. These have been used in different ways by different sites for such things as:

- natural (or preferred) language
- school
- area of residence
- year of intake
- course code
- sex
- ethnic origin
- subscriptions.

The site itself must choose how many of these optional classes it wishes to use, for what purposes, and what codes will be acceptable. Each of these fields has a maximum of six digits and abbreviations are constantly in use. They permit detailed analysis of patron records by the report program LPPXTR, using non-standard classification.

Use of the mail code

The mail code is used to indicate which name and address should be used for overdue and other system-generated notifications. The main codes are:

0   No notices are produced
1   Notices are sent to the patron at address 1
2   Notices are sent to the patron at address 2
3   Notices are sent to a person named on the first line of address 2 using the address in address 1 (e.g. the parent or guardian of a child)
4   Notices are sent to the department, residence or library address, entered as a short code in that field, but related to a full address on the system.

It is possible to run a batch program which changes all mail codes from 1 to 2 or vice versa. This allows academic sites to re-route all notices during vacation periods but to revert to college addresses during term time. An even more subtle use of the mail code allows some records to avoid the effects of this batch. Codes 5, 6 and 7 work in exactly the same way as 1, 2 and 3 but are unchanged by the batch and therefore described as 'locked'.

Finally, it is possible to use other mail codes to sort notices prior to printing. In this way different stationery can be used or notices destined for internal distribution (e.g. to staff) can be separated from those destined for the normal postal system.

Indexing the file

The usual procedure is to index the patron file on three keys; name, bar code number and a machine-generated ID number, and to do so online for all three indexes. Since the name field contains all the elements of the name in an inverted form, there is no need to use secondary filing keys.

There are two alternative filing policies which can be adopted, word by word or letter by letter. It is also possible to arrange for surnames commencing with 'Mc' to file as though they were spelled 'Mac'.

Searching the patron files

The database can be searched online by any of the three keys: the patron identification number (search command B), the name (N) or the I.D. number (#). Any new additions or amendments to the file may be indexed online by all keys.

When undertaking a search, the system will display a range of up to ten brief entries whenever the search results in either multiple hits or fails to make a direct match. This listing of brief entries included only the name field until an enhancement in Release 10.2 allowed the option of displaying the first line of the address. This does, of course, assist greatly in checking common names in a large database (see Figure 7.2). Release 21.4 for the 9000 has included a new option, likely to be of interest to academic sites, allowing for the display of title (Mr. etc.); department (or library or residency); statistical class; privilege class and agency, rather than the first line of the address. Release 21.4 also allows the library to choose whether to display up to ten entries from the index in the event of no direct hit being made, or whether to display only two entries; the one previous to the search string, and the one following it.

```
109 ONLINE CIRCULATION SYSTEM 21-02-91   DISPLAY: full/all   ACCESS LEVEL: 3
FUNCTION: USER QUERY/UPDATE   TIME 17:29   PRESS 'HLP' FOR HELP

COMMAND:FND  SUBCOMMAND:   SEARCH TYPE:  BROWSE KEY:N  DIRECTION:+  AMT:01
SEARCH STRING: WESTLAKE, D

5 MATCHES:

  0 WESTLAKE, DAVID ANTHONY JOHN        9, FIRST AVENUE,
  1 WESTLAKE, DEBORAH ANNE              72A, VICTORIA RD
  2 WESTLAKE, DENISE JOYCE              2 DALLEGA CLOSE, DAWLEY PARADE,
  3 WESTLAKE, DUNCAN                    AUTOMATED SYSTEMS, LEVEL 5,
 >4 WESTLAKE, DUNCAN ROBERT             LEVEL 5, CENTRAL LIBRARY,

Enter choice for FND: F
              Enter 'S'  to get new search string
              Enter 'Q' to go back to command level
              Enter 'H'  for help
```

Figure 7.2   Name index from a patron search

In the event of there being no direct match, the first entry displayed is the one immediately preceding the point where the desired record would have been filed. All the displayed entries are identified by numbers and can thus be selected for further examination. Alternatively the searcher can browse forwards or backwards within the index in batches of seven entries. At this point, the display can be either the full entry or a partial one. In the latter case only the name, number, agency, privilege and statistical class fields are shown. The command FUL will result in the remainder of the entry being displayed (see Figure 7.3). The advantage of the partial display is that there is much less data to transmit than for the full display, and it is often all that is necessary. When an entry is displayed in full, all the fields, whether set by the operator or the system, are visible but details of items on loan and financial records are not.

Should there be only one direct hit on a perfect match, the system automatically displays that entry in partial or full display, whichever option has been compiled, without the need to use the index. Having selected an entry, browsing backwards or forwards in that display mode is possible, one entry at a time. However, it is not possible to move back to the index from an entry. It is possible to browse by jumping a certain number of entries each time by using the browse command in conjunction with the amount field of the command header.

```
109 ONLINE CIRCULATION SYSTEM 21-02-91   DISPLAY: full/all   ACCESS LEVEL: 3
FUNCTION: USER QUERY/UPDATE   TIME 17:31   PRESS 'HLP' FOR HELP

COMMAND:DSP  SUBCOMMAND:   SEARCH TYPE:  BROWSE KEY:N  DIRECTION:+  AMT:01
SEARCH STRING: WESTLAKE, D

NAME:          WESTLAKE, DUNCAN ROBERT              (MR.      )
STATUS:        OL NORMAL                                       BADGE: 20112 000004407
PRIVILEGE:     ADULT          STATISTICAL:  ADULT   LIBRARY  : .       AGENCY:  STF

ADDRESS1:      LEVEL 5, CENTRAL LIBRARY,
               HIGH STREET, UXBRIDGE.                POSTAL CODE: UB8 1HD
ADDRESS2:      9, IVER LANE, COWLEY,
               UXBRIDGE, MIDDLESEX.                  POSTAL CODE: UB8 2JD
MAIL CODE:     4 PHONE:                              BUS: UX 50703      EXT: 3703
REGISTRATION DATE: 09-07-84       EXPIRY DATE: 31-12-99    LAST USE: 28-12-90
BIRTH DATE:    00-00-00
NOTE:

QUALIF :  RES                    SEX    :  M         YRBRTH :  54
P.LANG:   .                      SCHOOL:  .          UNUSED :  .
```

Figure 7.3   Full display of a patron record

```
109 ONLINE CIRCULATION SYSTEM 21-02-91   DISPLAY: full/all   ACCESS LEVEL: 3
FUNCTION: USER QUERY/UPDATE   TIME 17:33   PRESS 'HLP' FOR HELP

COMMAND:DSP  SUBCOMMAND:   SEARCH TYPE:   BROWSE KEY:N   DIRECTION:+   AMT:01
SEARCH STRING: WESTLAKE, D

NAME:       WESTLAKE, DUNCAN ROBERT           (MR.        )
STATUS:     OL NORMAL                                     BADGE: 20112 000011519
PRIVILEGE:  STAFF             STATISTICAL:  ADULT   LIBRARY :  .     AGENCY:  STF

Ref   Shelf              Library      Item
Num   Location           Location     Barcode        Type   Status

 1 $a  636.708           STORE        001354577      ANF    Due      13-02-91
 2 $a  LITERATURE:82>    UXADLT       010522826      ANF    Renew    Due 26-02-91
 3 $a  LITERATURE:82>    UXADLT       007189829      ANF    Renew    Due 26-02-91
```

Figure 7.4   Brief bibliographic records within a patron record

Further details in relation to a patron can be viewed following the display of a full or partial patron record by use of other commands. CPY (usually a function key) will lead to an initial display of up to ten brief records of items on loan, items returned that day, returned items with outstanding fines and any active holds (see Figure 7.4). If there are more than ten records to display, the system automatically sets the command CON, for continue. Release 21.4 has improved the amount of information available here; it is now possible to display 24 characters of the title field for each item, rather than the classmark and item level shelfmark. CUR displays a full record of any of the above (see Figure 7.5). HDT permits display of any hold records.

After examining a patron record, use of the command FIN (usually a function key) will access the fines records of the patron; HLD permits a hold to be placed; UPD or UPD FUL allows the details to be amended; ISS (on some terminals CHG) allows an issue (or charge) transaction to be carrried out without the membership card; REN (a function key) allows renewals of all outstanding loans; NAT (non-active transaction) displays any transaction records which are no longer current but which have not yet been garbaged by the system. Thus it can be seen that once a patron record has been selected it is possible to display all relevant details and carry out various operations quite quickly.

Adding or updating patron records is done from within the patron subsystem. It is easily achieved, with the required commands usually issued by means of a suitably programmed func-

```
109 ONLINE CIRCULATION SYSTEM 21-02-91   DISPLAY: full/all   ACCESS LEVEL: 3
FUNCTION: USER QUERY/UPDATE   TIME 17:34   PRESS 'HLP' FOR HELP

COMMAND:CON  SUBCOMMAND:  SEARCH TYPE:  BROWSE KEY:N  DIRECTION:+  AMT:03
SEARCH STRING: WESTLAKE, D

NAME:        WESTLAKE, DUNCAN ROBERT              (MR.    )
STATUS:      OL NORMAL                          BADGE: 20112 000011519
PRIVILEGE:   STAFF           STATISTICAL:  ADULT    LIBRARY :  .        AGENCY:  STF

ISSUE TRANSACTION REFERENCE NUMBER:   003

ITEM:        30112 007189829         COPY NO:  1
ISSUED:      17-12-90  11:52 at TERMINAL  17 Uxbridge Library
RENEWED:     05-02-91  14:47 at TERMINAL 109 Library administration
IS DUE:      26-02-91  24:00
STATUS:      CURRENT, RENEW:  1

CLASS £:     $a 828.914
TITLE:       $a Let your mind alone!
AUTHOR:      $a Thurber $c James
IMPRINT:
SUBJECT:
```

Figure 7.5 Full bibliographic record within a patron record

tion key. (The function keys' values are set by the program LPLANG, and can be relatively easily changed.) A template is presented to the operator, with some fields such as the user privilege already displaying a value, which can be altered if required. Once all the data has been entered, the system prompts for a barcode to be wanded in, and after checking its validity, the operation is complete. The newly created patron record is immediately available for use.

Previous versions of the Geac system have never been able to handle dates beyond the end of the current century. Release 21 has at last addressed the problem of the new century; hitherto it was not possible to set a borrower expiry date beyond 31st December, 1999, but now this is possible, with some modification to the 9000 itself. The field for the expiry date remains a 2-digit year, but now if years between 28 and 99 are entered, the 20th century is assumed, as normal, whilst if 00 to 27 is entered, the assumption is that this relates to the 21st century, and the operator is warned to this effect. The date of birth field has been expanded to a 4-digit year where all four digits of the year must be entered, thus once again allowing for the registration of borrowers born before 1928.

Bibliographic query

This subsystem bears a considerable similarity to that for patron records; the screen layouts are very similar and searches and commands work in similar ways. However, the data held is more complex and there is considerably more indexing; each of the major bibliographic fields are larger than the limited sizes of those for patrons. The indexes also use secondary sorting keys. There are seven fields commonly used within the main entry but there are a large number of local variations. The seven common fields are:

- Classmark
- Author
- Title
- Subject
- ISBN
- Imprint
- Notes

A form of tagging is used within some of these fields to identify subfields which can then be subjected to independent indexing. Thus, within the title field the subtitle can be identified (by the tag $b) and given a separate entry within the title index.

There are also several additional, optional fields which can be used for statistical analysis much as in the patron system. These have been used by sites to indicate such facets as:

- Provenance of the entry
- Cataloguer
- Academic level of the text
- Language

The system itself sets other fields such as date of creation, date of latest update, location of terminal responsible for creation or update.

There are several other fields which apply, not to the bibliographic entry, but to the individual item. These include material type (one of the major parameters), price, bookseller, number of copies in a set, shelf location (or local classmark) and library code. Further optional fields are available at the copy level to aid detailed analysis of stock, or for other purposes.

The material type is used by the system for many of the

standard listings and can be used by the report program LPEXTR. It is also used by the tables to determine the loan periods, renewal periods and fines levels for items. In the Hillingdon installation over 30 different material types are in use within several agencies but in large federal systems there can be many more.

Indexing facilities

Indexes can be built online for a large range of different searches:

    Author
    Title
    Classmark
    Local Classmark (very useful in categorized libraries)
    Subject
    Author/Title combination
    ISBN/ISSN
    LC card number (or BNB number)
    Publisher
    Accession number
    Subject classification
    Subject element
    Bindery Name
    Bindery bundle number
    Geac record source number (GRSN)
    Reserve collection professor
    Reserve collection course
    Reserve collection details

Local enhancements to these indexing facilities are possible. For instance, in the London Borough of Camden the publisher index has been modified to pick up subfields from the author field, resulting in a 'People' index for biographees.

Indexing can be done online, as a batch process or by copying the entire index at the start of day and updating one version offline at the same time as the other is being used online for searching. Each version can be applicable to specified fields so that online indexing could be adopted for title and ISBN for instance, but other files could be left for overnight indexing. Each of the various options has advantages and disadvantages and each has a different requirement in terms of disc capacity and processing power. It should be noted that where indexes are updated online, it is still necessary to rebuild them and reorganize them on the disc at intervals. This is carried out overnight along with other index rebuilding work for other files. Local circumstances dictate the choice of indexing practice and there is now a considerable range of options. Having opted for one technique, it is perfectly possible to change should circumstances alter, providing the system has been adequately configured.

Whilst it would be easy to say that all indexes should be built online at all times in order to achieve the fullest advantages of an online system, this has to be tempered with the practical realities of life. The site must determine how important it is for each index to be perfectly built and what cost there might be in response times or equipment to protect those times. For instance, it is known that in public libraries where classmarks such as F, Fiction, Romance, etc. occur in thousands or even tens of thousands, any attempt to build classmark or shelf location indexes online will result in degraded responses each time an entry with one of these classmarks is added or updated. The site must therefore determine how important it is for that index to be up to date or whether an overnight rebuild will be adequate. The author chose to build overnight to prevent occasional response time 'spikes' at issue counters.

Within the actual indexes there are several other options which can be chosen. For example, each index can have a separate list of stop words which are ignored for filing should they occur as the first word or, alternatively, wherever they occur. Space rules can be applied to determine whether spaces and punctuation are made significant or ignored, thereby applying letter by letter or word by word filing policy. This policy can be applied differently to each index. Numbers can be filed in correct numerical sequence in author, title and subject indexes. Mc can be set to file as Mac in the author, title and subject indexes if it appears as the first word.

Searching the bibliographic files

The subsystem is accessed by the command QRY (a function key), which displays a command header virtually the same as for the patron system. As with the patron subsystem, the default mechanism is used to set the command to FND and can be used to select a particular search type.

The first significant difference between the two subsystems

is in the number of search types that are available. Instead of the three choices of the patron system the bibliographic system offers searching on each of the indexes listed above (each with a one-character search type code):

- Author (A)
- Title (T)
- Subject (S)
- Class mark (C)
- ISBN (#, generally, but X at Camden where LPLANG has been used to provide a local variation)
- Item i.e. individual barcode number (I)
- Local Class Mark (Shelf Location) (M), etc.

Searching works in the same way as for patrons: a single direct hit will display an entry in detail (unlike a patron search the detail presented is not quite complete as there is insufficient space within one screen, see below). As with the patron search, a multiple hit or a mismatch will display up to ten entries from the appropriate index, or if preferred, only the previous and next entries to what has been searched for. When searching the classmark index, in similar fashion to the patron subsystem where the first line of the patron's address is displayed, the author is shown for each entry. This is a considerable improvement over what went before, which was that the searcher was presented with a screenful of classmarks, probably all identical. With Release 21.4 this facility has been extended, so that it is now possible to display author after title when doing a title search; title after author when doing an author search; title after classmark in class search (unless the previous option to display author after classmark is retained); title after publisher in publisher search; and title after subject if doing a subject search. This should represent a very considerable improvement over previous releases, and brings the usefulness of the circulation system up to approaching the level of the OPC.

The initial display of an entry can be either a partial one or a full entry. Partial entries are the more normal since they comprise the class, author, title, ISBN and imprint fields (up to a preset number of characters each) plus a statement relating to the number of copies in stock and the holds which have been placed since the record was created (see Figure 7.6). This figure for holds can be misleading since inexperienced users tend to assume it relates to outstanding holds. It also ceases to be

```
109 ONLINE CIRCULATION SYSTEM 21-02-91   DISPLAY: part/all   ACCESS LEVEL: 3
FUNCTION: BIBLIOGRAPHIC QUERY/UPDATE   TIME 17:36   PRESS 'HLP' FOR HELP

COMMAND:DSP   SUBCOMMAND:   SEARCH TYPE:   BROWSE KEY:T   DIRECTION:+   AMT:01
SEARCH STRING: GEAC

CLASS:     $a 022.9
AUTHOR:    $a Westlake $c Duncan R. £a Clarke £c John E.
TITLE:     $a Geac $b a guide for librarians and systems managers

ISBN/ISSN: $d 0566052156
IMPRINT:   $a Gower $b 1987
NOTE:

COPIES:  5      HOLDS:  14
STATUS:  *OL*
```

Figure 7.6   Partial display of a bibliographic record in Circulation

effective after 255 holds as the count then no longer increases due to the limitation of space within that part of the file. However, the hold counts on the entire file can be analysed and titles with high counts printed out. The counts can then be reset to zero; thus it can be used to give, for example, an annual picture of titles in demand.

Having accessed a record, further commands can be issued, often by way of a function key to see information about copies of that title, such as where it is located, what its material type is, whether it is in the library or if on loan when it is due back, who it is on loan to, where and when the transaction took place, what holds are outstanding against each item, and so on.

Several system-derived fields are maintained. Cumulating counts of the number of times an item has been issued or discharged (reshelved), though of only passing interest to someone searching the database via a terminal, are extremely useful when allied to the system's powerful report program generator. This allows statistics or listings to be produced on items which have issued for more or less than a specified number of times. The report program generator can also produce stock-taking lists by searching the last activity field. The reshelve count makes it possible to keep records of use of reference material, provided that users are requested not to reshelve items themselves but to allow staff to do so, having first 'discharged' them.

Adding or updating a bibliographic record

As described in Chapter 9, there is an entire cataloguing package which can be used to add MARC standard records by direct keyboarding or by data transfer from external sources. Many records are also created in the Acquisitions system and transferred into Circulation, as described in Chapter 10. Within the circulation package it is also possible to add new records to the file. The system displays a template for completion by the operator. Certain fields can be made mandatory or the contents subjected to limitations of format. Checks on the validity of ISBNs are made on completion of the template, and on the validity of bar codes assigned to items on completion of the addition of a copy.

On completion of the template, the system then prompts the operator to add a copy, at which point data relating to that item as a unique entity is created, such as its bar code number, its location, material type, price, etc. It is possible to have a field to hold details of that item's own copy specific classmark, called the Shelf Location. This is of particular value in libraries whose stock is categorized, allowing the bibliographic record to have a standard classification number, but copies to have their own local identities (see Figure 7.7). Although the system prompts

```
109 ONLINE CIRCULATION SYSTEM 21-02-91   DISPLAY: part/all   ACCESS LEVEL: 3
FUNCTION: BIBLIOGRAPHIC QUERY/UPDATE   TIME 17:37   PRESS 'HLP' FOR HELP

COMMAND:DSP  SUBCOMMAND:   SEARCH TYPE:  BROWSE KEY:T  DIRECTION:+  AMT:01
SEARCH STRING: HOW TO MAKE A WIDELIFE GARDEN

CLASS:    $a 719
AUTHOR:   $a Baines $c Chris
TITLE:    $a How to make a wildlife garden

ISBN/ISSN: $d 0241114489 $a 0241118700
```

Ref Num	Shelf Location	Library Location	Item Bar code	Mat Type	Status	
1 $a	PLANT LIFE:719	MFADLT	003124218	ANF	Ret 19-02-91	
2 $a	PLANT LIFE:719	UXADLT	003129423	ANF	Due 08-03-91	
3 $a	PLANT LIFE:719	OGADLT	005916033	ANF	In Library	
4 $a	719	SRADLT	006383001	ANF	In Library	
5 $a	PLANT LIFE:63>	UXADLT	006015967	ANF	Due 14-03-91	Renew
6 $a	PLANT LIFE:63>	HDADLT	006395260	ANF	Due 05-03-91	

Figure 7.7 Brief copy display of a bibliographic record in Circulation

for a copy at this point, it is not mandatory to add one, and copies can be added to bibliographic records at any time. Many sites not using the Acquisitions package add the catalogue record at the time of placing an order, only adding the copy some time later, when the item finally arrives. With the advent of Release 21 of the Circulation software, the maximum number of copies that can be linked to a single bibliographic record has risen from 255 to 999.

A new feature with Release 21 is the capability to add blocks of item records to the system, rather than laboriously have to re-key duplicate data for many copies on the one bibliographic record. The command (ADD BLK) allows an initial item to be created with the associated item level details, and then any number of item bar codes may be wanded to allow the creation of multiple items all having the same details. In the likely event of adding numerous copies, for several branches, it is optionally possible to amend the location code and material type for each copy, but without having to re-key everything.

Updating a bibliographic record is similar to adding one, but there is also a facility which allows for the updating of a single field rather than the entire entry. This technique has the advantage of speed as a lesser volume of data is transferred to the terminal and back again and the unchanged fields are not subjected to verification procedures.

Copy details can be updated either by effectively updating all fields, or through library maintenance changing just the location or material type. Copies can also be marked missing, under a variety of different 'categories', such as 'Reported lost by borrower' or 'failed Shelf Check'. Should the item reappear, the missing status will be automatically removed when its bar code is wanded.

Bibliographic records can be removed from the database in a variety of ways. Individual copies can be 'Deleted', with the possibility of later reinstating them, or completely 'Erased'. Deletion is possible even when there are transactions still linked to the item, whereas to erase a copy it must be free from any transactions, and located to the agency where the erasing is being done. A program called LPITER can be run to convert deleted items without transactions into erased ones. In the London Borough of Camden this has been modified to permit the selective erasure of ancient items which have not been issued for a long time, even though they have not been deleted. Release 21.4 allows for the removal of an item record from one bibliographic record, which can then be added to a different bibliographic record without having to re-key such data as material type, location etc.

The full bibliographic record can also be deleted, which will remove it from the Public Query side of the system, but it will still exist and be accessible on the staff side. Full bibliographic records are completely removed by another garbage program, which will only remove records to which there are no copies linked. Other criteria for keeping the record, such as how recently it was added to the database, can also be specified.

The Public Query module

Once an online database has been created for staff use, it can be made available for public use with relative ease. Geac saw the advantage of this from the outset and made available an online catalogue using the data contained within the bibliographic subsystem. In the same way, the data from the patron database was also made available with the added check that each patron could only view their own entry. For this purpose the bar code becomes a physical password which cannot usually be input by keyboard but only via the light pen, a very sensible arrangement in the light of legislation on data protection.

Like all elements of the Circulation package, Public Query can be permitted or denied to each individual terminal. It is therefore possible to offer it as one choice among many on those terminals assigned for staff use, or to make it the only choice available to those terminals assigned exclusively to public use. Alternatively, it is possible to arrange that Public Query is apparently the only function which is available but to permit access to the other functions by use of a password, usually a bar code. This latter mechanism gives all the security necessary, yet makes it possible to use public terminals for staff activities in the event of such a need arising.

Searching the Public Query module

The Public Query module is menu driven for ease of use. There is an initial simple menu which offers the choices of searching the bibliographic file (i.e. the catalogue) or the patron file. It is also possible to display a separate News Screen using a free format editor file which is available as another menu choice.

This option is discussed more fully in Chapter 11. Selection of any service requires a single numeric key to be depressed, followed by the SEND key. It is possible, as an alternative, to assign function keys to each selection choice. Each subsystem has its own menu which can offer simple instructions and a further set of choices.

A catalogue search

Like staff access to the bibliographic files, searches can only be undertaken on a limited number of keys, usually author, title, author/title combined, class, subject and ISBN, though it is possible to have local variations using any of the other indexes listed in the previous section. Release 21 has seen the introduction of extra indexes for author, title, and subject keywords. In conjunction with the ability for the site to have much more control over the appearance of screen displays through SMAN, this should remove many of the objections to Public Query when comparing it to the full OPC. Full MARC records, and the ability to carry out Boolean search operations will not, however, be possible in Public Query, so the OPC module is not made obsolete by these improvements. The Public Query module is an immediate improvement on traditional catalogues because it is kept completely up-to-date with stock holdings and shows the loan status of each item.

For each search the system displays the nearest matches, regardless of whether there is a direct hit or not. The nearest match or direct hit, if one exists, is displayed as the third of five brief entries containing author, title and class. Alternatively, it is now possible to have the nearest match displayed at the top of the screen. A choice of actions is then available; these are listed in a menu at the foot of the screen. This offers such choices as browsing in either direction, returning to the main menu or selecting one of the five brief entries for fuller display.

The fuller display carries most of the data input by the cataloguer and is easily sufficient to identify the majority of books. At this stage it is possible to select more detail relating to the copies of the book. The brief entry details are then displayed at the top of the screen and the standard one-line entries, showing bar code number, location and loan status are displayed below. Up to a maximum of 13 copies can be displayed on one screen. Unlike the staff query facility, the loan status does not carry any references to holds; missing items are indicated but not subdivided by reason; items in transit are shown only as though they were on loan; items returned earlier in the same day are listed only as 'In Library' rather than indicating time of return. There are no references to borrower details, either by name or number, except for the date of return of any outstanding items.

One additional extra option which can be permitted is to authorize the user to place a hold. To do this the terminal should be fitted with a light pen, as the bar code can then act as a form of password to prevent unauthorized placing of holds on another member's ticket, though it is possible to allow keyboarding of the number. A simple menu choice allows the user to activate the hold subsystem and instructions are given as to how to carry out the transaction. It is also possible for a user to cancel (or terminate) a hold but this must be done through the patron side of the Public Query module to avoid one user cancelling holds for another.

Despite the advantages to be gained from the use of the Public Query module as a catalogue, the author would issue one small word of caution. The module accesses the same bibliographic records as does the Circulation package itself. At present there is no way to prioritize this access (as there is for the OPC module) and it is therefore possible to find that heavy use of the public terminals could slow down responses of the circulation terminals. In those libraries where there is heavy use of the holds system, it is noticeable that public searching on titles with exceptionally long waiting lists (resulting in long transaction chains) results in poorer responses than normal. Having issued that caution, it should be noted that a large number of existing sites have used the Public Query module for some considerable time without this difficulty.

Others have encountered problems, so to overcome them Geac invented a system called ZQPUBL, which is to all intents and purposes the same as mainline Circulation (ZQHUGO), but accesses the security copy files instead of the constantly changing live files. As a compromise it is successful, but it does have the effect of losing the up-to-the-minute accuracy of item availability, based as it is on the state of the files at the end of the previous day. It has only proved necessary on particularly busy 8000 sites; it is not expected that the much more powerful 9000, with its multi-threading capability, will need such a compromise solution. The very large English county library systems at Essex and Suffolk are operating Public Query, with self-service holds, and maintaining excellent response times, as witnessed by the author in late 1990.

The Public Query module for the 8000 does not have anything like the sophistication of the true Geac OPAC, nor does it look so attractive. Public Query software on the 9000 is more sophisticated, however, including as it does keyword indexes, although there is no Boolen combination capability. The Screen Manager project on the 9000 should also enable sites to tailor the appearance of the system to their own requirements much more effectively.

A patron search

If the user elects to search his or her own records, the system first displays an instruction for the user to 'use the light pen to wand their membership card' (patron badge in sites which have used Geac's standard screen overlays). Only if this is carried out is it possible to examine details from the patron database, and then only for records relating to that one person.

This simple device makes the Public Query module almost perfectly acceptable to UK users from the point of view of the 1985 Data Protection Act. Several sites have considered permitting the keyboarding of the membership number on the premise that the use of check digits prevents entry by an unauthorized individual. This is being considered, in particular, by those academic sites where access to the databases can already be achieved using dial-up interfaces or Local Area Networks, which thus cannot accept messages from non-existent light pens. The ability to key in bar code numbers is also required if the placing of holds by remote users is wanted. As a way of making this more secure, it has been suggested that a second, confidential 'PIN' number will be required for each user.

Once access is gained, the user is first presented with informative messages by the system. These relate, generally, to holds awaiting collection and overdue books. They mimic the messages given to staff at circulation terminals but are usually expanded to full sentences rather than the abbreviated messages more appropriate to staff use. In addition to these messages, a menu is displayed at the foot of the screen (see Figure 7.8). The choices offered can be selected by a single character code (followed by the SEND command) and are:

Personal details i.e. Name and Address (P)
Books on loan (B)

Holds (H)
Information messages (I)
Overdue books (V)
Fines payable (F)

The final choice is to exit (X) to the main menu of the Public Query module.

```
109 GEAC LIBRARY SYSTEM   21-02-91  17:39   Function: Show your Library Activity

            * You have Overdue books! Please bring them Back!



Choose from this list, enter here:                    Then press 'SEND'.
  P - Look at name, address & other data    I - Look at Information messages
  B - Look at Books you have out            V - Look at your overdue books
  H - Look at your Holds                    F - Look at your payable Fines
  X - Exit to main selection menu
```

Figure 7.8   Initial patron display within Public Query

Within any of the elements of the module, the degree of detail offered to the user is impressive. Books on loan are given not only author, title and class details but the issue records show the date, time and specific terminal of issue and the date due for return. Time is shown to the nearest minute. Hold records show the current status of each hold as 'outstanding', 'in transit' or 'available'. Fines records give the same detailed records for the return of each item as for its issue plus references to the amount of fine originally levied less any amounts subsequently paid. The only elements which are not displayed are a few of the system-set fields within the main patron record and the notes field.

This part of the module seems excellent in every way. It has now been operationally tested in both academic and public libraries and has been found to be very popular with users. Not only does it allow them to confirm their personal details, as held by the library, but it also avoids the need to interrupt staff to discover if an item on hold has arrived or whether the member has reached their borrowing limit. The self-reservation facility is also working very successfully, and when coupled with automatic shelf checks to remote libraries is a very efficient way of handling routine work with the minimum of expensive staff involvement.

Loan transactions

There are three main loan transaction functions: issue (or charge), discharge (or return) and renewal (or re-issue). All have a function key assigned to them and can be operated in a variety of ways. In each case the normal practice is to press the appropriate function key and then to use the light pen to record the relevant bar code numbers. However, it is possible to permit the use of the keyboard rather than light pen to input the numbers.

The system can be compiled so that once a particular transaction has been carried out, the last patron and bibliographic record accessed can subsequently be called up for additional transactions. Thus, having discharged items from a patron, it is possible to enter the issue function and the system automatically calls up that patron's details without the need to wand the membership card. Should a membership card be placed in a card holder at any time, or should the XXX function key be pressed, this will cancel any such previous record and the transaction must be commenced from the start. A time-out can also be arranged to cancel previous records after a defined number of seconds. Care should be taken in the use of the time-out: if it is set too long then errors may be made; if it is set too short the system could forget patrons before the operator has moved from discharge to the financial subsystem, which can be very frustrating when collecting fines payments.

The issue function

The entire operation to issue an item usually takes only one or two seconds to complete. Within that time the system confirms the status of both patron and bibliographic record; checks that the patron has not exceeded borrowing limits either overall, or for that particular material type; updates the last activity dates of both; updates the circulation count for the item; calculates the due date by reference to the patron privilege, material type of the item, terminal specific rules and list of closed dates for the library; records the transaction against the patron; records the transaction within the catalogue; records the transaction for statistical analysis; and finally checks that the item was not on hold.

Several new features have appeared in Release 21. Users had long been asking for a count of items issued or renewed, in similar fashion to that provided at the discharge stage, and this is now possible to serve as a check for the counter assistant that all items have been wanded and the bar codes accepted by the system.

Some libraries issuing sound recordings wish to regularly check the quality of stylus being used by their patrons, and it is now possible for the system to prompt terminal operators that such a check is due for the current patron. Having made the check, the patron's record is updated with the date, so that after a pre-set period the system can again prompt the operator by referring to that date.

It has previously been possible to configure the tables such that the number of loans can be limited by the patron type, and the material type. For instance, it is possible to permit adult borrowers to have an overall limit of ten loans, within which perhaps six may be books, and a maximum of four may be audio items. Junior borrowers on the other hand might perhaps be limited to five items, none of which may be video recordings. Release 21 expands on this flexibility by permitting the number of loans to be limited according to the agency (or library) from which they are borrowed. Exceeding the limit for the particular agency will result in an error message to the terminal operator, with the ability to over-ride if needed.

The discharge function

When an item is returned to the library, the operation is somewhat simpler, commencing with the command DIS. However, it is still possible to carry out a special transaction in that a discharge can be backdated. This particular facility is used when, for some reason, discharges are not carried out on the original date of return and the operator wishes to avoid creating a fines record, which could be incorrect. Though such occurrences are normally rare in online operations, they can arise in the event of system failure or if the library operates a returned book posting box on closed days or after normal hours.

The discharge procedure is simplicity itself, the item bar codes simply being wanded. If no special message results, the system can be compiled to display the date on which the item was due back and a cumulative total of items discharged in this particular batch in the top righthand corner of the screen.

Complications arise only if there is a message to be output. These fall in to three main categories:

Item belongs to another library or location within the system,
Item is required for a hold,
or, Item has outstanding fines.

In the first case, the system outputs a message indicating the home location of the item, 'Ship book to [library name]'. This message can be directed to a mini-printer as well as the terminal carrying out the transaction, so that a physical routing slip is produced. While this appears to have advantages, this routing slip is not very large and the author would always recommend a large routing slip, even if this means resorting to pen and paper.

Whenever the system generates a shipping message, it also creates a transit record. This is, in effect, a form of issue, though it is kept separate from normal issues for statistical purposes. The book is 'issued' to one of a set of special patron records and a predetermined 'loan period' is assigned. The item is then shown in the bibliographical files as being 'In transit' from the 'issuing' library and on loan to the receiving library, with an appropriate due date. The precise location of all items in transit can therefore be ascertained at all times. Furthermore, any items which do not arrive within the specified period become the subject of 'overdue in transit' notices. These overdue transits are very easily ignored, but this is not to be recommended, as long chains of transactions can build up against the special patron records, with consequent serious effects on response times.

Long transaction chains for transit records have caused bottlenecks in several sites, with resulting poor response times when accessing items forming part of such chains. Partly to help resolve this problem, and partly to allow for the fact that in multi-threaded mode several terminals could now access the same transit record at the same time (such as discharging books just received from the daily van delivery), Release 21 has made significant changes to the way transits are handled. Formerly there were 256 transit 'patrons', relating to each possible terminal group. Transactions for copies put into transit were charged against the relevant 'patron' in order to be shipped on. With Release 21 there are now 1024 transit 'patrons', relating to one per theoretical maximum number of terminals, and the transit (and incidentally Reshelve) patrons are now identified by the *terminal* creating the transit or reshelve.

The result of this change is that there will now be many more transit transaction chains, each shorter than the ones likely under the earlier system, and concurrent access to the same patron record by multi-threaded circulation is now possible.

It is perhaps worth mentioning, at this point, that there is an alternative to this need to return items to a home location. The Geac Circulation software permits the designation of items as being dynamic or non-dynamic. This system uses one of the optional fields within the item level of the bibliographic record. In the latter, more normal circumstance, items have a fixed location which results in shipping messages. If, however, an item is designated dynamic, its location is transitory. If it should be discharged in a library other than its designated location, no shipping message is output. Instead the location of the item is changed to that where it has appeared; the catalogue record is updated online and the item can be shelved correctly without further action.

In the case of an item required for a hold, two alternative messages are possible, depending on whether the hold was placed for pick-up at the library where the book has just been discharged or elsewhere. If the hold is local, the message 'Hold for [patron's name]' is output. If the hold is at another library, the message is 'Ship for hold at [library name]'. A transit record is created and a routing slip is required as for the earlier example. Further details of the hold system operations are contained in a later part of this chapter.

If fines are outstanding on an item when it is discharged, the system can be compiled to display the amount payable in the top right hand corner of the screen. Immediately below this figure is displayed a cumulative total for the patron being dealt with. For the first discharge of a batch of overdue books, this total is obviously the same as the individual charge; but for subsequent overdues the two figures show the individual charge and the cumulative figure. However, it should be noted that, at this stage, the system does not indicate any fines owed by the patron from discharges carried out at another session: these are only displayed when the operator enters the financial subsystem. Fines need not be collected at this stage but will be recorded in full detail until the patron pays the appropriate amount.

A new facility in Release 21 permits the terminal to display the last three item bar codes that have been discharged; a useful check for busy operators that they have in fact been discharged.

The system can be compiled to have this facility automatically turned on when entering discharge, or it can be left to the individual operator as to when it is used. Whatever way the system is compiled, the operators are able to choose when to use this facility.

The renewal function

Renewals are carried out using the command REN which calls up a screen closely resembling the issue transaction screen. Transactions can be carried out simply by wanding item bar codes; the membership card is not required as the system already knows the patron in question. As an alternative, the item number is frequently input via the keyboard, as described earlier, since renewals are often the result of a telephone call. In these circumstances, the use of check digits within the construction of numbers has proved to be a valuable safeguard since callers misquote numbers with amazing regularity.

When an item has been renewed, the system responds with messages similar to those found on issue. However, during renewal one additional message is frequently seen, 'There are more holds for this item'. The software permits sites to specify the actions to be taken at this stage: renewals could be permitted automatically; renewals could be prevented; or a combination of both. The software offers a choice: to continue with a normal renewal for the standard period; to cancel the renewal; or, to continue the renewal but to offer a reduced loan period. The software can be set to default to one of these three choices and, if the third choice is selected, it can be set to default to a predetermined loan period which can be altered if necessary. In this way, telephone renewals can be taken for reserved items without either offending the caller or seriously inconveniencing the patron who placed the hold.

In addition to the renewal of individual items, bulk renewal of all items out to a patron is also possible. The system displays the bar code number of each item, asking if it is to be renewed, so the option exists to not renew some of the patron's loans. It is also possible to cease bulk renewal partway through a list by typing 'X'. This feature would be much improved if it were possible to identify the items by title, especially in cases where the renewal is not allowed, perhaps because the pre-set number of allowed renewals has already been reached. It would also be better if all the items were renewed without the operator having to confirm each one, as this can be quite a time-consuming process when dealing with a large number of items. For some reason not clear to the author, the UK Registrar of Public Lending Right frowns on the practice of renewing items in bulk.

Within the tables it is possible to prevent the renewal of selected material types, a possible method of dealing with the problem of taking rental charges for non-book material. The software also allows for a limit to be set on the number of times an item can be renewed by the same patron. This is achieved because the system counts renewals against the original transaction and stores this count. Once the limit is reached the system displays a message to the effect that the renewal limit has been reached and that no more renewals are possible. Early warning of this limit at the previous renewals is given, but still there exists the possibility for dispute with patrons wishing to continually renew their loans. As the final refusal to renew cannot be over-ridden, the only way to prevent such disputes entirely is not to set a limit at all, or to set a limit high enough to be avoided by all but the most persistent renewer.

Fines subsystem

The Geac Circulation package contains a very sophisticated fines subsystem which controls the records relating to fines and their payment. The system allows for the levying of fines by various methods: hourly; daily; weekly; periods of grace when fines do not apply; extra charges for the cost of notices; maximum levels per item; and so on. The level of fine charged per item is determined within the tables by reference to three facets: the privilege status of the patron concerned; the material type of the item which is overdue; and, the terminal or location from which the item was borrowed. It is thus possible to set up a policy which applies two different levels of charge for the same type of patron (depending on the material type) but to have these over-ridden by another policy relating to a specific library.

Within the tables, it is also possible to indicate individual days which should be excluded when fines are calculated. These are usually days when the library is closed, but it is possible to indicate other such days even though the library is operational (e.g. open for only part of the usual hours). These days can be set for individual agencies within a network and need not apply to the whole network. Thus, if each library within a network has been designated as a separate agency, each can be treated separately.

Display of fines records

As was described in the section on Discharge, fines payable on an item are displayed on discharge along with a cumulating total for the current group of items. When all the items for an individual patron have been discharged, and if fines are outstanding, the operator must call up the financial system records for that patron by pressing the function key marked FIN. At this point further detail is available, ranging from brief summaries of monies due to very detailed information showing 'chapter and verse' on when and where items were borrowed, when renewed, when returned, and the money due from each of these possible stages. What is lacking is a good summary screen within the financial subsystem; an excellent one exists in the patron subsystem, from where information about fines is available, but not the ability to pay them, so it is a pity that despite numerous requests from users it has not been copied in the financial system itself.

Collection of fines

Payments can be collected to cover all amounts which are payable (i.e. the discharge has taken place) but not for amounts owing on items still incurring fines. These payments can be for the full amount or for only part of the amount, or for only one of the items on which fines have been incurred. Alternatively, some or all of the amount could be waived and the amount due modified. If no payment is made the records remain on the system.

Bill for replacement

In the event of an item being lost or damaged, a bill for replacement can be generated. The Financial subsystem must be accessed and the patron's details displayed. The system performs checks and provides prompts to allow an amount to be entered and for a processing fee and fines to be added to that. An interesting feature of this system is that the record of the bill for replacement can remain permanently on the patron's financial record even after the amount has been fully paid. It is then possible to refund replacement costs if the item is found subsequently.

Multiple patron discharges

One problem, which arose with earlier versions of the fines subsystem, related to the discharging of a batch of items which were returned as a single unit but which were borrowed by more than one person (e.g. members of the same family). Because the system only recognizes each person separately, it is not possible to cumulate the fines of two or more borrowers. Equally it is not possible for the system to recall more than one active patron from its memory. It was therefore a frequent occurrence that fines were collected only for one patron, but recorded against others as uncollected, only to be discovered some time later. Whilst the system was keeping perfectly accurate records, it was not making the collection of fines a simple operation, nor was public relations aided by the rediscovery of ancient fines records.

More modern software deals with this problem at the discharge stage by indicating whenever there is a change of patron at a time when there are uncollected fines from a discharge belonging to the previous patron. This allows the operator to recognize the problem and to divide the batch of items or to collect the fines from each item separately. It has the added advantage of warning staff should they fail to collect fines and go on to the next patron. Whilst a considerable improvement over the previous situation, many sites feel this is still a cumbersome approach as it would be preferable to present the patron returning the family's books with one big bill at the end of the discharge session, rather than several little ones which the operator has to manually add up.

Control of fines

As has already been described, the system can maintain records of the fines transactions at each terminal; subsequently these can be audited. The relative proportions of fines collected and modified can be monitored and records of each individual modification operation (detailing item and patron as well as terminal) can be listed. Thus the whole of the library's fines income can be subjected to much more rigorous scrutiny than was previously possible.

Additionally, it is possible to use the overnight processing routines to produce warning notices to patrons who have allowed their fines to reach high levels. Most overdue systems rely on the period of time since issue, to act as the trigger for overdues. This is the basic principle of the Geac system but it is also possible to have another notice indicating the level of fines. In many automated libraries the limit on the number of items on loan has been increased and it is now likely that a significant level of fines can be reached before the traditional overdue notice is generated. The extra notice is therefore another useful public relations tool.

Not only can notices be generated on the basis of total fines owing, but stops can be activated automatically should a limit be reached. In these circumstances the system 'suspends privileges' and outputs that message whenever the patron attempts to carry out further transactions. This stop can be over-ridden by the operator, if this is permitted within the tables, but it does usually prevent such a patron from continuing to borrow. It is also the final mechanism for bringing to book those patrons who continually claim to have insufficient cash to pay their fines. Eventually these mount up until the suspension limit is reached. Because the financial system operates throughout a library network, it also prevents a patron from moving from one library to another should they incur fines of too high a level.

Overdue recovery subsystem

The Circulation package can produce two different types of overdue: one based on elapsed time from the date on which the item was due for return; and the other based on the volume of fines outstanding against the patron. It can also produce notices for the recall of items or to inform patrons that a hold is awaiting collection. Additionally there is a system which allows the library to produce a bill for replacement should a patron lose or damage a book.

In all these cases it is possible to produce up to five different notices and each can carry a different message selected by the library as part of the setting up procedure. Although not exactly in the same category as the policy parameters, as described in Chapter 6, the criteria by which overdue and other notices are produced must also be determined as part of the setting up procedure of the Circulation package. The notices are controlled by a program called LPRULE, one which soon becomes familiar to the person responsible for input of the wording of the notices. This is because the actual wording has to be entered for each individual agency. Since there can be up to five different notices for each of the notice types this may seem a clumsy process, but the logic behind it is that the wording can then be different for each agency. For instance, one may wish to have a completely different message on overdues to users of a housebound readers service, or a college library, and so on. This facility is particularly useful for networks of a federal nature, since each unit can maintain its autonomy.

Each agency can have a general message at the top of all its notices; the wording of each specific notice can vary; the severity of the messages at the bottom of each notice can be increased. One can decide the wording for up to eight levels of severity message, although to use all eight would be taxing for anyone's imagination!

The Geac system is extremely flexible and it is possible to change the layout, the message or the timing of any notices to suit operational requirements. Geac staff will assist in this process, but it soon becomes apparent that they are not essential and many sites carry out such changes without reference to the supplier.

There are certain limitations to the notices. Firstly, in the standard layout, it is not possible to display the details of more than five items on any notice due to lack of space. Secondly, it is not possible to combine two types of message on one piece of stationery. Nevertheless, the system is extremely flexible and reliable. Variations in the production of notices abound (e.g. Camden have a version which permits up to 11 items to be listed), and it is likely that any site with a great enough need could arrange to have this need met, though there may be a cost implication to this.

Recall notices

Whereas most of the notices are generated automatically by the system, following parameters set by the library, recall notices are generated following specific individual commands. Recalls are usually created in circumstances where a hold has been placed on a title, and a copy – especially if there is only one – is overdue or will become overdue shortly. It is perfectly possible to devise software which would generate automatic recall notices on all items which have outstanding holds and which fall overdue, but this is not necessarily the most desirable action. In the case of there being multiple copies and only one hold such a recall would seem unnecessary; human intervention allows for action to be taken which is appropriate to the circumstances.

It is perfectly possible to use the recall system to send notices prior to the due date of items but this is not common practice. More usually they are used when placing holds and noticing that a copy is overdue. Alternatively, monitoring of titles on waiting lists or regular checks on the time taken to satisfy holds will bring to light titles on which a recall would be useful. Each individual item must be subject to a recall instruction; it is not possible to instruct the system to issue blanket recalls for all copies of a title.

Methods of output

The most common form of output of notices is simply to print them on to standard computer listing paper and to separate the perforated sheets by hand and place them in envelopes. To improve the image of the library, the listing paper can be pre-printed with a logo and/or certain standard messages, though the Geac system can actually produce all the messages that are required as part of the notices.

In public libraries, where the number of overdues can reach mammoth proportions, this task of inserting notices into envelopes and franking them can become excessive and is never a popular job when all the overdues from an entire library network are centralized. To overcome this problem, several libraries have used the services of computer stationery suppliers to produce notices in the form of datamailers (see Figure 7.9). Geac now offer appropriate formats of output to accommodate these. In essence the notice is already sealed inside a form of thin envelope which has a carbon film on certain areas. It is therefore possible to print the address on both the envelope and the internal notice simultaneously but to print the details of the items concerned only on the inside. Yet another variation allows for a complete copy of the notice to be produced by another carbon for examination by staff before posting.

It is also possible to output notices on continuous format postcard stationery. However, from the samples seen it would appear that the postcards cannot carry as many as five items and that three may be the limit.

Usual practice is to generate overdues using the program

040008

London Borough of Hillingdon Libraries

From Central Library, High Street,
Uxbridge, Middlesex. UB8 1HD.   TEL: UXBRIDGE 50714

MR EXAMPLE BORROWER

18 EXAMPLE ROAD,
WEST DRAYTON, MX.

Membership No: 002227776
Date: 20 02 91

Fines increase daily for all overdue items on loan to Adult borrowers. A 32p fee is also charged for sending each reminder.

CLASS MARK	AUTHOR AND TITLE	DATE DUE	BARCODE NUMBER
POP	Brown Bobby Don't be cruel	23-01-91	009578144 O'DUF CASS
First overdue notice			
FEATURE	Once upon a time in America Vide	09-01-91	010539382 O'DUF A.VID
Second overdue notice			

Despite a previous reminder, the above item(s) have still not been returned or renewed. Please give this matter your urgent attention.

Figure 7.9 Example of a data-mailer

LPOVER in order of agency, subdivided by patron name or number. In the case of datamailers it is necessary to separate notices to staff or other patrons which could be sent by other means in order to save expenses by using cheaper listing stationery. One solution to this is to use the mail code within each patron record to separate such special categories. This acts as a sorting code and it is then possible to output notices in mail code order, changing stationery as necessary. Another alternative, not currently available, would be to output notices by patron privilege class.

Holds subsystem

There are several different types of hold available within the Circulation package: copy specific; agency specific; district wide; system wide; pending and priority. A compile option within the software can be used to set a default to whichever of these is the most frequently used. In this case, the basic command HLD will then be sufficient, otherwise a subcommand is required (e.g. SYS, CPY). It is possible to use the tables to exclude certain material types from the holds system so that a system-wide hold would apply to all copies except certain excluded types. Indeed, updating a copy's material type to one on which holds are not permitted has the effect of terminating any holds already on that copy. This is a useful feature for those libraries using system-wide holds where terminating holds on one copy does not mean terminating the holds altogether. There are circumstances where it is required that the holds on a particular copy are removed, and updating that copy to a material type not for holds is a good method of doing so.

Holds can only be created from within the bibliographic query system or from within the Public Query module. In both cases the precise bibliographical entry on which the hold is to be made effective must be displayed before the command is given.

Placing a hold

When the HLD command is given, the system first responds with a message indicating the availability of copies of the title. These messages range from an indication that a copy or copies are currently available on the shelves of a library or libraries within the network (Geac's term is consortium), to the earliest date at which any copy is due back. These messages are accompanied by a request for a patron number.

Release 21 of the Circulation software includes the long awaited facility to allow holds to be placed even where no copies yet exist – an essential requirement in many public libraries where long waiting lists for popular authors' new titles accumulate long before the books are published, let alone are received at the library. This is achieved by recording the fact that a hold has been placed in a special file, so that when the first copy is added the pending hold is created against that copy.

It is possible to insist that the number is only input via a light pen (normal practice for the Public Query module) but the use of the keyboard is usually permitted for staff terminals. Once the number has been input, it is checked as it would be for an issue transaction, relevant messages are output, and the patron's name and number are displayed along with a template. The latest release of Circulation, Release 21, for the 9000 family, permits the imposition of a limit of from one to 99 holds per borrower. Alternatively, the number can be left unlimited, as before.

In placing holds, it is possible to set expiry and activation dates. The use of an expiry date is obvious but the activation date is less so. Its use is infrequent in public libraries but it is much used by some academic sites. To prevent items arriving too soon the activation date can be set to ensure that the holds arrive at approximately the right time, though some intelligent guesswork is required. This is particularly useful should someone wish to place a hold on a title with a waiting list, yet wishes to avoid the possibility of the item arriving whilst they are away on holiday, thus necessitating rejoining the queue at the back. A second use is in the reservation of several titles in a sequence. In the case of a trilogy, for example, it is possible to place three holds to be active immediately, after two weeks and after a month, respectively. With any luck the three titles will then arrive in sequence just as the reader is ready for them.

It is possible to place a hold at one library for collection at another, either because the patron is visiting a library which is not normally used, or because there is some quirk of administration which results in one library inputting holds for another. This latter can occur when holds are processed for part-time or mobile libraries at another site. It can also arise when generalized requests for books on a topic are circulated. In the author's own library network such generalized requests are frequently broadcast on the message transmission system (see later in this chapter). Providing the patron number and name are circulated with the request, other libraries can find appropriate items on their shelves, place the hold with the correct pick-up location, and discharge the item to create the transit record, etc. This facility is much appreciated by junior members, anxious to obtain books for schoolwork.

It is not possible to move holds up or down the queue once it has been formed; only to go to the head of the list by virtue of a priority hold. The use of the priority mechanism is generally reserved for rare occurrences. Holds can either have no priority, in which case they are treated in strict chronological sequence; or they can be given priority, in which case they are allocated the next available copy. A priority hold would capture a copy of a title which had previously been put into transit for another patron, providing that the copy concerned had not yet been allocated to the hold shelf and the patron notified. There are problems with the use of priority holds in that two libraries could effectively keep queue-jumping each other by repeatedly placing priority holds, and the author recommends that it is treated with some caution. See the end of this section for an outline of how this position might change in the near future.

Waiting lists

It is common practice at some sites to prefer to make most holds system-wide. This is particularly true in smaller public library networks which possess multiple copies of the same title and wish to deliver the first available copy to the requesting patron. In these circumstances, long transaction chains can be created against bibliographical records. It is not unusual to find that there are over 50 copies of a particular title and that over 200 active holds need to be maintained: this combination creates a chain of 10,000 transactions. The system cannot easily cope with the creation of such long transaction chains online; or, to be more accurate, the system can create the chains but response times can run to several minutes, particularly on an 8000.

Geac's resolution to this problem is a program known as LPHFIX which allows such holds to be placed as though they were system-wide but identifies them as possible 'trouble makers' and treats as copy-specific holds in the first instance. The mechanism for doing this is to check the existing summary of outstanding holds and should this exceed the number of copies available the special procedure is put into operation automatically. The overnight procedures are then used to expand their effect to the remaining copies without giving rise to response-time problems during normal operations.

LPHFIX must be operated in conjunction with another special batch program, LBNHLD. The main function of this program is to extend holds to additional copies of a title. It is invaluable when additional copies of a title are added to stock after holds have been placed on earlier copies. Without LBNHLD these subsequent copies would only be caught for holds placed after their addition to the circulation database. By using LBNHLD the earlier holds can be extended to cover all new copies. Apart from its value in the case of extra purchases, it is most useful when a site is in the process of retrospective conversion and new copies are continually being added to the database. Again, the future plans for holds as outlined at the end of this section should make this mechanism obsolete.

Displaying hold information

Once a hold has been placed, the transaction can be viewed from either the bibliographic or the patron database. In either case the CPY command will show brief details of the hold: in the bibliographical record the term 'Act. Hld' appears with a count alongside each copy, when system-wide holds are active. In the case of copy specific holds, 'Cpy Hld' is used, and so on. Holds which are not yet active are additionally identified by the term 'Pnd Hld' (for pending hold). In the patron records a brief one-line entry records the transaction. Similarly the command HDT will display full details of the hold from either side. Finally, the command HSM displays a brief listing of the outstanding holds for each copy.

Capturing an item for a hold

Items are only captured following a discharge, though a message indicating that an item is on hold is displayed during issue and renewal transactions, so that the borrower can be asked to return it promptly. When a held item is discharged, the message 'Ship for hold at [location]' or 'Hold for [patron name]' is displayed (as described in the section on discharge). In the former case, a transit record is created: in the latter case, the item is immediately located to the Hold Shelf of the library.

Items in transit are subsequently discharged from transit at the pick-up point in order to achieve the same status. This status is immediately visible in any of the databases, including the patron record of the person for whom the hold has been captured.

In the Geac Circulation package, all holds remain active until the patron has actually collected the item, or until the expiry date is reached. Only at that stage does the system record the hold as satisfied, and sets the status as such, so that the hold transaction can be garbaged on the next run. This permits one subtle element within the software. If a copy has been captured by the system to satisfy a hold, and is placed in transit, the system will subsequently capture a second copy provided that this second copy is discharged at the pick-up location specified. The system recognizes that this will speed up the delivery of the title and therefore substitutes it for the first copy. When the transit item arrives, a message is displayed to return it to its home location or to forward it to the next hold in a list. With this one exception, the system never stops more than one copy of a title for the same patron. Should the item have been placed into transit and not arrived, turned up elsewhere and found by a borrower wishing to borrow it, previous releases would retain that transit until the item was again discharged. This caused confusion and difficulty, but in Release 21 if such an item is issued the hold in transit is cleared, meaning the system can again trap the first available item to satisfy the hold.

If a mistake is made and more than one hold is placed for the same patron, the system recognizes this when the first copy is collected. All other outstanding duplicate holds are then terminated.

Notifying the patron

There are three separate ways of informing the patron that a hold is available for collection. Firstly, the system itself can output a message to the patron, either at a circulation terminal or via the Public Query module. Such a message can be given immediately after the receipt of the item at the pick-up location but requires the patron to be active on the system. Many patrons soon realize that this is the quickest way to discover the status of their request and they frequent the library to check on arrivals.

The second method is for the system to produce 'hold available' notices as part of the overnight processing. Once an item becomes available, the system can generate a notice, much in the same way as for an overdue item. The notice can specify the item(s) and the pick-up location and carry any other standard messages. The production of such notices can be delayed for a number of days if patrons are in the habit of attending the library frequently, but this cannot be applied differently for different patrons. Using this delaying tactic notices can be produced, and postage charges incurred, at a lower rate since the system does not generate the notice if the patron has already collected the item concerned.

Finally, the automatic notice can be suppressed and the library can substitute its own manually produced notice. This technique permits notices to be sent a few hours earlier than the overnight process and allows staff to intercept those for regular visitors. Otherwise it has few advantages over the automatic version.

It is possible to indicate at the point of placing a hold whether a notice is required or not. This works by a prompt message appearing at the end of the operation, immediately after the 'Hold Placed' message has been displayed. A message 'Suppress notice, N' appears which assumes that no suppression is required. The 'N' can be changed to 'Y' to suppress the notice and the procedure carried out as explained above. By use of this option, staff placing holds can eliminate the notice and its associated costs in circumstances where a patron is a frequent visitor or when it is known when delivery is due to take place. It is also possible, by using the Cash Management system (see later in this chapter), to automatically prompt for a hold fee. At the time the hold is placed the system asks if a hold fee is required; if it is the operator is prompted for it when the item in question is collected. In Geac's future plans for the holds subsystem as outlined later, the ability to charge for holds according to library policy will be considerably enhanced.

Issuing a hold

When a patron collects a hold, the system can generate a message to that effect. This acts as a reminder to collect any fee due if the Cash Management system is not in use. The author has found that this particular message causes irritation to counter staff and slows down operations. This is particularly true when a patron calls to collect a reserved item as the system will first respond to the patron input to inform staff that holds are available, to be followed by a second message when the item is issued, and often a third if other users are waiting for the same title. Fortunately it is possible to suppress this message.

Problems arise should the person collecting the item not actually be the same one against whom the hold was registered. The software is designed to prevent the incorrect issue of items from the hold shelf, and it must be remembered that the system precisely allocates each copy to a specific patron. However, in the public library situation, it is a common occurrence that another member of a family calls to collect a held item. To circumvent the restrictions normally imposed, the software has been written to first issue a warning but to then offer an opportunity to continue. Following this offer is a second offer – to retain or cancel the original hold for which the item was provided.

Terminating a hold

Holds are automatically deleted when they are collected by the patron but can be terminated for other reasons. They can be automatically terminated if they have not been supplied by an expiry limit. They can also be terminated by direct command within the patron or bibliographical database or from the Public Query module.

If an item remains uncollected after being on the hold shelf for longer than a locally determined time period it is deemed to have lapsed and the hold is terminated. This can be accompanied by the production of a special notice, known as a lapsed hold notice, to draw the attention of staff to the need to reshelve or return the item to the home location, though many sites rely on staff to identify these items and have suppressed the notice.

Automatic checks

The advantage of an automated system over a manual one is that it can carry out regular checks on the databases to inform staff of problems which may be arising, or to prompt action. The Geac holds package has several such features.

Firstly, the system can produce lapsed hold notices to parameters specified within the tables. The hold can then be discharged from the hold shelf and a message will indicate to which location it should be sent next. One disadvantage with this part of the software is that, at present, once a lapsed hold notice is produced the system resets the loan status of the item to 'In Library', prior to any staff action. The item could, of course, be in an entirely different library, as a result of the hold, and the databases become misleading.

Secondly, the system can be checked to detect any large waiting lists building up against particular titles. It is possible to run a batch program known as LBTHLD as part of the overnight processes, which checks the ratio of active holds to copies for each title and lists those in excess of a specified level. Thus, extra copies can be ordered of titles in heavy demand across a network.

Thirdly, the batch program LBHLDS (previously LBOHLD) can report at intervals on those holds which have been outstanding in excess of a specified number of days. Such delays could be a result of long waiting lists, but could equally result from one patron keeping the only copy of a title overdue or because copies have been stolen or lost in transit. This automatic check is again a feature of the overnight processing. In the event of such an item becoming overdue a recall notice can be generated in advance of the usual time limit for overdues.

Finally, it is possible to arrange for the system to generate shelf check listings or online messages for items which are on hold but for which copies exist on the shelves somewhere in the network. In this way it is possible to permit patrons to place their own holds without the difficulties that may arise through lack of understanding of the way in which the system operates. The London Borough of Camden have a specially written program to produce an interlending list. This is a shelf checklist of items reserved during the past X days which should be in the library at another branch. Branches check the shelves against this list and discharge all items found. The first to find the book is rewarded with the 'Ship to' message and sends the item off to satisfy the hold, whilst those finding the book afterwards will simply be prompted to reshelve it.

Efficiency of the holds system

There is only one way to determine the efficiency of a system such as this: that is to quantify the time taken to deliver holds. The author can only speak for its operation within his own network, as other sites have different policies which produce different results.

In the Hillingdon network, with its 17 branch and single

mobile library, the following figures have been collected in annual surveys covering large samples. The figures for 1990 are:

Supplied the same day	1%
Supplied within 1 day	13%
Supplied within 3 days	40%
Supplied within 7 days	60%
Supplied within 14 days	70%
Supplied within 30 days	79%
Supplied within 60 days	90%

The majority of the remaining items were either newly published titles which were not yet available; subject to long waiting lists for which policy had dictated that no further copies were to be purchased; or, items which were not in stock and which had been sought through purchase or interlending agencies. In short the Geac system seemed to deliver virtually every held item within 30 days and a very large percentage much earlier than that.

In quoting the above statistics, it should be emphasized that Hillingdon insists on operating on a system-wide basis for all holds other than specific copies required for administrative purposes. This policy was adopted in the knowledge that it would provide the quickest delivery service and accepting that it would burden the transport system. It is also of importance that the transport service operates on an almost daily basis to all libraries in the network.

Hillingdon has also adopted a rigorous practice of trying to locate copies on shelves, via the bibliographic database, and using the message transmission facility to request shelf checks. This accounts for the high percentage of holds satisfied within the first two days. This is, after all, one of the major advantages in having a sophisticated online circulation system. The effect of such an efficient service was to increase the number of requests, which rose from an already high level of 50,000 per annum to over 75,000 per annum within one year of converting to Geac.

The need for separate bibliographic entries

In a public library situation, it is often the case that a patron requires a particular format of a title (e.g. hardback as opposed to paperback; large print as opposed to normal size text). If system-wide holds are to be applied as a matter of policy, it becomes essential to distinguish these different formats. This can be done by entering each as a separate bibliographical entry within the database. While this helps to speed up the delivery of the right version of the title, it has a negative effect on searching the catalogue, since it results in the duplication (or even triplication) of records. It is also an important factor in the calculation of file sizes for the various bibliographic databases, and should not be overlooked.

Patron-placed holds

Several Geac sites already operate patron-placed holds via either the Public Query module or the OPAC. In both cases the option to give the command HLD exists when a single bibliographic entry is being displayed. Patrons selecting this command are then requested to wand their membership card and the system repeats the usual hold prompts. As described later in this chapter, placing a hold in Public Query, as with the staff side of the system, will, if required, automatically generate an online shelf check message to a site where the required item is known to be available.

Future plans

The holds subsystem has always been amongst the most impressive parts of the Geac Library system, but has developed little over recent years. Suggestions from existing users, and requirements in specifications from potential customers have prompted Geac to put in considerable effort to rewriting the holds system. At the end of February 1991 the author was given a large document outlining plans in this area for the near future. The detail in the document is most impressive; Geac's standards of documentation have certainly improved recently! Whilst it is not appropriate to rehash that document here in any great detail, the following summarization may be of interest.

The most significant change is to remove the 'chains of reservations' from the item level to the title level. Currently all holds are linked to single copies, or 'sets' of copies, such as all those belonging to a terminal group, or all copies in the system. Under the new approach, reservations will be linked against the title. In order to achieve this a new file, called **RESV is needed, and **STUD and **CALL (the borrower and bibliographic files) will have some minor changes made to them.

The new holds subsystem will allow many new features, but principally these will be:

- It will be possible to place holds against titles without copies in an identical way to those with copies. Release 21 of the Circulation system finally addressed the problem of placing holds for which no copies yet existed, but this would appear to be bringing the way all holds are handled together in one procedure.
- Holds will extend automatically and in real time to new copies of the title if appropriate, presumably eliminating the need for the batch programs LBHFIX and LBNHLD.
- The ability to place 'multi-edition' reservations for a user. Previously it was not possible to trap the first available copy of title, regardless of edition.
- The ability to update virtually all information for a hold, such as its pick-up location, expiry and activation date, scope (i.e. system wide, terminal group, etc.), priority, and so on.
- The ability to define hold priorities from 0-9. Currently, a hold either has no priority, or full priority.
- Further recognition of the importance of charging for holds, with the ability to charge at the time the hold is placed, at the time the notification is sent (i.e. user is only charged if hold was successful), or at the time the item is actually issued.
- Other benefits from the new design will be considerably improved information on holds to allow for more sophisticated statistical analysis, such as average supply times; the ability to limit the number of holds any user may have outstanding; no limits on the number of items for a hold; and the ability to archive completed reservations. Materials bookings, as a species of hold, are also affected by this rewrite to a lesser degree.

In addition to the planned changes outlined above, other enhancements are still under consideration. In particular, the ability to alter the position of a reservation in the queue has been asked for by many users, and this complex problem is receiving attention.

Message transmission

One of the facilities of the Circulation package is a message transmission system. This may not be of too much value in a single site library but is both valuable and economic within multi-site networks. It can be used in two modes, for a single message between two terminals or for a broadcast message from one terminal to all others in the network. In the case of single messages there is also the opportunity to save the text being transmitted and to re-transmit it to a subsequent terminal or terminals. This facility allows the use of the dedicated telecommunications link (for which there will be no additional charge) in place of the normal telephone line for which an expense will be incurred. It is not, however, an electronic mail facility. Geac's Electronic Mail package is described in a later chapter.

Sending a message

The command MSG (a function key) gains access to the message transmission system and displays a screen which is mostly blank save for a limited matrix. The cursor moves to the foot of the screen to await a further command. The command SND moves the cursor to the head of the screen where there is a field labelled 'Term', meaning terminal. In this field the terminal number of the recipient is entered as a three-figure number. If it is desired to broadcast a message to all terminals, this field is completed with the word ALL.

When the recipient has been identified, the cursor moves automatically to the beginning of the blank area, where the message can be typed in free text. The screen takes only a maximum of 40 characters per line and there are ten lines available for each message because in this mode the typeface is quite large. This is generally sufficient for most messages, but if more space is required the message must be transmitted in two parts.

After entry of the text, the SEND key completes the operation. The text of the message is retained and the system responds with 'Message sent'. This is generally very quick for messages to a single terminal but can take several more seconds for a broadcast message which is, in effect, a large number of separate transactions. For this reason, broadcast messages can slow down response times at periods of peak use.

If a second transmission of the same message is required, the operator need only type the SND command and the next terminal number to repeat the process. If, however, the MSG key is pressed the text will be cleared from the screen.

Receiving a message

When a message has been received at a terminal, a capital 'M' appears in the top lefthand corner of the screen, partly overwriting the terminal number. This indicator cannot appear on an idle terminal but is displayed when the screen is refreshed. Though only small, this symbol is highlighted and is easily seen. It appears in all the modes of the Circulation package including the Public Query module.

The command MSG calls up the incoming text exactly as transmitted but with the terminal number and location code of the sender and the date and time of transmission at the top (see Figure 7.10). Because the same command calls up incoming messages as well as setting up a terminal for transmission, it is usual to receive any incoming messages before transmitting. This can be avoided, however, by typing the command MSG SND in preference to using the function key, or by using the program LPLANG to assign the full command MSG SND to the MSG function key when used with the shift key. This will bypass incoming messages and allow access directly to the transmission procedure.

Once a message has been received, the text will be cleared by the next transaction. There is no facility for storing messages and rereading them. The only mechanism for this is to use screen image or other printers. However, it is possible to retransmit an incoming message, with amendments if necessary. This is used constantly in Hillingdon to report on the outcome of requests for shelf checks. The bibliographic details are supplied by the original transmitter, the results of the check

```
109 ONLINE CIRCULATION SYSTEM 21-02-91
FUNCTION: MESSAGE VIEWING

MESSAGE: FR:001 ADMIN 21-02-91 17:43 –
SCR PLEASE: SPORT– 796.815 CROMPTON, P
KARATE TRAINING METHODS. THANKS. DRW




XXX TO QUIT
```

Figure 7.10 Received message

are appended, and the message retransmitted in the same way as explained in the preceding section.

Automatic messaging

A recent feature of the Circulation software is the introduction of an automatic messaging facility, whereby a shelf check request is sent to a library holding a copy on the shelf of a title for which a hold has just been placed. The terminal receiving the message is the one with the lowest terminal number in the terminal group holding the required item. The message tells the operator where to send the book (which may well be a different library to the one in which the hold is placed), and whether it has been sent from a staff teminal, or a public one as the result of a self-service hold being placed. Such messages can also be sent to designated 'polled' printers.

Clearing the message file

Messages which are not collected are usually cleared each time the Circulation package is brought up. This means that the message transmission system cannot be treated exactly as one would treat an electronic mail facility. There is a danger that some messages would not be collected; this is particularly true in a library network where each library has a different set of days on which it is open. This is the case in Suffolk County Library Service, so there the message file is only cleared once a week. This is particularly necessary, as the automatic messaging facility does not take account of closed days for small libraries.

Message broadcasting in BPS

A drawback with the modular character of the Geac system is that the functions available in one module are usually not available in another. Such is the case with message transmission in Circulation, which is not accessible from other modules without physically switching into the Circulation package. Cataloguing staff, spending all day using the BPS Cataloguing system (described in Chapter 9), will therefore be unable to benefit from Circulation's message transmission facility. BPS does have, however, a message transmission facility of its own, with some advantages over Circulation's, and some aspects that would appear to be less good.

It is possible to send a message from whatever BPS function one is in, simply by typing the command 'BRO'. The terminal number to which the message is to be sent is then specified, and a message of up to 145 characters entered in the string field. Recipients of messages are advised that a message awaits their attention by the code 'MSG' in highlighted text on the top line of the screen the next time they press the Send key, and the message can be read by typing the command 'RCV'. The advantage of this approach would appear to be that the operator can send and receive messages from whatever function they are currently accessing, without losing the record they were working on, whereas the Circulation version is a completely different function, accessible only by leaving the current function. However, a disadvantage would appear to be that it is possible only to send to a specified terminal, rather than also having the ability to broadcast to all terminals.

It is pleasing to this author to see that Geac have now extended the concept of messaging to a module other than Circulation. UK users have for some time been asking for a similar facility to be included in the Soft Backup module (see next chapter), which would have a very practical application in advising operators that they should cease using Soft Backup and switch to 'live' Circulation, so that Soft Backup could be taken down and the records downloaded to the main files. At present, system managers have the choice of either warning all sites by telephone, or simply taking the Soft Backup package down, with resulting confusion and a break in service at the branch libraries.

Reserve room operations

Reserve room operations allow items to be placed in special locations for a time specified by the library, and permit the temporary alteration of their loan characteristics, most commonly the use of a shorter loan period. The system was created to handle the need within academic institutions to make up special collections of material to support certain courses. Items are first transferred to the reserve and then subsequently issued to one of up to 3000 courses.

Creating and updating a reserve course record

To set up a new course the Reserve Query subsystem is first

accessed by using the command RES. This produces a command header similar to the patron query system. Adding a record is much the same as in Patron Query, with screen templates looking similar, although there are several different fields. These are:

(i) Course (a name or number up to ten characters):
(ii) Professor (name of a person associated or responsible for the course, up to 15 characters long plus three initials);
ID number (optional identification number up to 13 characters);
Details (further information held on two lines, each of 35 characters);
Office (address details for correspondence held on two lines, each of 35 characters).

On completion of the record the system responds in the same way as for the addition of a patron and a bar code can be linked to it, although in some circumstances this is not essential. Hillingdon libraries have for some years used elements of the reserve subsystem to handle loans of project collections to schools, without the need to add bar codes.

Updating reserve records is equally similar to Patron Query.

Searching the reserve course files

Although the reserve records share the same file as the main patron file, **STUD, it uses separate indexes to enable searches to be made for courses, professors' names, and details. Searching by bar code number and ID number is also possible. Commands such as CPY and CUR can be used to display brief or full details of items reserved for a course.

Creating and updating a reserve course list

To allocate items to a course the Reserve Query function is used to find and display the correct course record to which items are to be linked. This is done with the request function (command REQ), which presents the user with a new template for completion with a new, temporary location and material type, an activation date and an expiry date. It is possible to have these fields set by default, but the defaults can be over-ridden.

Once these fields have been set up, the system prompts the operator to wand item bar codes to link items to the course. Once the initial parameters have been set up the use of the procedure is relatively quick, and a large number of items can be assigned to a course in a relatively short period. Items can be removed from the course individually, or, with care, in bulk.

Circulation of reserved items

Items which have been reserved for a course using a date in the future circulate as normal within the library. Once their activation date has been reached they can be captured on discharge. Items which are reserved to be immediately active can be added to the course by discharge following the request operation.

Once items have been captured for a course they are subject to new loan parameters according to the location and material types they have been assigned. These remain in force until the item's reserve course details have reached the expiry date, at which point they revert to their original state, or they may be captured for another course. An item can be subject to several different reserve course requests, but these cannot conflict.

Examples of the reserve subsystem in use

The reserve subsystem is a sophisticated tool, but one that is a little daunting at first acquaintance. It is perhaps for this reason that more users do not exploit it, which is a shame, as with a little imagination it can prove very useful in situations not envisaged when it was first written.

In Hillingdon Borough libraries the reserve room has been employed for several years to keep track of loans of project collections to schools. These collections are put together in the Schools Library Service, usually from their own stock, but sometimes drawing on the stock of children's branch libraries. The project will have been requested by a teacher, who will be teaching a topic for a school term. The Schools Library Service wanted to be able to link the loans of on average 50 items to individual teachers, but at the same time to be able to identify where the individual items were and where the projects themselves were.

The reserve subsystem permits all this quite elegantly, with little effort. In Hillingdon, children's books will have materials such as 'Junior Fiction' and 'Junior non-fiction', which to a teacher responsible for checking the items against a list when returning the project is not very helpful, but it is a simple matter to temporarily change the material type for these items to 'Book' for the duration of its time in a project. On return to the Schools Library Service, the material type and location automatically revert to normal as it is discharged, without staff needing to know what they should be. In Hillingdon the process stops with the REQ command to link the item to the course; it is not discharged into the course, nor is it subsequently issued.

Teachers appreciate the inclusion of a list with the box of materials they receive, and the Schools Library Service appreciate the facility to chase items not returned with projects. Both requirements have been met by the creation of reports, using the Geac report generator program, GLUG.

The London Borough of Camden was faced with the need to quickly create a Schools Library Service when responsibility for schools in the area was passed from the Inner London Education Authority to the local authority. Again the reserve subsystem was chosen to enable the compilation of topic lists, which can be flexibly varied to meet changing needs. By maintaining such lists effort is saved when the topic is next requested, and teachers are able to view the lists from remote terminals (Hayes, 1990).

Camden have expanded on Hillingdon's ideas, and by changing several screen displays through the use of LPLANG have made the system more user-friendly. For example, the Course field has become the Key Stage/Year Group field; the Details is now known as Formats, and the Office field now holds Details. The Lecturer field is suppressed. Expiry dates for transactions have been relabelled 'review date'. The entire Reserve subsystem has been renamed in Camden as 'Topic Query'.

In Camden items are linked to topic records using the LNK command in much the same way as REQ. Items are then loaned from the topic to teachers using the normal issue procedures, with the end-of-term due date being generated automatically. Reminders, generated by use of GLUG, are sent to teachers *before* the end of each term.

Teachers can access the topic query system via the Public Query system using public enquiry terminals at branch libraries, and it is hoped in time to be able to allow them to dial into the system from PCs in schools.

Camden have a long history of changing the appearance

and wording of the system to suit their requirements, and using the multi-lingual facility LPLANG the Reserve Room subsystem has been transformed from a standard product to one which closely reflects Camden's own style. When the Screen Manager project is complete, such tailoring of the system will no doubt become commonplace.

The relatively straightforward adaptation of the Reserve Room subsystem to the needs of Schools Library Services shows that it has potential for other services too; in Essex County it is being assessed for its suitability for handling loan collections in Elderly People's homes.

Materials booking

There is a system within the Circulation package which allows certain items to be booked for future use. In one sense it is a simpler form of reserve system in that it can be used to define precisely the period for which a booking is required but without the ability to change loan parameters. It can be used to prevent the issue of an item to another patron for a period which will overlap with the booking and to prevent conflicting bookings. This is distinctly different from a hold with a pending activation date, when it is possible for one patron to be issued an item only hours before the pending hold becomes active, and for that patron to have the item issued for a long period.

The bookings system is also useful for the booking of heavily used reference material, as a record can be maintained of the demand and a 'diary' maintained of the future bookings.

In a public library context the system would be useful for the booking of playsets and music works for performance by local societies. Bookings can be made well in advance of the actual date when they are required and the items will then be flagged should they appear for an issue which would conflict with the booking.

A further use of the system relates to the booking of materials which are not bibliographical. By creating pseudo bibliographic entries in the circulation database for items such as projection equipment, lecture rooms, squash courts or football pitches, the Geac system can be used to control lettings. Where the library has an OPAC, it is possible to use the materials booking system as part of the circulation software but to exclude the entries from the public catalogue. This has particular advantages if the items available for bookings are only available to a restricted clientele.

When used in conjunction with restrictions of patron types and material types it is possible to create a system whereby only authorized users can book certain items.

Placing a booking

The system uses the tables to define whether a particular item is bookable or not by referring to the material type. It is possible to define material types as being available for booking or not available. Thus, within one title record some items may be available whereas others are excluded from the bookings system.

To create a booking the bibliographic record is accessed in the normal way and the command MBK given. At this stage use of a subcommand will restrict the booking of items in several ways, as with normal holds:

TGP restricting the booking to items in the terminal group where the booking is being placed;
LIB making the booking applicable on the first copy within the agency;
SYS making the booking system-wide;
CPY making the booking specific to an individual copy.

Following the booking command the system prompts for the patron's bar code number, and then prompts for shipment types, pick-up locations, and the start date for the booking. At this point the system checks to see if there is sufficient free time between bookings to permit this new one, and in the event that there is no free slot large enough to accommodate the booking the system outputs a warning. When a slot is offered it is then possible to define the booking period by indicating both a start and finish date and time. In so doing the shipment type and pick-up location can be changed, the default period can be accepted or another substituted, the next free slot can be displayed if the one offered is not suitable, or a booking can be forced against the system warning.

Displaying bookings information

Bookings can be displayed which relate to the entire system or are restricted to the terminal group, agency or copy. A summary similar to the holds summary displays bookings in chronological order, giving start date and time, end date and time, patron name and bar code number and copy allocated. Detailed information on bookings are brought to the terminal in chronological order, interfiled with holds.

In addition to these two displays which mimic the holds system there are two other bookings displays. The command DAT will display a daily schedule of bookings for a date specified in the search string field. The command CAL (for calendar) will result in a display of a monthly summary of bookings. The calendar indicates the number of bookable copies, the number of bookings for each date, and whether bookings are only for part of the day.

Archival issue records

Many libraries require a system which will allow them to recognize when a patron borrows an item which they have borrowed previously. This is usually required by public libraries which maintain records of loans to housebound patrons unable to visit the library, who receive a door-to-door service. As these patrons cannot make their own selection, and since they often have well-defined reading tastes, a system is needed to avoid offering them books they have already read. A written record on the book's date label is one way of checking, but a double check mechanism through the Geac circulation software helps avoid mistakes.

Housebound patrons are registered with a special privilege status. At the issue stage, the patron's ticket is wanded in User Query, rather than in Issue, and when their record is displayed the command CHK (check) is issued. Once this command has been accepted item bar codes are wanded, and the system checks each against an historical record of loans to that patron. Only patrons with the housebound privilege accumulate archival records of their loans.

It is also possible to list the patron's archival loans, giving guidance on the kind of material that person has already borrowed, and providing a useful general picture of their reading tastes.

Such a facility would also be of use to academic and special libraries wishing to maintain records of previous borrowings by selected patrons. It is unlikely ever to be required for a library's entire membership, but if such a facility is contemplated it must be remembered that there will be significant and ever-growing disk storage implications. For this reason if no other, it is sensible to keep the number of patrons affected by this facility to a minimum.

Inter-library loans

It is possible to use the Geac Circulation package to handle the recording of loans of material to and from other libraries outside the network. Outgoing material can be easily treated since all that is necessary is to use a separate privilege type for any other libraries which have been registered for the purpose of borrowing. This privilege status can be used to determine rules for loan and renewal periods, fines and overdues. It is perfectly possible to record all external loans to one pseudo borrower but this should be treated with caution. Firstly, it still necessitates some form of manual record as to the precise whereabouts of the loaned items. Secondly, and more importantly, it is likely that a large number of transactions will build up against this patron and this could lead to response time degradation whenever it is used. The latter is less likely to cause trouble with a 9000 machine, but it would still seem unwise to allow extremely long chains to develop.

In Hillingdon the technique adopted is to register each individual library which borrows items rather than each library authority. While this means that a considerable number of additional patron records have to be created, it also means that the system can generate overdue notices automatically and that items can be posted or sent via the regional transport system, addressed directly to the library concerned. When requests are received at the central requests services section, holds are placed for the library concerned and messages transmitted to libraries which have items on their shelves. The owning library merely discharges the item to discover the details of the requesting library, carries out the issue and calls up the patron record to discover the full address for labelling the parcel. Returned items are discharged in the normal way.

Incoming items can be treated in a variety of ways, ranging from the maintenance of entirely manual records to the complete cataloguing of the item so that overdues and issue records can be maintained automatically. This latter option can present difficulties for sites that use the public query module for their catalogue. In Hillingdon, with its two databases, incoming inter-loan items are catalogued in the Circulation system but flagged to prevent transfer to the OPAC. Cataloguing is not in full, but author and title details are entered for overdue purposes.

The inter-loan reference number is entered as a pseudo ISBN or accession number, allowing staff to call up the record by author, title or request number. When an item is returned to its home library a note is added to the record relating to the date of return should there be any need to refer to this later. The record is retained on the database for two years, and then discarded in a standard 'garbage run' of redundant records.

Statistics of the number of items borrowed from external sources can be obtained by the use of specific material types: in Hillingdon's case loans from the LASER regional bureau and the British Library Document Supply Centre are recorded separately. Loans to other libraries can be obtained via the programs which analyse loans by patron privilege type.

As outlined above, the Circulation system can be used to satisfy many of the inter-loan problems libraries face. It is not a specialist inter-loans package however, and over the years various attempts have been made to specify a package that will give libraries better control over such loans. Of particular interest is the ability to automate the *requesting* of material from other libraries, which requires the ability to know which libraries have the desired items, and being able to ask for them. The English County systems of Suffolk, Norfolk and Essex are exploring ways in which they can cooperate in a networked fashion on the provision of loans between their systems, using the Geac communications product TRAX.

As an alternative to putting a lot of effort into the development of a sophisticated inter-loans package within the Geac system, several academic sites interface with commercially available systems, such as TinLend (Lambert and Hallam, 1988). Also possible is an interface with a system developed by the University of Lancaster, (Stuart, 1987) and Lancashire County Library service is successfully using this in a simplified version.

Bindery management subsystem

The Bindery Management system allows items requiring binding to be sent to a central binding station or to a 'Binding preparator' and then subsequently to a binder.

Creating the records

It is necessary to create a pseudo patron record for each binder, binding station or preparator within the system or with which the library has dealings. The privilege status BINDER is used for the first two and this prevents those patron records from being accessible through the normal patron query system. Another status should be used for preparators so that items in their possession can be accessed in the normal way. Items for binding should first be issued to the preparator; at this point they are still within the normal library system and can be accessed. It is assumed that items will remain with the preparator for some time before the next part of the operation, hence the need for them to be issued so that control is maintained over their whereabouts.

The next phase is for the preparator to collect the items into bundles and to 'issue' them to the binding station or binder. This is achieved by calling up the bindery management system (using the command BND) then calling up the appropriate patron record as though within the normal patron query system. Once the record is displayed the command ADD BUN creates a patron bundle. This copies the details from the previously displayed patron record, which can be updated as necessary. In particular, the expiry date must be updated to the date at which the bundle is expected to be returned from the binder. Once the bundle patron is ready the command RQS (to request a transaction) is used to allow the bar codes to be wanded or keyboarded into the record. The system then prompts for records. Geac suggests that bundles be limited to a maximum of 50 items as larger units become more demanding of processing time, although with the 9000 this is probably less critical. As each bar code is wanded the system continues to display the bindery name and bundle number and adds short bibliographic details for confirmation. It also allows details to be entered relating to standard binding codes (a default is possible to the one most commonly used), and makes available an item-specific note field in which free format binding instructions can be entered. On completion of each detailed item record a binding slip can be printed.

At any point it is possible to summon the patron bundle again and add additional items to it. This will usually be done while the bundle is on issue to a binding station rather than to a binder. It is also possible to summon a patron bundle and to transfer the entire details from a binding station to a binder.

Searching the records

Within the bindery management system it is possible to search by binder's name or bundle number. Once a bundle has been accessed the command CPY displays a summary of the items within the bundle; CPY DTL displays additional details; CUR displays details of the creation of the individual record and any notes.

Within the normal query systems and the Public Query module, items within bundles attached to binders or bindery stations show as being 'In Bindery'.

Return of bundles

When items are returned by the binder it is only necessary to discharge them in the usual way. This will record the return of the item and result in any appropriate shipping message. The system continues to keep records of all items within a bundle, showing return data, until all items within that bundle have been discharged. When this occurs a message is displayed and the bundle records are made available for garbaging on the next overnight garbage run.

Reports

Several overnight batch programs are available to support the system. LBRET will list details of every bundle that has been completely returned, but since it works on the garbage collect it must be run before the collect is carried out. LBRET1 sorts the data by binder, and LBRET2 sorts by discharge date and time. LBOVRB reports on bundles which are overdue, including those where only a single item has not been returned from a bundle. LBCURB reports on current bundles, and LBREPB reports on all patron bundles. LPEXPB reports on binders that have no current transactions.

Cash Management subsystem

The Cash Management system is relatively new, first appearing with Release 10.2 of the Circulation software on the 8000 machine. The software at that time was not however particularly fully developed and there were difficulties with the security of the system that inhibited its use. It has been significantly improved for the 9000, and the author has seen it in use in the Suffolk County Library service.

Using this system, it is possible for a library to keep records of its cash receipts for such items as fines, membership fees, photocopying fees, reservation fees and sales. Not only does the software create records which can be listed and analysed centrally, but each library within a network can examine its own records at any time via any terminal – providing the correct level of permission has been assigned. It is therefore possible to display cash summaries at the end of daily operations for reconciliation with cash in hand under each of the headings in use. The nightly reporting program LBCMS produces a library by library summary, and clears down the daily totals, so that when looking up details online, the current day's totals are inevitably the ones displayed.

As its name implies, this system helps with management of library finances; it is not a system of keeping patron accounts. The totals that are updated are those for categories of money, rather than recording the indebtedness of individual patrons. To illustrate this point, renewals of items with a material type attracting renewal fees (such as video cassettes) will prompt the operator for the relevant fee. The operator can either accept payment, in which case the relevant total will be automatically updated, or waive the fee. No automatic record that the patron owes a renewal fee is made, although a note can be manually added to the patron's record.

User registration fees, issue fees, renewal fees and fines are automatically transferred into the Cash Management subsystem. There are other payment categories, such as photocopying charges, where the amounts can, or often must, be manually assessed and the relevant total updated. It is possible to disallow the manual updating of a block of payment categories, and it is wise to assign such categories to the first ones in the list.

Fines

The system requires no additional action on the part of the terminal operator when collecting fines, except that the full procedure for modifying or waiving fines must be implemented in order to ensure that records are accurately maintained. Waive fine payments can be automatically recorded in a single predefined category for 'waived fines'.

Fine payments can be automatically accumulated in predefined categories based on the material type of the item which generated the fine (e.g. fines for adult material can be gathered in an 'adult fines' category and those for junior material gathered in a 'junior fines' category).

Loan and renewal fees

It is possible to set up tables to prompt for payments by material type. Issue and renewal fees can then be automatically accumulated in predefined categories based on the material type of the item.

The system will display a prompt in the Issue and Renewal functions, defaulting to a set fee for each material type, at which time the fee can be either paid or waived. Waived lending fees are recorded in a single predefined category for 'waived lending fees'. If no fees are required for particular material types, no prompt is given.

As explained above, the system will prompt for a renewal fee, but if the patron is not present, as with a renewal by telephone, there is no automatic mechanism for recording the fact that a renewal fee is owing, and the fee has to be waived. Manually updating the patron's note field will ensure that the fee is taken on the patron's next visit to the library; presumably a separate category for 'deferred renewal fees' is necessary.

Particular patron privilege classes can be exempted from paying lending and renewal fees altogether by setting a bit in the patron privilege bit table, but the system is not able to charge fees for a particular material type to one category of patron, but not another.

Membership fees

The system can prompt for a fee when a patron is enrolled or the expiry date is reset, and then record the payment in predefined categories dependent on the patron privilege class (e.g. registration fees for patron privilege classes permitted to borrow audiovisual material can be gathered in an 'audiovisual registration fees' category). Where no fees are required for particular privilege classes, no prompt is given. Many libraries, whilst making no charge for initial membership do charge for replacement tickets, but unfortunately the system does not deal with this separately.

It is possible to have up to six different amounts for issue, renewal and membership fees, to permit different levels of fee at different libraries, in similar fashion to allowing different loan periods or fine levels library by library.

Reservation fees

It is possible for reservation (or hold) fees to be automatically accumulated in a predefined category. For those material types requiring hold fees a bit is set in the reserve room table (as is the bit determining whether a material type is holdable). As with other fees, it is not possible to charge some privilege classes and not others, unless the 'exempt' privilege classes are totally exempt from all fees other than fines.

When a hold is placed it is possible to suppress the hold fee. The automatic prompt for hold fees is made in the issue function when the hold is collected, although a refinement would be to permit a choice of whether to prompt at issue, or at the time the hold is placed, with the ability to defer payment until the item is issued.

Other income

Apart from the above sources of income, it is possible to set up other accounts for income from any source, up to a total of 255 categories. Each of the additional categories can be given a name and reference number within the tables by the library, and each can have a default amount set. It is therefore possible to collect income from photocopiers by calling up the category and responding to the prompt, although with frequent transactions this is time-consuming, and it is likely to be the case that at the end of the day the category is updated to reflect the entire day's takings. Access levels or passwords control who is permitted to add and subtract amounts from these categories.

Reports

Cash Management payments are recorded by category and terminal number. The CAS command displays the categories and totals for the terminal and terminal group, which will be of use to library staff reconciling their tills at the end of the day. Managers with appropriate access level or password authorization are also able to see totals for the whole system.

An offline batch LBCMS automatically collates the amounts

per category on a daily/monthly/quarterly/yearly basis, producing a printed report sorted by terminal group within agency (Figure 7.11).

Geac.CBCMS2 SAXMUNDHAM LIBRARY		Date: 04-12-90		Page:1
Terminal group: SAXMUNDHAM				
	Day	Month	Quarter	Year
LOAN FEES : records	0.00	0.00	3.20	5.08
LOAN FEES : cassettes	0.00	0.00	0.00	0.64
LOAN FEES : CD's	0.00	0.00	3.76	10.26
LOAN FEES : Story Cass's	0.00	0.00	3.20	6.36
FINES : records	0.00	0.00	2.88	6.62
FINES : cassettes	0.00	0.00	0.00	0.64
FINES : CD's	0.00	0.00	3.76	4.23
FINES : Story Cassettes	0.00	0.00	0.64	1.28
FINES : Books 2 week	0.00	0.00	92.12	280.96
FINES : Books 4 week	0.00	0.00	53.85	1,353.26
FINES : Books 6 weeks	0.00	0.00	2.43	4.28
BOOK REQUEST CHARGES	0.00	0.00	38.22	107.19
FINES WAIVED	0.00	0.00	0.00	2,307.12
LOAN RATES WAIVED	0.00	0.00	1.28	1.88
MAT TYPES – NO FINES SET	0.00	0.00	0.00	0.28
Totals	0.00	0.00	205.34	4,090.08

Figure 7.11 Display of income accounts within Cash Management System (Reproduced with permission of Arts and Libraries Department, Suffolk County Council)

The present Cash Management System is a considerable improvement over its predecessor, but there is still scope for greater flexibility in being able to charge differing fees according to differing privilege class. With libraries being driven into ever more commercial ways, and consequently needing to be ever more accountable, a sophisticated system for handling the not inconsiderable sums of money concerned is becoming increasingly necessary, and this part of the Geac system goes a long way towards achieving this.

Help system

Throughout the entire Circulation package there are help screens which can be accessed using the function key marked HLP or giving the command HLP in the command header in association with a sub-command such as HLD (see Figure 7.12). This will display a simple screen of assistance relevant to the function which the operator has selected.

```
109 ONLINE CIRCULATION SYSTEM 21-02-91   DISPLAY: part/all   ACCESS LEVEL: 3
FUNCTION: BIBLIOGRAPHIC QUERY/UPDATE   TIME 17:45   PRESS 'HLP' FOR HELP

COMMAND:FND   SUBCOMMAND:   SEARCH TYPE:T   BROWSE KEY:   DIRECTION:+   AMT:01
SEARCH STRING:

All hold transactions are created by placing 'HLD' into the COMMAND field. There
are two kinds of hold transactions: Copy-specific and multi-copy.
Copy-specific hold transactions are added by placing 'CPY' into the SUBCOMMAND
field and the reference number of the copy into the amount field. Only that item
can satisfy that hold transaction.
On the other hand, a multi-copy hold transaction places holds on many copies.
The first of these copies to become available will satisfy that multi-copy hold
transaction. The valid subcommands for multi-copy hold transactions are:

TGP  – Place holds on all copies in your terminal group (terminal-group-specific)
LIB  – Place holds on all copies in your library (library-specific)
SYS  – Place holds on all copies in your system (system-wide)
ILL  – Place an ILL hold. See your Terminal Operator's Procedure Manual

If you enter no subcommand, you will create a default hold transaction. When
the system asks you for the requesting user, either wand the user badge,
or enter LST for the last active user
record.
```

Figure 7.12 Help screen for the Hold System

All commands can be displayed using the subcommand HLP. Thus HLP HLP will give access to the first element of the entire help package (see Figure 7.13).

A particularly useful feature of the help system is the ability to examine the rules set up within the tables (see Figure 7.14). Questions about which patron privilege classes may borrow which material types, and for how long, or what is the correct abbreviation for an entry in a field are all relatively easily answered. The more complex a system becomes the more queries will arise as to 'Why did it do that?' and to be able to answer the question from the terminal is important. As library policies change, they are immediately accessible to all, without having to depend on frequently changing documentation. This is not to say that documentation and staff manuals are unimportant; far from it. Rather, the help system is an essential back-up to adequate training and manuals.

```
109 ONLINE CIRCULATION SYSTEM 21-02-91   DISPLAY: part/all   ACCESS LEVEL: 3
FUNCTION: BIBLIOGRAPHIC QUERY/UPDATE   TIME 17:46   PRESS 'HLP' FOR HELP

COMMAND:CON   SUBCOMMAND:   SEARCH TYPE:   BROWSE KEY:   DIRECTION:+   AMT:00
SEARCH STRING:

More complete help text is available in the following areas if you enter 'HLP'
into the COMMAND field and the indicated subcommand into the SUBCOMMAND field:

HLP  -  This help text
CMD  -  The available set of commands
cmd  -  Complete information concerning the command 'cmd' and its subcommands
SCR  -  Detailed information concerning the screen format for this function
TYP  -  Six-letter codes for the valid material types
LOC  -  Six-letter codes for the valid item locations
TNM  -  Six-letter codes for the terminal groups and libraries by Terminal Number
TGP  -  Six-letter codes for the valid terminal-group locations
LIB  -  Six-letter codes for the libraries in your consortium
PRV  -  Six-letter codes for the user privilege classes
STA  -  Six-letter codes for the user statistical classes
RES  -  Six-letter codes for the residency classes
OPB  -  Six-letter codes for the user record optional fields
OPC  -  Six-letter codes for the bibliographic record optional fields
OPI  -  Six-letter codes for the item record optional fields
```

Figure 7.13 Help screen for available help commands

```
109 ONLINE CIRCULATION SYSTEM 21-02-91   DISPLAY: part/all   ACCESS LEVEL: 3
FUNCTION: BIBLIOGRAPHIC QUERY/UPDATE   TIME 17:50   PRESS 'HLP' FOR HELP

COMMAND:CON   SUBCOMMAND:   SEARCH TYPE:   BROWSE KEY:   DIRECTION:+   AMT:01
SEARCH STRING:

MATERIAL TYPE    2         SHORT AF      LONG ADULT FICTION BOOK
                                         ----------------------------------------POLICIES----------------------------------------
USER            CLASS      LOAN          RENEWAL         FINE         MAT TYPE LIMIT

1               ADULT      21 days       21 days         5p           No Limit
2               JUNIOR     21 days       21 days         No Fine      No Limit
3               STAFF      21 days       21 days         No Fine      No Limit
4               DISAB      21 days       21 days         5p           No Limit
5               HB.IND     28 days       28 days         No Fine      No Limit
6               HB.HME     91 days       91 days         No Fine      No Limit
7               HB.HOS     31-12-91      31-12-91        No Fine      No Limit
8               SCH T      21 days       21 days         No Fine      No Limit
9               SCHOOL     91 days       91 days         No Fine      No Limit
10              DEPCOL     31-12-91      31-12-91        No Fine      No Limit
11              LASER      91 days       28 days         No Fine      No Limit
12              GLASS      91 days       28 days         No Fine      No Limit
13              ILLOAN     91 days       28 days         No Fine      No Limit
WOULD YOU LIKE TO SEE MORE USERS FOR THIS MATERIAL TYPE      Y
```

Figure 7.14 Help screen for part of the system rules

Provided as it is as part of the standard circulation software, with its early history in North American academic libraries, the text in the help system is not always exactly as individual sites would wish. Whilst it is possible to make limited amendments to the text using LPLANG, as has been done to great effect in the London Borough of Camden, true customization of the help system to suit individual site requirements is not easily achieved. There are two sources of light at the end of this particular tunnel, however. The new Community Information system, described in a later chapter, permits sites to very easily compose their own help screens, and it would not appear too difficult to introduce such a facility into the Circulation system. The other source for hope is the Screen Manager project, whereby sites will have much greater control in the appearance of all aspects of the system. At the time of writing the author understands that this project is almost completed on the Circulation package, and will soon be released as a new product to users of the 9000.

Library maintenance routines

The Library Maintenance function allows authorized operators to perform several functions, including:

1. Creation and amendment of authorized passwords, and the assignment of one of three levels of authority for each element of the Circulation package.
2. Bulk amendment of bibliographic data.
3. Bulk deletion or re-instatement of stock.
4. Viewing the loan periods set for the agency to which the terminal being used belongs.

Password authorization

Within the Circulation package passwords or access level bar codes have to be registered. This registration specifies three levels of increasing freedom of action (above the default level 0, which bars access) for each of the following subsystems:

- Circulation transactions
- Fines transactions
- Patron transactions

- Bibliographic transactions
- Hold transactions
- Messages
- Cash Management, and
- Library maintenance itself.

It is therefore possible to achieve a reasonable degree of flexibility. For instance, one could allow individuals to create and update patron records but deny them the same freedoms within the bibliographic database.

Bulk amendment of bibliographic item data

This facility is of considerable use when it is required to alter the item level details of stock in bulk since it is accomplished by a few simple commands followed by the use of the light pen to identify the items concerned. Having given the command DTL from within the Library Maintenance function, a template is displayed, offering the ability to amend the primary and secondary location and material type. All the items concerned are then updated simply by wanding their bar codes, or keying in their item numbers.

Bulk deletion

In a similar way to bulk amendment it is possible to delete items in bulk, using the unsurprising command DEL. As with bulk updates, the bar code is wanded or the item number keyed in, and the system responds with a message to the effect that the item has been deleted. It will not permit the deletion of items which have transactions linked to them, even non-active transactions waiting to be garbaged off overnight, nor will it permit the deletion of the last copy of a title. Both these conditions must be dealt with from Bibliographic Query.

Library Maintenance can also be used to restore deleted items in bulk, by using the command REV.

Viewing loan periods

The command SLP, when used within the Library Maintenance function, allows the terminal operator to see the different loan periods set up in the tables for the agency to which that terminal belongs. Used in conjunction with the help system, this facility is sometimes of use in answering queries as to why the system has issued a particular item to an unexpected date.

References

Hayes, D. (1990), 'School topic list management in Camden', *VINE*, October, pp 26–29.

Lambert, P. and Hallam, S. (1988), 'Inter Library Loans using TINlend,' *Vine*, **70**, May, pp. 8–14.

Stuart, I.M. (1987), 'A multi-user Inter Library loans system from the University of Lancaster library,' *VINE*, **68**, November, pp. 3–10.

8 Back-up systems and portable terminal operations

There are three back-up circulation systems available at the present time. The most common system relies on PCs linked to a group of terminals to protect the basic circulation functions in the event of c.p.u. or telecommunications failure. The second form of back-up system relies on the portable data capture units, using the Psion organizer, normally associated with mobile library services, which can also support a basic offline circulation function.

In both these cases the data is captured offline and is subsequently downloaded to the c.p.u. when the fault is rectified. Downloading from the mobile library unit is achieved via the PC, from which it is onwardly transmitted to the c.p.u. in the same way as data stored on the PC in normal back-up operations. Both methods receive error messages from the c.p.u. as part of this downloading procedure so that staff can take any necessary action. The PC needs to be attached to the circulation software within the system tables, and the configuration file through SPCNFG. Release 21 of the Circulation software for the 9000 family allows a PC device to behave either as a back-up micro or a normal Circulation terminal without the need to register two separate devices, as was previously the case. This is achieved by giving the device all the required permissions, including that of a back-up device (MBU) in the tables, and in the configuration file specifying all the required onlines, whereas previously an MBU could only access Circulation.

Multi-terminal, PC back-up

The usual configuration is for the PC to be daisy-chained to the terminals within a library; the PC therefore requires a Geac daisy-chain board. Since the system can only protect the ability to continue with a basic form of circulation, it is usually located in close proximity to those terminals which it is intended to 'drive'. In sites that also operate public terminals, or that have terminals available for functions other than issue and discharge, Geac recommends a form of daisy-chaining excluding these terminals. The arrangement is to connect these terminals first in the line after the modem, followed by the MBU and finally by the circulation terminals (see Figure 8.1).

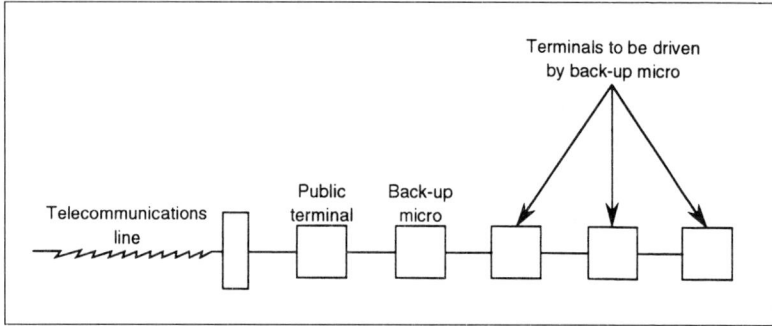

Figure 8.1   Diagram of the wiring sequence of terminals + back-up micro

In the event of a failure, the back-up system is activated and the PC controls the downstream circulation terminals, which are effectively cut off from the remaining terminals, modem and c.p.u. In the meantime the other terminals remain able to 'see' the c.p.u. and will indicate when the service has been restored. This layout has an added advantage for sites operating packages other than circulation in that, should the problem relate only to that package, it is possible to operate circulation in back-up whilst simultaneously maintaining a full service of, say, community information on the other terminals.

There are four programs required to operate the back-up procedures fully, and all are held on the PC's hard disk which is also used to store any captured data. The back-up system has been made much more user-friendly than used to be the case by the introduction of a PC-DOS menu system for the easier running of these programs.

The first program, LPBACK1 is run every day to prepare the system for use, by entering a series of due dates. For the majority of the time that is the only program that is used, the others only coming into play when the back-up system is needed. Once the due dates have been entered, the PC can be used as a normal terminal or for any other PC software, ready to be called upon in the event of a crisis.

The second program, LPBACK2, is run when the back-up system is in use. It drives its slave terminals, and records transactions onto the PC's hard disk. In addition to recording the borrower number and item number for each transaction, it also 'date stamps' them with the date and time. Once activated, the back-up system puts up a menu offering issue, discharge, renewal, fines transactions and help on the screens of all the appropriate terminals. The function keys representing these choices are still active and the terminals act, to all intents and purposes, as though there were no difference (at least as far as the borrower is concerned).

Once online service is restored, LPBACK3 controls the downloading of captured data to the c.p.u. It is at this point that difficulties can arise, even it seems on a multi-threaded 9000 series machine. The PC is able to send data to the c.p.u. at a considerably faster rate than is usual when bar codes are wanded manually, as the terminal operator pauses between each item to locate bar codes and perhaps chat to borrowers, a liberty not permitted the PC. Artificial pauses have been introduced into the software to some effect, but it is inevitable that downloading may cause a deterioration in response times if allowed to proceed unchecked. This is partly due to the intensity of transmission mentioned above, but also because the period after a spell in back-up is extremely frantic with libraries desperately clearing up the mess left by being denied access to the c.p.u. for any length of time. Where the back-up session was caused by a communications break to a single branch no difficulties arise, but if it was a complete c.p.u. breakdown in a large County system there may well be trouble. For this reason, despite their normally excellent response times Essex County Library service restrict downloading to one PC per area at any one time. Apart from the danger of slowing the system itself, there have been problems with the speed at which data downloads, but this would now appear to have been cured, and Geac claim recovery rates of 50-100 records recovered per minute.

Once the downloading procedure has been completed, the fourth program, LPBACK4 is run to examine any error messages generated by the c.p.u. The PC screen is used to display the details of the offending transactions, and staff can then take any necessary action, including checking the online system, to rectify anything which requires that level of attention. An option within LPBACK4 allows all of the transaction records to be viewed, rather than only those generating error messages, and this can be useful in circumstances such as when the wrong due date has been entered in LPBACK1 and all items have therefore been issued to a ridiculous date, requiring renewal to the correct date.

Though the back-up system attempts to take over from the online system in the three major transaction functions, operational practice is often to use it only for issue unless the normal service is out of action for a very long time. The reason for this is that the time involved in clearing up the messages after a spell in back-up is usually quite lengthy, even for a short break in normal service. Staff in the author's own library prefer to delay discharging items until the service is restored, when responding to online messages is quick and easy. Only when the volume of returned books becomes a problem do staff prefer to consider discharging in back-up.

Likewise, there are problems in operating the fines system in back-up. The software assumes fines are unpaid unless instructed otherwise. Unfortunately there is no easy means of calculating fines without the online system and mistakes can arise where patrons are undercharged. If the back-up system were used properly this would result in the system maintaining a record of the missing amount. Whilst this is perfectly accurate, it can lead to subsequent awkward confrontations. At the author's library it is seen as preferable to delay the discharge until the online system bcomes available and then to indicate that the fine was paid in full.

Mobile Library Unit operations

The Geac portable library unit is a hand-held data capture device, primarily intended for use in mobile libraries, non-automated service points, the bulk relocation of material, and stock-taking. It can however be used as a back-up in a library where the live and PC back-up systems are unavailable, perhaps because of power failure, since it can be run off battery or mains power.

The unit consists of a Psion organizer with a datapack, a light pen, and a Comms Link for downloading to the PC. As with the PC version, it is able to record issues, returns, renewals and fines payments. Operation is in many ways similar to using the PC-based back-up system, in that due dates are entered, and data is trapped and downloaded. The obvious difference of course is that this is a stand-alone device; it is not driving slave terminals.

The unit does make life a little easier for staff however, in that it is able to recognize from its internal clock when due dates may need changing because the current date has changed since the due dates were last amended. It will add to the due dates the number of days since the last change, giving the operator the option of accepting these, or entering something different. The operator is also able to manually enter a relatively small number (less than 200) of traps into the unit for borrowers or items, which for a mobile library may well be sufficient.

When used for issue/discharge operations one datafile will hold approximately 600 records. When the file is almost full, all that is required is to exchange it for a new pack, an operation that takes only a few seconds.

When connected to a Psion printer, details of the current transaction can be printed, perhaps for giving to the borrower as a form of receipt.

Choosing the recovery option on the Psion's menu allows the operator to download to the PC (for which the Comms Link must have already been attached), to view the transactions in the datafile one by one on the Psion's screen, or to see statistics. The statistics include issues plus renewals, renewals alone, discharges, fines and total value of fines collected, as well as the number of borrower tickets wanded. Whenever the unit is started up the option to clear existing statistics is given. It is usual for sites to have at least two Psion units, to allow for downloading of data to be achieved using one, whilst the other is in use collecting new transactions.

Other applications for the portable library unit

The Psion unit has also been developed to be of use in situations where it is not convenient to take a terminal, and where all that is required is a data capture mechanism. Software on the Psion unit allows bulk updates to be performed, by allowing the user to enter location and/or material type information in the form of a six character or less name, followed by wanding a number of item bar codes. Should there be several batches of updates to do, the parameters can be changed, which will affect all subsequently wanded items until another set of parameters is entered. Upon recovery, the locations and/or material types for the items will be changed on the live system. Bulk updates data may be held on the same datafile as data from the Mobile Library software, and recovered at the same time.

Stock-checking is also possible using the portable unit. Data is collected simply by wanding item numbers, which when recovered indicates to the system that those items physically exist. It is then simply a matter of producing a list of items which are presumed missing because they were not wanded, and not on loan or in transit or on the hold shelf. If the operator enters the location at which the check is being carried out, information can also be provided regarding those items whose location on the system files differs from where they actually were wanded. Downloading of this data is also possible with data recorded by the Mobile Library software, or the bulk update software.

Soft back-up

The third back-up system, Soft Backup, is an online system used when the 'live' circulation is unavailable, but the c.p.u. and telecommunications links are working normally. This situation will occur when there is some software fault with the circulation system, or when it cannot be brought up because it is still running essential overnight programs. The advantage of this system, where it is possible to use it, is that the setting of all due dates and downloading is handled by the system manager, relieving branch library staff of the responsibility and allowing them to get on with the pressing tasks involved in recovering from a period without access to the live system. The system is in fact two packages; one to control terminals in back-up mode, called ZQSOFT, and another called ZQBACK to restore transactions captured in back-up to the main circulation files. It follows that the recovery can only take place when the live circulation system has been brought up.

The options available are the same as in PC back-up, with the addition of the need to identify the agency that the terminal belongs to. If this is not done, transactions recorded on it will be rejected.

At the system centre end of the operation, four due dates

for each agency are entered, daily if required, or just before the system is used if this can be anticipated. This can be quite a tedious procedure if done manually for branches with differing due dates, but where all branches have the same due dates a batch program handles the process very quickly.

Having brought the soft back-up system up and down, the transactions recorded are backed up onto tape for security before running the recovery program, which is simply achieved by running ZQBACK. An improvement in the 9000 operating system is the ability to monitor how the recovery is progressing by keeping track of the record numbers as transactions are recovered; 8000 users simply have to check periodically to see if it has finished.

Once the recovery has been completed, a range of error reporting programs can be run, reporting on all transactions, rejected transactions, and different types of transaction, as required.

As with much else in the Geac system, a little imagination can adapt a standard feature into a useful additional facility without the need for large development effort. When Essex County Library service were converting their database from their previous automated Telepen system, the issue records for each library were downloaded as it 'went live' into the soft back-up transaction file **SOFT, and then transferred into the live circulation system using ZQBACK in the usual way.

Back-up catalogues

The principle of back-up for catalogues is probably not seen as so critical as back-up for circulation functions for many libraries, so consequently is less standard. Sites operating Public Query from Circulation are in difficulty if Circulation is not available, unless they are 8000 sites with ZQPUBL, which accesses the security files. OPC users are able to continue to provide a catalogue without circulation, although unable to provide status information on item availability.

If the entire system is unavailable however, catalogue information can only be provided if it has been produced in alternative formats. For many years some sites have produced their catalogues on microfiche, largely as the only form of public catalogue, but it would certainly be possible to produce fiche catalogues for use as back-up catalogues in the event of failure.

The limiting factor is likely to be whether the cost and trouble involved is worth it for what one hopes is relatively infrequent use.

The attractive alternative to microfiche, which Geac are expected to make available in 1991, is to produce the catalogue on CD-Rom. As with fiche it is perhaps unlikely to be produced purely as a back-up, but those sites where it is produced for non-automated libraries, or for supply to other organizations such as local schools, may well consider making a few extra copies with each run for use as back-up catalogues in automated libraries to be money well spent. It is understood that the Geac CD-Rom product will be capable of being networked to several workstations, which may make it an attractive alternative to the existing online catalogues in some circumstances, with the inevitable benefits of colour, windows and advanced searching procedures.

9 The Cataloguing module

Introduction

Cataloguing on the Geac system varies to a certain amount, according to the standard of catalogue required. The catalogue can be created entirely in Circulation, with a reasonably high number of access points, as briefly described in Chapter 7. Chapter 10 describes the Acquisitions package, and it is perfectly feasible to create an adequate catalogue from here, with perhaps some additional input in Circulation. None of these methods can handle MARC data however, and it is with the production of a MARC-based catalogue that this chapter is primarily concerned.

Why MARC?

MARC is required by sites wishing to use the OPC online catalogue described later in this chapter. The usual way to achieve this is by cataloguing in MARC, or buying in MARC records, but it is possible to automatically create MARC records from Circulation records if required. Sites wishing to create their catalogues from bought-in records usually buy them in MARC format, although again this is not essential. Sites wishing to provide Boolean search facilities can only do so from the OPC, so again a MARC record has to be created.

The bibliographic control system

Previously the method employed in creating MARC records was the MARC Record Management system (MRMS), which was described in some detail in the first edition of this book. No attempt is made here to repeat that, because MRMS is to all intents and purposes a 'frozen' product. It was a somewhat cumbersome cataloguing system, and was unable to provide for the requirement of many users that individual fields should be edited, so with the development of the new 9000 series of machines came the development of a new system – the Bibliographic Control System (BCS). This chapter attempts to describe most of the facilities possible with BCS, but it is an extremely complex system, of which the author has unfortunately no practical experience (other than the OPC element), so this should not be relied upon as a complete guide to the package. I have no doubt omitted some extremely important functions which are of immense value to cataloguers, and if I have I must apologize, and plead ignorance in mitigation. I have drawn heavily on Geac's BPS user's guide for this chapter, which I found to be an excellent piece of documentation; an area that has not always been Geac's greatest asset. I am also grateful for comments from David Easton at Edinburgh University Library, which was the Alpha site for BPS in the UK, and Jim Craig at Glasgow University. I have attempted to include criticisms of the package where these seem common and justified, but it should be stressed that cataloguing staff in the sites I consulted agree that this system is a very considerable improvement over MRMS, and it is to be expected that further developments will address many of the problems currently in existence.

BCS consists of a number of different programs, but the two most important are the Bibliographic Processing System (BPS), which is the cataloguing element, and the Online Public Catalogue (OPC). Features of BCS include the ability to load records from several bibliographic vendors, authority control, support for all MARC formats, and up to 20 access points (indexes) for search and retrieval of data, with Boolean searching possible against the three keyword indexes. As one would expect, BPS permits original cataloguing, copy cataloguing, the creation and maintenance of detailed holdings, the creation of cross references, and the generation of management reports. Dewey and LC are handled as standard, but the author understands that the system is as yet unable to correctly sort classmarks from some local classification schemes in the online system or lists.

In addition to the online system and the ability to produce printed listings, it should also be possible to produce a catalogue on COM fiche. Unfortunately, neither Edinburgh or Glasgow Universities have been able to do so, citing a combination of cost and technical difficulties.

As with the other major packages, BPS can be customized through the judicious use of compile options (CCPs). Using a program called FPTBLD the library defines its own MARC tables and formats. This allows the library to describe or prescribe each MARC table, MARC field, variable length subfield, fixed length field offsets, and the prompts which appear in the online system for each of these. For each fixed length field the character positions, length and allowed data of each offset is defined, and for each variable length field a set of screens permits complete field/subfield definition – valid, mandatory, repeatable subfields, indicator lists, etc.

Anything the system can 'produce' from a MARC record is referred to as a product. Such products include indexes, record displays, citation and index screen displays. The definition and content of these products is determined by the sequence, tag number and subfields of MARC fields as defined in the master 'products' file, over which the library has considerable control.

MARC formats are defined by one of the library's MARC tables, of which there can be several for different record formats required for books, serials, audiovisual material, etc. Fields can be assigned as repeatable (e.g. tag 650 – Subject Added Entry Topical Heading could be used several times in the same record), mandatory – enforcing something to appear in for instance tag 245 (Title Statement), or prompted. Prompted fields are automatically displayed when starting to add a new record.

As with Circulation, the ability to produce reports is provided by Report Writer software. This allows the library to define any report, choose which database to work from, and employ Boolean operators for complex selections. Although potentially powerful, the Report Writer is complicated to set up. It is reported as taking quite a long time to run, requiring the online system to be down for part of the process, which must therefore be scheduled into overnight batch jobs.

Proof lists can also be produced, for quality checking of catalogue records before they are completed. This facility is not yet as valuable as it should be, with users commenting that the very text one would wish to proofread is omitted. It would seem that the list works on records as they are transferred to the core files, which if there are errors in the cataloguing is one stage too late. To generate a proof list is a two-stage process, with the first stage carried out by human intervention from a separate online system. Previous versions have been more useful, and possible to run entirely overnight without human intervention.

BPS provides extensive edit and display capabilities for bibliographic and authority records. There are three display formats for individual records: full MARC format, full public format or a partial public format. Cataloguers themselves may display a complete record, a particular version of a record, an individual field, a record leader, a field by field comparison between two records, a record linked to a record currently on the screen, a record memorized for quick referral, or a field previously captured for later insertion into another record.

Cataloguers can also edit bibliographic or authority records by adding a field, changing a field, copying one field into another within the same record, deleting a field or complete record, inserting a field from one record into another, renumbering a field, creating a record, or checking a field or a record for errors.

BPS also permits online control of bibliographic data through linked authority records. Cataloguers are able to create, search or edit authority record for personal or corporate names, subject headings, and series/uniform titles. The creation and maintenance of 'see also' relationships between authority records is possible, as is the ability to perform a global change throughout the authority and bibliographic files. A refinement that is desired by users is the ability for the more sophisticated amongst them to be able to perform large-scale changes across the database for all records found that satisfy a set of criteria. Large-scale changes, such as the offline updating in bulk of stock locations, as one might wish to carry out when closing a branch library, are not possible.

Core and work files

The authority and bibliographic files are each made up of a core file and a work file. In other words, the files include a bibliographic core file, a bibliographic work file, an authority core file, and an authority work file. The core files hold the most complete and up-to-date version of a record. Core records are intended to be validated by staff with the highest level of cataloguing expertise in the library, or loaded directly into the core files after automatic error checking. It is these core files that make up the online public catalogue.

If a record needs to be modified, the system copies the core record to a work file, which contains records under revision and newly created records not yet validated. A core record remains unaffected by changes made to its work version until a staff member validates the work record. After validation, the work record is flagged for transfer to the appropriate core file (authority or bibliographic). It is possible for the cataloguing supervisor to initiate the transfer of the validated work record into the core files, but in practice this task is usually left to the system manager, who will schedule the job to its most suitable time.

Current/in-process records

When a record is searched for and displayed, the record as it displays on the screen is called the current record. As soon as this record is edited or linked, it becomes known as an in-process record. Similarly, a new record in the course of creation is an in-process record. It is only possible for the operator to have one record in-process at any one time.

At the time an operator has a record in-process it is possible to validate it, accept it, postpone further work on it until later, or erase it. Postponing or accepting an in-process record has the effect of creating a work record, replacing the previous work version, or creating a new work version when no previous version exists. Accepting a record indicates that it is catalogued but requires checking by a supervisor before release into the core file. A postponed record indicates the record is not yet completed.

When an in-process record is validated, it becomes a work record, waiting for the Work to Core transfer. This transfer, a program called ZQLMST, moves the record to the core files, replacing the previous core version if there was one, or creating a new one if not. Another transfer program, ZQCIRC, transfers the records from BPS into the Circulation module. It is these transfers which have caused operational difficulties in some cases, and the duplication of data, particularly holdings information, has been wasteful of disc space and generally inefficient. These problems were to be addressed by a project called the Integration Project, which foundered due to the extreme complexity of the work involved. This caused much dismay amongst Geac users, and the concept has resurfaced under the name of the Holdings and Pieces Management Project, described later in this chapter.

The maintenance of two separate databases (three with Acquisitions) is undoubtedly a disadvantage, although there are definite benefits too, for peformance is likely to be better if users are not all accessing and manipulating the same data at once. That said, the operational difficulties involved in reliably transferring large quantities of data on a regular basis have led to real problems. In particular, the transfers from BPS to Circulation have given Edinburgh University many problems, although it would appear that these have now largely been eliminated in newer releases of the software at newer sites. The logic employed by the transfers is felt by some users to be too stringent with too many records rejected as incompatible. It is felt by some that only data not addressable by the operator should be subject to rejection, but at present this is not the case, with control numbers, for example, unable to be changed. As evidenced by the recent moves towards integration within Geac, there is clearly recognition that these are not inconsiderable problems which are being addressed in some measure at least.

Searching

Searching in BPS is similar to Circulation's search facility, but with much greater flexibility, and consequently some greater complication. The operator, having issued the command 'FND' then has two other fields to complete on the command line – Parm A and Parm B (see Figure 9.1). In Parm A the index to be searched is entered, such as the Title index (TIL), Title Keyword (TIK), or personal name authority (NAA). Parm B is used to restrict the search further. For instance, a search of the title index is achieved by entering TIL in Parm B, and then by entering 'X51' in Parm B the operator can search only for 'geographic subject headings'. If Parm B is not used in this way to restrict the search, it can be used to set the MARC format display. BPS defaults to full MARC display, but it is possible to specify full public display, or partial public display if desired. The line below the command line is used for the operator to enter the search string, as with Circulation. The system normally treats the search text as though it were only the start of an index entry. For example, the search string 'SPACE' will result in an index display of 'SPACE', 'SPACECRAFT', SPACES', etc. Exact matches can be specified by prefacing the search string with an = sign, e.g '=SPACE' will result only in entries with 'SPACE' as the subject.

Another way a search may be restricted is by use of the 'SET' command to set a session's profile. Using this command the operator is presented with a screen allowing the specification of 'search qualifications'. The operator can choose to search

```
Command : FND Parm A: SUB Parm B: X51
String    : canada history
```

Figure 9.1 Screen header from BPS system (Reproduced by permission of Geac Computers Ltd)

only work or core records for bibliographic or authority files; search only on validated index entries; restrict author searches to one of personal, corporate name or conference name; restrict title searches to uniform or collective titles; restrict ISN searches to ISBN, ISSN or ISRN; restrict searches to a particular book location; or restrict searches to records which belong to a particular owner group of cataloguers. Searches can also be restricted by date of publication; a range of dates is possible, such as >=1972 will look only for records published in 1972 or after, <=1980 will search only for records published in 1980 or before, or =1987 will look only for records published in 1987.

A search resulting in only one exact match will cause the relevant record to be displayed. Any more than one exact match, or no exact match at all, will result in the relevant portion of the index being displayed, from which a record can be displayed, or the index may be browsed. The search cannot be further refined from this point; if a different search type or search string is required, the process must begin from scratch.

Boolean searching

Unlike the Circulation module, BCS has a Boolean search facility, which works on the title, author and subject keyword indexes. As would be expected, it is possible within one Boolean search to search all three keyword indexes.

The familiar Boolean operators 'AND', 'OR' and 'NOT' are permitted, and the search can also be prequalified using the 'SET' screen described above. If no operator is interposed between two statements, 'AND' is assumed. Word proximity, to join two words together into a phrase is also permitted, as are nested expressions which the system extracts before continuing with the rest of the search string.

Boolean searches are infamous for being greedy of processing power, particularly when searches are involved or badly framed. The BCS is compiled by the library to prompt the searcher after a specified period with a question as to whether the search should continue. Should a search contain too many keywords, perhaps as a result of injudicious truncation, the system will cancel the search. 'Too many' in this context is over 64. Should a search be so general as to produce more than 500 citations, the system will stop searching at that point.

The Boolean search facility is limited by the fact that it only consults the keyword indexes, so does not include authority records. The system may have been compiled to build keyword indexes only from core records, in which case Boolean searches will not be able to retrieve work records. Nonetheless, the Boolean facility is greatly appreciated, and when used in conjunction with the 'SET' capability allows for considerable flexibility and precision in searching. Users the author has spoken to are agreed that the Boolean facility responds surprisingly quickly.

Displaying records

A detailed record will appear in one of the three formats already mentioned; full MARC, full public, or partial public format. BPS defaults to displaying a record in full MARC, whereas OPC defaults to full public format. For each format, the library defines which fields will display, and how, by means of the BTPROD product files. From the full record, individual fields can be displayed on their own if required. Should there be several occurrences of a field, the required one can be specified.

Having retrieved a record, it is possible to browse successive or preceding records. If still in the index or a 'hit list' of citations, browsing through them is also possible.

The record as displayed is the bibliographic record only. Holdings, which are held separately, must be requested. The system is able to perform 'clever volume handling', whereby volumes are displayed in the correct order, i.e. V1, V2, V3 and so on, instead of the usual computer trick of displaying V1, V10, V100, V2, V20, V200 etc.

As previously explained, records can exist as work, core, or in-process records. Core and work records are held on disk, whereas current and in-process records exist only in memory. It is possible to switch between these versions to allow comparisons to be made, without losing the unfinished work. It is also possible to return to the record previously in-process before the one currently in-process. In-process records can also be 'memorized' by storing in memory buffers whilst another record is examined, and then recalled from memory for completion.

Editing records

The term 'editing' in this context includes adding, changing and deleting records. It is possible to edit either the complete record, or individual fields. As previously explained, records can be core, work, authority or holdings records. Before BPS allows any editing command to be used, it first checks the operator's security parameter settings against those for the record to be changed. Each user has the set of commands which may be used defined by system administrators, and each command set is linked to a particular MARC format or MARC table. In this way, it is possible to permit a cataloguer to change monograph records, but perhaps not personal name authority records. Owner groups also exist, by which each record in the database belongs to a single owner group, but cataloguers may belong to several. If a record belongs to an owner group other than the one the cataloguer is currently signed onto, the system will not permit changes to be made to that record.

It can be seen that considerable control can be exercised over who is able to edit what, although from this author's experience of the less severe security system in Circulation, such levels of complication are often difficult to keep track of. The point is that should very stringent control over cataloguing staff be required, with BPS it is possible.

Editing at record level

When creating a new record, the first task is to select the MARC format required, by entering the relevant code for the MARC table. This is necessary because as mentioned earlier, different tables are defined for different types of material, such as books, serial, audiovisual material, etc. Having specified the table name, the system displays a template for the fixed fields at the beginning of the record. The exact fields, and the prompts/labels within them will depend on how that table has been set up. Having completed that template, a second template is displayed for completion of the variable length fields, again according to how that particular MARC table has been set up. Once this template has been completed, any desired additional fields can be added to the record.

It is often possible to save time by copying an existing record, rather than having to create a record from scratch. This facility is of value when cataloguing new editions of works, or several volumes in a series.

Editing at field level

Rather than editing an entire record, it is also possible to edit specific fields, having first displayed the record to which they belong. Extra fields can also be added, or unwanted fields deleted. Fields can also be renumbered or copied, or moved, and may be captured and memorized for insertion into another record.

Authority control

BPS can handle authority records for personal, conference and corporate names, subject headings, and uniform/series titles. The authorization of a heading involves linking the actual heading in the bibliographic record to the established form of that heading in the authority record. The cataloguer determines and controls which authority records to link to.

In the BPS system, it is possible to create, edit and search authority records for personal names, conference names, corporate names, subject headings and uniform titles. 'See also' relationships between authority records are constructed and maintained, as are 'see' and 'see also' references for the public catalogue. It is also possible to make global changes of all occurrences of a heading by changing the authority record.

There are two parts to handling authorities in BPS. Firstly, they are handled as records: searching for them, displaying them, creating them, etc. Secondly is the concept of authority control: the linking of bibliographic records with the appropriate authority records. The handling of authority records as records follows the same rules and procedures as other records, but within authority control some extra functions are available.

Having created an authority record, in much the same way as creating normal bibliographic records, it can be edited, or made subject to global changes. If a change is made to an established heading in an authority record, this change will automatically be repeated in every field linked to that record. This global change takes effect when the record is transferred to the core files, and if many linked headings are likely to be affected, such transfers are best run when the BPS system is down.

The BPS authority system works by putting the onus onto the cataloguer. The cataloguer must decide that a record should be subject to authority control, and search for a suitable authority record to which to link the new record. Having searched for an authority record, the new bibliographic heading is either linked to a suitable authority record, or if none exists the cataloguer can create one. At the point of creating the link, the relevant data derived from the authority record is copied into the correct field in the new bibliographic record. In other words, the BPS system does not check new catalogue records for matching the authority file; the file is used to generate 'approved' headings as records are built up.

Save file

Each terminal using BPS has its own temporary file, called a save file. This is used to hold records that have been memorized for later comparison, or insertion of fields into other records. The save file is also used for the printing of records, either by a printer directly attached to the terminal, or to a designated one elsewhere on the network. The last record worked on or displayed can be printed, or the memorized one, or the current, or in-process record may be printed. Multiple records can be added to the file for printing together if desired.

A useful feature of this facility is the ability to print the spine label for a book by first finding and displaying its holdings record, and then issuing the command 'SPI'. BPS then constructs the spine label on screen from the relevant fields, allowing the operator to amend it if necessary before printing. Multiple copies of the spine label may be printed. Similarly, an item's bookplate may also be printed, and yet another command will cause the printing of both spine labels and bookplates.

Holdings

The way the Geac system handles holdings is under considerable review, and intended changes, which will have the effect of creating a more fully integrated database, will be described shortly.

Currently, however, the Circulation and BPS systems maintain their own separate holdings records, in addition to the separate bibliographic records already described. In Circulation the relevant files are called **COPY, **ITEM, and **CTXT. In BPS, the relevant files are **HOLD and **HSPL.

Once a bibliographic record has been created, holdings information is then added to it. This record is used for all holdings information about that bibliographic record; each new item is added to the holdings record as extra fields (tag 966 for detailed holdings, and tag 930 for summary holdings). The holdings record is linked to the bibliographic record via the **GRSN (Geac Record Sequence Number) file. The bibliographic record and the holdings record share the same GRSN, which is how the link is effected.

The previous version of Geac's MARC cataloguing system, MRMS, maintained holdings records as 966 fields within the main bibliographic record, which in public libraries led to very large records in many cases. Amendments to holdings records are often frequent, and in this system caused many difficulties due to the large amount of processing required.

It had long been apparent that the maintenance of at least two separate holdings and bibliographic files was inefficient. With the 8000 system there were also advantages in that staff and public were accessing two different files, easing bottlenecks at the c.p.u. by spreading disk accesses over several different drives, but with the far more powerful 9000 this is much less necessary. Consequently, a scheme to reduce the need for such duplication was drawn up, and given the enticing title of the 'Integration Project.' Unfortunately, due to the very great development effort required, this project never progressed beyond the planning stage, but Geac have recently unveiled plans to resurrect the most important elements of it, which they have called 'Holdings and Pieces Management'. The development costs for this project have been funded by ten customers in North America, and the author understands that the work is almost complete.

This project is designed to merge the holdings records for Circulation and BCS to create an integrated holdings database. The effect of this will be improved maintenance of holdings avoiding the problems indicated above, and to minimize the need for movement of data between applications. As an 8000 system manager of several years experience, this author can vouch for the desirability of reducing the need for transferring data around the system. Transfers will in future be restricted to bibliographic records.

The number of holdings supported on a single bibliographic entry will in future be virtually unlimited, which will prove attractive to public library systems in particular. Academic libraries also hope to benefit in this area in dealing with periodicals, which have never been particularly well handled. Although all the volumes and parts of a journal can be linked as 966 tags to a core record, it is not possible to 'jump' through the list to, say, Volume 49 part 5. Rather, one has to page through all the parts up to the desired one before finding whether it is in the library or on loan. It is to be hoped that any new work on holdings management will address this problem. Many public libraries are increasingly interested in moving their stock in bulk from branch to branch, and informing the BCS system has always been difficult when dealing with very large numbers of such movements so eliminating the need for transferring this data is especially important.

All holdings management will continue to be possible in either system, but the work of writing to the holdings database will be done by the Circulation database manager. Bibliographic data will continue to exist in separate files, so that changes made in the Circulation database will not affect the BCS database. A useful byproduct of what may be considered this disadvantage is that libraries will continue to be able to maintain records in Circulation which do not appear in the OPC, such as materials booking and reserve items.

Other benefits from the new software will be the ability to delete or erase all holdings attached to an item in one operation, rather than separately as at present, and software to handle 'Bound-withs'. This will allow the user to specify that an item is bound-with another item during the adding of copies. When displaying this item, a note that it is bound-with another item will be displayed.

A source of criticism from customers has been the inability to identify the date of addition or amendment of item information in the Circulation database; this project will include the creation of fields to hold this information for each item, allowing for better management information.

Whilst this is still some way short of full integration, especially as it continues to leave data in the Acquisitions system on its own, the removal of duplication of holdings information for those sites using both BCS and Circulation will be very welcome.

The OPAC

The OPAC was first made available at the Elmer Holmes Bobst Library of the New York University in 1983. The author has seen the module operational at some of the academic sites in the UK, where there are different options in use, but the majority of his experience is gleaned from close contact with the OPAC at Hillingdon, where it was first made publicly available, throughout the borough, in September 1983.

The OPAC forms the second part of the Bibliographic Control System, and is known in Geac as the OPC, so throughout the rest of this chapter it will be referred to as OPC. It is usually accessed via the Inter-Online Communications (IOC) package which connects the various parts of the system, but in cases where the OPC is the only package to be made available there is no necessity to force users through this intermediate step, and the system simply reverts to the initial Introduction screen at the end of a search, rather than the main system menu.

If the main system menu is used, the relevant choice for the OPC must be made, followed by depressing the SEND key. One of the author's greatest complaints about the Geac system is that the need to use the SEND key, which is so important for users to understand, is not spelt out at the first screen the user encounters. Once beyond that screen the various packages make it perfectly clear that SEND is important, but by that time one assumes the user has been lucky enough to find that out. Regrettably, many users give up in frustration before achieving this breakthrough. The main system menu (known as the TCP screen) is in fact easily amended to include this vital piece of information, (see Figure 9.2) and it is to be hoped that Geac will soon include it as part of the standard offering.

Having found the way into the OPC the user may be presented with one or more pages of news, a facility common to all the packages for public use. These news pages can be suppressed, which is the option followed in Hillingdon, as it was felt to be frustrating for users to be constantly forced to read the same news every time they use the package, so they are given the option of choosing to read the news through the special facility in the Community Information System (see Chapter 11).

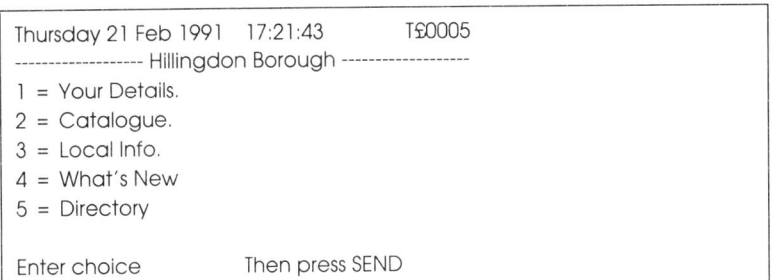

Figure 9.2 Terminal Control Program main menu (Hillingdon public version)

Function keys

Following the news pages, there is a simple screen which explains the use of the major function keys (see Figure 9.3), including those for help. It is perhaps worth pausing here to explain that the OPC has two levels of help available to users. For those very inexperienced users who cannot follow the abbreviated instructions on the standard display screens, there is a Help key, which leads to the display which explains, in extremely basic terms, what should be done next and what the options are for the precise point in the search that the user has reached. A second function key, labelled Advanced Help, is for use by proficient searchers, explaining time-saving techniques such as command chaining, thereby converting a menu-driven system into a command-driven one. As with Circulation the text of the help screens can only be altered with difficulty, although it is possible, and at Hillingdon much customization to the appearance of the OPC has been achieved. It is to be hoped that a similar facility to that offered in the Community Information system, will soon be made available to sites using the OPC. Alternatively, the Screen Manager project should provide satisfactory results.

Another function key, usually labelled New User, but changed at Hillingdon to Introduction, takes the user to an explanation of the system, with basic instructions as to how to use it.

There is also a function key assigned to the command code for Previous Screen, and this command will allow the user to retrace the search steps up to six times. At present, browsing and certain other commands can only be achieved by the input

```
109 Hillingdon Libraries.      - GEAC LIBRARY SYSTEM -      *INTRODUCTION


    This is the GEAC ON-LINE PUBLIC CATALOGUE

        At any stage you can:

        Press f1 for INTRODUCTION
        Press f2 for HELP
        Press f3 for ADVANCED SEARCHING
        Press f4 for COMMAND HELP to explain available commands
        Press f5 for PREVIOUS SCREEN
        Press f6 to START AGAIN
        Press f7 to EXIT from the catalogue


Now press SEND to begin:
```

Figure 9.3   OPAC initial help screen

of a typed three-letter command code followed by the SEND key. It is possible to reassign function keys to these commands using LPLANG and thereby reduce the operation to only one keystroke rather than four. The Public Enquiry Terminals, now sadly defunct, had a simplified keyboard with only eight function keys. An Elite terminal has 16, and using LPLANG a value could be assigned to all of them twice, as the shifted key counts as a separate key. Thirty-two function keys would be misleading, even to staff, but there is scope for making greater use of function keys in academic institutions, as research has shown (Mitev, 1985).

Beginning a search

After the introductory screen, pressing the SEND key leads to the OPC main menu, which offers a varying number of choices, depending on which options have been compiled. Figure 9.4 shows the main menu offered to users at Edinburgh University Library, although since this was captured by dialling into the system over the Joint Academic Network (JANET), Carriage Return has been substituted for SEND. Choice is indicated by keying a single reference number, or the associated three-letter code, followed by the SEND key.

```
271 EDIN.UNIV.MAIN LIB.   - GEAC LIBRARY SYSTEM -   ALL *CHOOSE SEARCH

    What type of search do you wish to do?

        1.  TIL   -   Title, journal title, series title, etc.

        2.  AUT   -   Author, illustrator, editor, organization, etc.

        3.  A-T   -   Combination of author and title.

        4.  SUB   -   Subject heading assigned by library.

        5.  NUM   -   Call number, ISBN, ISSN, etc.

        6.  BOL   -   Boolean search on title, author and subject.

        7.  LIM   -   Limit your search to a portion of the catalogue.

    Enter number or code, then press CARRIAGE RETURN
```

Figure 9.4 OPAC main menu (Reproduced by permission of Edinburgh University Library)

If any of the first four choices are selected, the system takes the user to an initial instruction screen, appropriate to that function, where an example is displayed; the user is invited to type his or her search. Figure 9.5 shows such a screen as presented to users at Hillingdon libraries, including locally relevant examples, which were felt to be important as the standard examples were imported from an academic American library and had little relevance to British public library users. If any of the last three choices are selected, there is an intervening menu giving alternatives within the search type in question, which then leads on, as before, to an initial screen for each type of search. The use of these sub-menus avoids the need to present the user with an overwhelming set of choices on the main menu.

A title search

A simple title search merely requires the user to type the title, or as much as is known, commencing with the first word. This is checked against the title index, in which are included subtitles, added titles, uniform titles, etc. A site-specified list of stopwords are ignored both for filing and searching. This stoplist can be as full as desired; in Hillingdon it contains very few entries. If there are a number of matches or if there is no perfect match, the system displays the relevant part of the title index (see Figure 9.6), giving each entry a sequential number. Thus, if

```
109 Hillingdon Libraries.      - GEAC LIBRARY SYSTEM -      *AUTHOR SEARCH

    Type the author you are searching for below.

    For people, enter last name first.

            eg. BRONTE, EMILY
            eg. TOLKIEN, J.R.R.
            eg. ROSS, DIANA

    For other authors, use normal word order.

            eg. HILLINGDON COMMUNITY HEALTH COUNCIL
            eg. BRITISH AIRWAYS
            eg. DIRE STRAITS


Enter author:                                       Then press SEND
```

Figure 9.5   OPAC screen for an author search

```
109 Hillingdon Libraries.      - GEAC LIBRARY SYSTEM -      *TITLE SEARCH

Your title: COMPUTER PROGRAMMING                    Matches 13 titles

                                                    No of entries in
                                                    entire catalogue
 1  Computer programming, Fortran                         1
 2  Computer programming in BASIC                         2
 3  Computer programming in BASIC 2nd ed                  1
 4  Computer programming in BASIC : a unique, teach-yourself cou>  4
 5  Computer programming in COBOL                         1
 6  Computer programming in MSX BASIC                     1
 7  Computer programming in Pascal                        1
 8  Computer programming languages in practice            1
 9  Computer programming made simple                      1
10  Computer programming made simple 2nd edition          1
11  Computer programming made simple 3rd edition          1

Type a number to see more information -OR-
    FOR - move forward in this list    BAC - move backward in this list
    CAT - begin a new search


Enter number or code: FOR                           Then press SEND
```

Figure 9.6   OPAC title index display

a search term were mistyped, the system may still offer the correct title providing it is not separated too far alphabetically. The user can then select an entry for display, browse forwards or backwards, or return to the main menu, using a function key or three letter command for this purpose. Experienced users can also type the relevant three-letter command for a different search type, circumventing several menus. For example, keying AUT/DICKENS would have the effect of performing an author search for DICKENS from this point. If one, and only one, perfect match is found on the original search, the system bypasses the title index and displays an entry for that title. The system can be compiled to display the brief record first (see Figure 9.7), with the user given the choice of also seeing the full record (see Figure 9.8), or *vice versa*. Brief entries include information about copies, including loan status, whilst full entries provide the complete bibliographic record.

At this point the system allows the user to browse in either direction looking at brief or full entries, depending on which format is currently being displayed, or allows the search to return to the title index

```
109 Hillingdon Libraries.      - GEAC LIBRARY SYSTEM -      *TITLE SEARCH

AUTHOR:      Maynard, J.
TITLE:       Computer programming made simple 3rd edition


Location            Item    Shelf Location         Copy    Availability

EA    /EAADLT       ANF     ELECTRONICS:001.642    1       In Library
HL    /HLADLT       ANF     001.642                2       On Loan      12-03-91 24.00
MF    /MFADLT       ANF     001.642                4       In Library
NW    /NWADLT       ANF     001.642                5       On Loan      02-03-91 24.00
UX    /UXADLT       ANF     001.642                6       In Library
UX    /UXADLT       ANF     ELECTRONICS:005.1      7       In Library
HE    /HEADLT       ANF     ELECTRONICS:005.1      8       On Loan      08-03-91 24:00


FUL  -  see full details              IND  -  see list of headings
CAT  -  begin a new search            TWO  -  see full shelf locations


Enter code:                                              Then press SEND
```

Figure 9.7   OPAC brief entry

```
109 Hillingdon Libraries.     - GEAC LIBRARY SYSTEM -      *TITLE SEARCH

        AUTHOR:          Maynard, J.
        TITLE:           Computer programming made simple 3rd edition
        IMPRINT:         Heinemann 1986
        SERIES:          Made simple books
        SUBJECTS:        Computer programming
        CLASS NUMBER:    001.642
        ISBN:            0434986070 * 0434984825


        BRF  -   see library and shelf locations      IND  -   see list of headings
        CAT -    begin a new search


        Enter code                                            Then press SEND
```

Figure 9.8   OPAC full entry

An author search

Author searches are carried out against the author index, which can be compiled to include added authors, illustrators, and so on. The search works in much the same way as for titles except that the index display lists authors and states the number of titles on the database for each (see Figure 9.9). As with the title search, if there is only one perfect match the system bypasses the index and displays the entry relating to the author (see Figure 9.10). As can be seen from the figure, the author entry is a listing of titles by that author. If there are too many to display on one screen, the system offers the choice of browsing forwards in the listing. If there is only one title by the author concerned, the system bypasses the citation list and displays the brief (or full) entry.

An author-title search

The third choice leads to a search using both author and title. For the experienced user, who knows that this search works against an acronym index needing only four characters from the author and title indexes, this is the quickest way to achieve a direct hit on a specific title. The search can be undertaken in two stages, for which the help screens duplicate the individual author and title search help screens. However, with command chaining it is possible to carry out a search from the OPC main menu in 12 keystrokes (e.g. 3/SMIT/INTR

```
109 Hillingdon Libraries.    – GEAC LIBRARY SYSTEM –    *AUTHOR SEARCH

Your author: DOWLIN                                    Matches 13 authors

                                                       No of entries in
                                                       entire catalogue
 1   Dowlin, Kenneth E.                                        1
 2   Dowling, A.P.                                             1
 3   Dowling, Alick                                            1
 4   Dowling, C.A.                                             1
 5   Dowling, Colette                                          2
 6   Dowling, Geoff                                            1
 7   Dowling, Gregory                                          2
 8   Dowling, Jeanette                                         2
 9   Dowling, Kevin                                            1
10   Dowling, Maria                                            1
11   Dowling, Marion                                           2

Type a number to see more information -OR-
   FOR – move forward in this list      BAC – move backward in this list
   CAT – begin a new search

Enter number or code: FOR                              Then press SEND
```

Figure 9.9   OPAC author index display

```
109 Hillingdon Libraries.    – GEAC LIBRARY SYSTEM –    *AUTHOR SEARCH

                                                        matches 20 entries

   Refs   Author                 Title
    13    Aldiss, Brian          Moreau's Other Island
    14    Aldiss, Brian          Non-stop
    15    Aldiss, Brian          The Penguin master quiz by Brian Al>
    16    Aldiss, Brian          The Penguin world omnibus of scienc>
    17    Aldiss, Brian          The primal urge
    18    Aldiss, Brian          Report on probability A
    19    Aldiss, Brian          Space, time and Nathaniel
    20    Aldiss, Brian          Trillion year spree : the history o>

Type a number to see associated information -OR-
   IND – see list of headings      BAC – move backward in this list
   CAT – begin a new search

Enter number or code: BAC                              Then press SEND
```

Figure 9.10   OPAC author citation entry

(SEND)). Even with a very general example such as that above, there are remarkably few hits for so few keystrokes. A single perfect hit will lead to the display of the record concerned; a multiple hit will offer a choice of entries (see Figure 9.11). Since there would be little point in displaying the acronymic index for searches which have no matches at all, the system displays a message 'Nothing found, try again'.

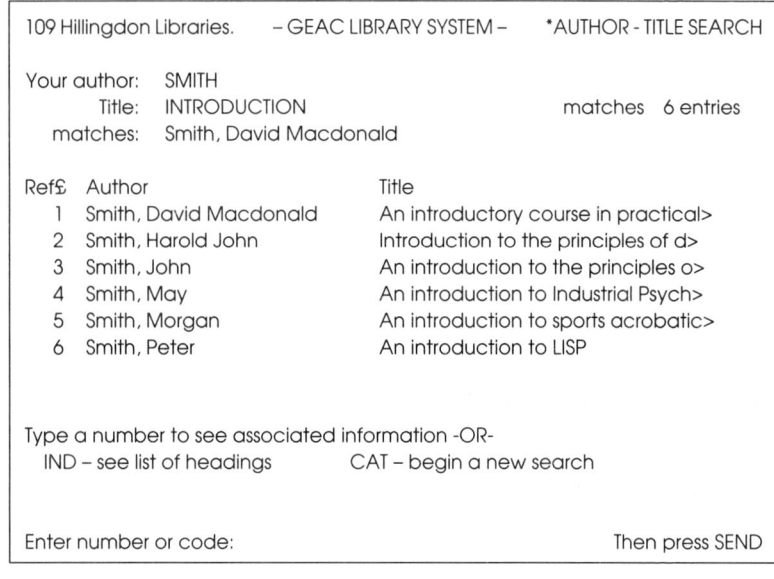

Figure 9.11   OPAC combined author/title display

A subject search

A subject search requires the user to input as a search term exactly the heading which was used by the cataloguer, to provide a direct hit. Fortunately, if there is no perfect match or if there are several index entries which match the search term, the system displays the relevant part of the index (see Figure 9.12), showing the number of titles to which each term has been applied.

Since the introduction of the OPC and the growing awareness of its potential, it has been possible to give subject headings which are of use to the public. This includes the use of subject headings for junior fiction material, which has benefits for staff and users alike. One other specialized use has involved Hilling-

```
109 Hillingdon Libraries.      – GEAC LIBRARY SYSTEM –      *SUBJECT SEARCH

Your subject:  DOG                                   Matches   49 subjects

                                                              No of entries in
                                                              entire catalogue
  1   dog                                                            2
  2   Dog and Duck public house, Denham                              1
  3   Dog behaviour                                                  1
  4   Dog breeding                                                   6
  5   Dog breeds                                                    12
  6   Dog care                                                       3
  7   Dog grooming                                                   2
  8   Dog health                                                     1
  9   Dog manuals                                                    1
 10   Dog racing                                                     2
 11   Dog shows                                                      1

Type a number to see more information -OR-
   FOR – move forward in this list      BAC – move backward in this list
   CAT – begin a new search

Enter number or code: FOR                               Then press SEND
```

Figure 9.12 OPAC subject index display

don's relatively large playset collection. Each play has been subject indexed according to the number of characters and their sex. This enables drama societies to search the database using these parameters to discover quickly the titles which will suit the available cast.

A number search

This choice leads to a sub-menu offering five choices: call number; ISN; Library of Congress Number; Government Document number; and Catalogue source number. In Hillingdon only the first two of these have any application, so the others have been suppressed. The call number (classmark) search is very useful. There are two effective classmarks in use: one is the bibliographic number which is applied to the catalogue entry as a whole (there can of course be added entries); the other is a copy-specific 'number' which indicates the shelf location. It is perfectly possible to classify a bibliographical entry by traditional Dewey but to allow the copies of the book to be shelved by some other number or alphabetic term. In Hillingdon this has been done to a considerable degree by the recataloguing of all items to place them into stock categories. The potential of the call number index might best be illustrated by Figure 9.13. Not only does the system allow the bibliographical and shelf location 'numbers' to be different, but each copy can have a different shelf location. In Hillingdon, the local college is linked to the catalogue which is able to accommodate the classification scheme used there as well as the public library's categorization scheme.

```
109 Hillingdon Libraries.      - GEAC LIBRARY SYSTEM -     *SUBJECT SEARCH

AUTHOR:     Alfieri, Vincent
TITLE:      The best book of Wordstar : features release 5


Location         Item      Shelf Location        Copy    Availability

UH   /UHADLT     UTCBK     651.8                  1      On Loan    13-03-91 24:00
UX   /UXADLT     ANF       MANAGEMENT: 651:8      2      On Loan    23-02-91 24:00



FUL  -  see full details              CIT  -  return to the list of entries
IND  -  see list of headings          FOR  -  see next entry in list
BAC  -  see previous entry            CAT  -  begin a new search
TWO  -  see full shelf locations
Enter code: FOR                                            Then press SEND
```

Figure 9.13   OPAC brief display showing mixed classifications

There is an important cost element to be considered when contemplating such an index, as there is an obvious requirement for disc storage capacity. Because the amount of data involved is considerable, it can also prove difficult to actually build the index in the first place.

A search against the class index works in much the same way as other searches, and for multiple matches or mismatches the index is displayed with a title count for each. Direct hits lead to the display of those titles with the classmark concerned.

Number searches can also be undertaken against ISBN, BNB and Library of Congress numbers, and so forth. One further element of sophistication allows gramophone record or cassette or CD manufacturers' numbers to be entered as control numbers.

A keyword search

There are three keyword searches on the Geac OPC: author, title and subject. In each case multiple hits result in the display of one-line entries and a hit count; a single perfect hit bypasses this listing and displays the entry concerned; complete misses produce the message 'Nothing found, try again'.

Author keywords are any words or names within the author field, for which purpose hyphens are treated as spaces. Such a search is useful when compound (especially foreign) names are concerned; it is no longer essential to provide 'see references' for such names as they can be discovered by searching under any component. Author keyword searches also bring together corporate authors whose names may be alphabetically separated but which cover a similar topic. For example, a search under 'library' would bring together titles entered under 'Library Association', 'American Library Association' and 'British Library'. Within keyword searches there is the added facility of righthand truncation, signified by the symbol #. This is not required in the other searches as righthand truncation is generally implied, but in keyword searching the desire to truncate must be indicated. Thus, an author keyword search for 'librar#' would additionally find 'Hillingdon Libraries' and so on.

Title keyword searching is perhaps the most significant step of all. Every word in every title is indexed, apart from a very limited number of stopwords which are site-defined. Though some words produce an excessive number of hits (the system count states 'More than 100 matches' in these circumstances), it is still possible to browse down the entire listing in a relatively short time. Title keyword indexing produces significant numbers of entries when used as an alternative to subject searching. Though false drops are common, especially in a catalogue with a high fiction content, this does not appear to be disconcerting to users.

Subject keyword searches work in much the same way as above but against the subject headings file. They therefore offer a way of bringing together all the headings on a given topic, despite their position in a subject string.

Boolean searching

Boolean searching was available to 8000 users, but was always likely to unduly affect response times. It has been considerably developed on the 9000 series, and from the author's admittedly brief experience of it, it works very efficiently. Sites offering this facility report a high level of satisfaction amongst their users, and have been pleasantly surprised that response times are so good, with impact on the rest of the system much less intrusive than feared. Those sites offering Boolean searching provide it as the sixth choice on the menu, rather than calling that choice 'Keyword' searching. Boolean searching in fact allows the user to search any or all of the three keyword indexes in a single search.

As with the other search options, the system displays instructions on how to perform a Boolean search, explaining the use of special symbols to denote the AND (& or blank), OR (/) and NOT (!) operators. The '-' is used to find two words together in a phrase, and parentheses are used to group words together in a complex search. Terminals directly connected to the system offer a menu-driven beginner's search, or advanced searching for the more experienced user, but unfortunately, because of screen handling difficulties, this is not yet available to users accessing the system remotely across networks.

Having entered a search and pressed the SEND key, the system searches each element in turn. As with the BPS system described earlier, where too many words will be retrieved a warning is displayed. The result is displayed as a citation list, from which the records can be displayed in a variety of orders (see Figure 9.14).

It is also possible to limit the search before beginning by taking choice 7, which acts in the same way as the SET command in BPS. Having typed 7 and pressed SEND, an intermediate menu screen lists the permitted ways of limiting the search (see Figure 9.15). Combined with the Boolean capability, this represents a very powerful catalogue searching tool. One drawback of this facility is that once set, limits remain in force until changed or removed. This can lead to confusion in an OPAC, where a user may be interested only in material published after 1975, and perform a search with satisfactory results. If the date limit remains set however, the next user may be unaware that the entire database is not being searched, and fail to find the required material.

Another choice that can be made available from the OPC main menu, but not illustrated here, is the ability to permit users to view their own records, rather than doing so via the Public Query part of Circulation. This has obvious attractions,

```
271 EDIN.UNIV.MAIN.LIB.    – GEAC LIBRARY SYSTEM –    LIM *BOOLEAN
                                                         RESULTS

£  WORD                   AUTHOR     TITLE    SUBJECT      TOTAL

1  GEAC                      0         1         0           1
2  WESTLAKE                 23         0         0          23

-----------------------------------------------------------------
Your search has found ONE CITATION

  DAR – display as retrieved         REV – Revise current search request
  DAT – display in author/title order CAT – begin a non-Boolean search
  DTA – display in title/author order DST – display in subject/title order
  ABS – advanced Boolean search      CMD – see additional commands

Enter Command, then press CARRIAGE RETURN
```

Figure 9.14 OPAC Boolean search citation list (Reproduced by permission of Edinburgh University Library)

```
271 EDIN.UNIV.MAIN LIB.    – GEAC LIBRARY SYSTEM –    ALL *LIMIT SEARCH

How would you like to change your search limits?

  1. LOC – limit to citations found in specific locations.

  2. LAN – limit to citations published in specific languages.

  3. MED – limit to citations of specified media.

  4. YEA – limit to citations published in specific years.

  5. ALL – remove all search limits.

  6. CAT – to begin a new search.

  -OR- Press RETURN to return to previous display

Enter number or code, then press CARRIAGE RETURN
```

Figure 9.15 OPAC search limit choices (Reproduced by permission of Edinburgh University Library)

integrating all public functions except Community Information into one package, and removing any possibility of unauthorized access to the Circulation module. That it has not been implemented in Hillingdon was partly due to some early bugs and display problems, but also because it was difficult to think up a name for the package describing both the catalogue and user details elements in 15 characters or less so that it could be intelligible on the main TCP system menu! This will not be a problem with sites where the only package accessed by Public Enquiry terminals is the OPC.

References

Mitev, N.N., Venner, G.M. and Walker, S. (1985), 'Designing an online public access catalogue: Okapi, a catalogue on a Local Area Network.', British Library Research and Development Department Library and Information Report No. 39.

Walker, S. (1988), 'Improving subject access painlessly: recent work on the Okapi online catalogue projects,' *Program*, **22**, 1, January, pp. 21–31.

Walker, S. (1988), 'Okapi: Developing an intelligently interactive online catalogue,' *VINE*, **71**, October, pp. 4–11.

10 The Acquisitions module

The Acquisitions module is designed to operate those library functions which control creation of orders, order file maintenance, receipt and financial records. Library acquisitions systems present a wide range of operative methods, unlike the Circulation functions, where patterns of operation are broadly similar. In addition there is differing practice in between the major geographical areas, North America, United Kingdom and Europe where the Acquisitions System is well-established. Now used by national, academic and public libraries in these areas, the module is designed to cater for a wide variety of acquisitions routines.

This flexibility results in a module which can appear complex, but in fact can be used for large library systems with multi-site selection and multiple copy ordering, or for single site, single copy ordering with equal success. Originally designed for North American academic libraries operating discrete acquisitions systems, the module has been modified to reflect developments in acquisitions practices in the ten years since its inception. This inherent and developed flexibility within the module allows its integration into these differing operative systems.

The aspect of planning the integration of the Geac system into acquisitions routines is an important one, and it is necessary in the initial stages to establish the interrelationship of different functions, and the resultant implications for management information. The software is very complex, but compile options and site specific features are available to effectively customise the package.

Databases and external communications

Data in the Acquisitions database can be used within any of the modules including Circulation and MRMS or BPS. In Acquisitions data can be transferred from the other databases to form the bibliographic details for ordering.

One of the major developments produced for UK libraries has been the provision of cataloguing facilities within Acquisitions, enabling records to be created which can form the basis of the order to a library supplier, and the eventual bibliographical record. Acquisitions to Circulation transfer, online or overnight, can then be set up, without utilizing the MRMS or BPS module. In addition, data from suppliers or other external sources can be downloaded into a Potential Requirements File (PRF). These records can be transferred to Acquisitions and enhanced to the required standard. This structural change is following the trend in acquisitions departments to utilize external data, and reduce in-house cataloguing.

Approval tapes from several library suppliers, such as Askews, Holt Jackson and Morley in the UK, and Blackwells and Coutts in North America, are now available. Some suppliers can provide data via electronic mail, for example JMLS in the UK. This system provides for the downloading of MARC records into the Potential Requirements File and for electronic ordering using BISAC (Book Industry System Advisory Committee) standard. Invoice tapes from suppliers can be downloaded and data can be transferred to external financial services departments, with full reconciliation, for issuing of cheques against invoices.

Westminster City Libraries have had success in creating their potential requirements file by electronic communication between their Geac 8000 and the booksellers T.C. Farries, by X25 over the British Telecom PSS network. Farries send a weekly download of data via their BT Gold Mailbox, which is then accessed by the Geac and transferred to the Potential Requirements file. Any existing record for a title in the PRF is overwritten to prevent any risk of an outdated record being used as the basis for an order. The system also works in reverse to allow automatic electronic ordering. Westminster have ceased to send printed orders to Farries; they are dispatched nightly to the Farries mailbox for subsequent capture by the Farries computer. All the file transfer is carried out automatically by the system as part of its overnight processing, minimizing costs and using free processing time. Similar procedures are available for accessing other booksellers' systems.

In addition, Geac are developing software to allow downloading of data from other external sources, such as databases available on CD-ROM, a number of which are especially relevant to Acquisitions. Records would be downloaded overnight, or transferred as single records online.

Online functions

There are nine functions available, all represented by a three-letter mnemonic on the initial main menu (Figure 10.1).

SEARCH QUERY	SRH	Searching the databases
REQUEST QUERY	REQ	Creating requests and orders
ORDER MAINTENANCE	ORD	Monitoring the order file
VENDOR QUERY	VND	Recording suppliers' details
BUDGET QUERY	BUD	Accounting functions
STAFF PRIVILEGE	STF	Maintaining staff records
CURRENCY	CUR	Maintaining currency exchange rates
INVOICING	INV	Maintaining invoice records
CHEQUE QUERY	CHQ	Creating payment records

The screen layouts and command structures are similar to those in Circulation; the complexity of the screens can be reduced by suppressing fields, and the development of Screen Manager will allow sites to arrange screens to their own requirements. LPLANG can be used to alter terms, some of which differ with national usage.

There is a Help subsystem as in Circulation, command driven, and command codes as well as main functions can be assigned to the programmable function keys.

```
M 1 ONLINE ACQUISITION SYSTEM 12-03-91

LOCATION: Z/ZB          TIME: 14:42

FUNCTION: TERMINAL MODE SELECTION

SRH   SEARCH QUERY      REQ   REQUEST QUERY
ORD   ORDER MAINT       VND   VENDOR QUERY
BUD   BUDGET QUERY      STF   STAFF PRIV
CUR   CURRENCY          INV   INVOICING
CHQ   CHEQUE QUERY      OFF   SIGN OFF
```

Figure 10.1 Acquisitions main menu

The following description of the use of the system is somewhat simplified, as many variations of input and usage are possible at each stage, but the basic steps of selecting an item, ordering, receipting and invoicing are outlined.

Search Query

This is used to establish if a copy of the item required is already in the library's stock, or if there is a bibliographic record held in the databases. There is a default for the sequence of databases to be checked so that the Acquisitions, Cataloguing or Potenials, and Circulation databases are searched in the specified order (see Figure 10.2).

If the bibliographic data for the item is held in the system it can be transferred to Request Query by use of the ADD command. This will carry across the bibliographic data and the class number, category and material type. If a record is found in Acquisitions the request can be updated, if it has not yet been made into an order, or another order can be created. If the item is not on any of the databases, it can be added as an original entry in Request Query.

```
1 ONLINE ACQUISITION SYSTEM 12-03-91   DISPLAY: part/all   ACCESS LEVEL: 6
FUNCTION: SEARCH QUERY   TIME: 14:43   SHERIDAN, MARGARET

COMMAND:DSP   SUBCOMMAND:CIR   SEARCH TYPE:ISN   BROWSE KEY: ISN   DIRECTION:+   AMT:001
ISN       :  0566055139                  CLASS # :
TITLE     :

AUTHOR    :

SERIES    :

MATCHING ON (ISN  ) FROM (CIRC  ) SYSTEM
LC CARD   :
AUTHOR    :  WATSON, Alan A.
TITLE     :  Forensic medicine: a handbook for professionals.

IMPRINT   :  Gower, 1989.
CLASS     :  614.19
ISN       :  0566055139
COPIES:  3      HOLDS:  0
STATUS:  *ON ORDER**VERIFIED*
  WK     PPR     BP
```

Figure 10.2   Acquisitions search query

Request Query

There is a distinction in the system between creating the request (or selection) for order, and creating the order for the supplier, which can be maintained to allow selection and ordering to be performed as separate functions. Search Requests can be printed overnight to assist in collation and verification of requests to order.

Bibliographic data transferred from Search Query or entered on the bibliographic screen in Request Query is augmented by the addition of the location for which the item is intended, and the funds which will be used to pay for it. In earlier releases these additions, and the subsequent process of converting the request into an order required the operator to use several screens; this has now been simplified and the number of screens required can be reduced. To describe the elements used to compile the order, the automatic sequence of building up an order is followed.

The first screen in Request Query is the Bibliographic Screen (see Figure 10.3). This will hold data transferred from Search Query, or data entered directly on this screen. The system at this point assigns a sequential request number to the request, or a request number can be designated. If a monographic series is being requested or ordered, a main record (series title) can be created, with linked information records for each volume title.

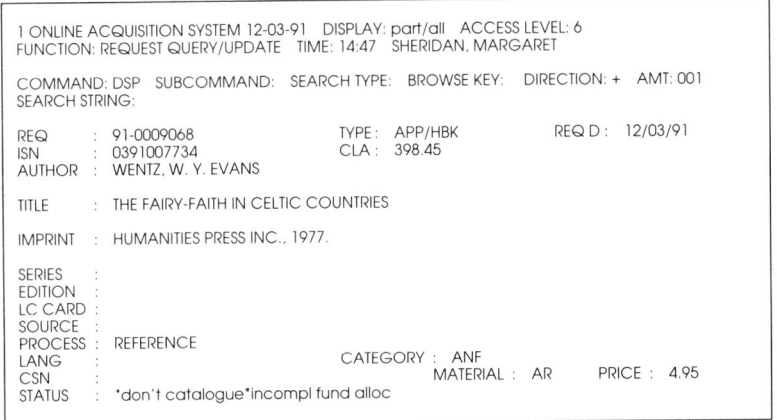

Figure 10.3 Bibliographic Screen in Acquisitions request query

Primary Request and Secondary Request Types are assigned; these are site-defined, and can be considered as facets of the information used to provide management information, as they are used for subsorting account and order reports. Generally, reporting on requests and orders will be required for the type of order, the format, the category of material, the location and the function, for example reference, short loan. Some sites may find that not all these aspects can be combined in the request/order types and the account structures, and may also need to use the Category or Media field to overcome this, and to use it as an additional subsort for reports.

The system prompts to the Miscellaneous Screen, where the item can be flagged as an urgent order, using the Rush Order field, if necessary (see Figure 10.4). The name of the searcher, selector and requestor appear on this screen, and these can be set as system defaults. Other defaults include location, vendor and accounts.

```
1 ONLINE ACQUISITION SYSTEM 12-03-91   DISPLAY: part/all   ACCESS LEVEL: 6
FUNCTION: REQUEST MISC/LOC QUERY/UPDATE   TIME: 14:47   SHERIDAN, MARGARET

COMMAND:UPD   SUBCOMMAND:MSC   SEARCH TYPE:   BROWSE KEY:   DIRECTION:+   AMT:001
SEARCH STRING:

REQ #     :  91-0009068  TYPE:  APP     /HBK           ACQ. PRIORITY:  1
AUTHOR    :  WENTZ, W. Y. EVANS                        CATALOGUE  :  N
TITLE     :  THE FAIRY-FAITH IN CELTIC COUNTRIES
RQUSTR    :  SHERIDAN, MARGARET
CANCEL REQUEST :  N      DUP ON ORD :  Y     LIB :  N
UNIT COST:  0.000.004.95    UK                         ACT :  26-03-91
```

Figure 10.4 Acquisitions miscellaneous screen

The next screen is the Location Screen, where the location and number of copies are entered. Up to five locations can be added on one screen (see Figure 10.5).

Using the automatic sequence, the next screen is for assignment of the Supplier or Vendor (see Figure 10.6), followed by the Fund Screen, which displays the total number of copies requested. Account numbers are entered and applied to a percentage of the total order or against a number of copies. A fund can be used to pay for copies for several locations, or several funds may be set against the copies for one location (see Figure 10.7).

```
1 ONLINE ACQUISITION SYSTEM 12-03-91   DISPLAY: part/all   ACCESS LEVEL: 6
FUNCTION: REQUEST MISC/LOC QUERY/UPDATE   TIME: 14:51   SHERIDAN, MARGARET

COMMAND:ADD   SUBCOMMAND:LOC   SEARCH TYPE:   BROWSE KEY: REQ   DIRECTION:+ AMT:001
SEARCH STRING:   910008910


REQ #    : 91-0008910  TYPE:  REP    /PBK         ACQ. PRIORITY:  2
AUTHOR   : WENTZ, W. Y. EVANS                     CATALOGUE :  N
TITLE    : THE FAIRY-FAITH IN CELTIC COUNTRIES
RQUSTR   : SHERIDAN, MARGARET
CANCEL REQUEST :  N       DUP ON ORD :  N    LIB :  Y
UNIT COST:  0.000.004.95    UK                 ACT :  00-00-00



LOCATION INFORMATION
  #   LOCATION    VOL   CPY
 001   A          000   001
 002   P          000   001
 003              000   000
 004              000   000
 005              000   000
```

Figure 10.5   Acquisitions location screen

```
1 ONLINE ACQUISITION SYSTEM 12-03-91   DISPLAY: part/all   ACCESS LEVEL: 6
FUNCTION: REQUEST VENDOR QUERY/UPDATE   TIME: 14:50   SHERIDAN, MARGARET

COMMAND:ADD   SUBCOMMAND:VND   SEARCH TYPE:   BROWSE KEY:   DIRECTION:+ AMT:001
SEARCH STRING:

REQ #    : 91-0009071  TYPE:  APP    /HBK        REQ DT:  12-03-91
AUTHOR   : WENTZ, W. Y. EVANS
TITLE    : THE FAIRY-FAITH IN CELTIC COUNTRIES
IMPRINT  : HUMANITIES PRESS INC., 1977.
STATUS   : *don't catalogue*incompl fund alloc

VENDOR   : JMLS          JMLS LIMITED
```

Figure 10.6   Acquisitions vendor screen

The final screen is the note screen, where instructions to the vendor can be entered, for printing on the order form, and any general and cataloguing notes can be recorded

The flexibility of the system supports several methods of selecting and ordering, in addition to the automatic sequence.

1   Requesting an item using the UPD MSC FUL screen on which two locations and two funds can be entered, with subsequent addition of vendor and authorization of the order.

```
1 ONLINE ACQUISITION SYSTEM 12-03-91   DISPLAY: part/all   ACCESS LEVEL: 6
FUNCTION: REQUEST FUND QUERY/UPDATE   TIME: 14:52   SHERIDAN, MARGARET

COMMAND:ADD  SUBCOMMAND:FUN  SEARCH TYPE:   BROWSE KEY: REQ   DIRECTION:+ AMT:001
SEARCH STRING:  910008910


REQ #     : 91-0008910  TYPE:  REP      /PBK          REQ DT:  12-03-91
AUTHOR    : WENTZ, W. Y. EVANS
TITLE     : THE FAIRY-FAITH IN CELTIC COUNTRIES
IMPRINT   : HUMANITIES PRESS INC., 1977.
STATUS    : *on order*ready for ord*vendor delay notice*don't catalogue*Acq Priority 2


FUND INFORMATION  (2 COPIES)
LINE     FUND #           #COPIES    APPLY     AUTH
001   A000-A2000-20000     001         Y         Y       BLACKBURN ANF REFERENCE
002   Z000-A2000-CT200     001         Y         Y       CENTRAL SERVICES SYSTEM COPY REF.
003   ZFS2-00000-00000     002  f      Y         Y       FS ADULT NON-FICTION ASSET ACCOUNT
004   0000-00000-00000     000         Y         N
005   0000-00000-00000     000         Y         N
006   0000-00000-00000     000         Y         N
```

Figure 10.7   Acquisitions fund screen

These two operations can be performed separately, or combined, and reduce the number of screens used (see Figure 10.8).

```
1 ONLINE ACQUISITION SYSTEM 12-03-91   DISPLAY: part/all   ACCESS LEVEL: 6
FUNCTION: REQUEST MISC/LOC QUERY/UPDATE   TIME: 14:53   SHERIDAN, MARGARET

COMMAND:UPD  SUBCOMMAND:MSC  SEARCH TYPE:FUL  BROWSE KEY:    DIRECTION:+ AMT:001
SEARCH STRING:


REQ #     : 91-0009073  TYPE:  APP      /HBK         ACQ. PRIORITY:  1
AUTHOR    : WENTZ, W. Y. EVANS                       CATALOGUE :  N
TITLE     : THE FAIRY-FAITH IN CELTIC COUNTRIES
RQUSTR    : SHERIDAN, MARGARET
CANCEL REQUEST :  N       DUP ON ORD :  Y    LIB :  N
UNIT COST:  0.000.004.95      UK                     ACT :  26-03-91


#     LOCATION      VOL   CPY
1                   000   000
2                   000   000


#      FUND #          #COPIES    APPLY     AUTH
1    0000-00000-00000    000        Y         N
2    0000-00000-00000    000        Y         N
```

Figure 10.8   Acquisitions miscellaneous full screen

2 Input of request and order as one operation using the Brief Screen. This allows all order details to be input on one screen, with up to seven locations and funds (see Figure 10.9).

```
NLINE ACQUISITION SYSTEM 12-03-91   DISPLAY: part/all   ACCESS LEVEL: 6
FUNCTION: REQUEST QUERY/UPDATE   TIME: 14:56   SHERIDAN, MARGARET

COMMAND: BRF   SUBCOMMAND:   SEARCH TYPE:   BROWSE KEY:   DIRECTION:   AMT:
SEARCH STRING:

REQ #    : 00-0000000    TYPE :  APP     /HBK         ORD LOC:  ZB
ISN      : 0843605723    CLA  :  642.56               MATL:    ANF
AUTHOR   : SEABERG, Albin G.
TITLE    : Menu design: merchandising and marketing. 2nd ed. Rev.

IMPRINT  : U.S. : Institutions/Volume Feeding Magazi EDITION:
ACQ. PRIORITY:  1    CAT:  N     ACT:  26-03-91      RQUSTR: SHERIDAN, MARGARET
VENDOR   : JMLS      UNIT COST:  0,000,010.00 UK     DUP ON ORD: Y    LIB: Y

 #   LOCATION    VOL   CPY            FUND #         COPIES   APPLY   AUTH
001               000   000     0000-00000-00000      000       Y       N
002               000   000     0000-00000-00000      000       Y       N
003               000   000     0000-00000-00000      000       Y       N
004               000   000     0000-00000-00000      000       Y       N
005               000   000     0000-00000-00000      000       Y       N
006               000   000     0000-00000-00000      000       Y       N
007               000   000     0000-00000-00000      000       Y       N
```

Figure 10.9 Brief screen in Acquisitions request query

3 Several agencies adding locations and funds for the same item, using the separate locations and fund screens; a central order unit can add the vendor and authorize the order.

When all the detail required for ordering has been entered the request can be authorized for overnight printing, or generated online. Full bibliographic details including class number and heading, where provided at the time of ordering, are printed out, and locations can also be printed on the order form, for direct delivery by the vendor.

After the order is printed the Request Query file can be interrogated by vendor, or invoice information can be displayed after receipt, just as in Purchase Order Maintenance, but monitoring of the progress of the order and receipting of items are carried out in Purchase Order Maintenance.

Purchase order maintenance

Receiving in Purchase Order Maintenance records items supplied against the order for specific locations (see Figure

10.10). At this stage the item bar code can be wanded in for overnight transfer to the Item File, or this can be bypassed and the bar code wanded in when the item is received at the requesting library.

```
1 ONLINE ACQUISITION SYSTEM 12-03-91   DISPLAY: part/all   ACCESS LEVEL: 6
FUNCTION: PURCHASE ORDER MAINT              TIME: 15:01   SHERIDAN, MARGARET

COMMAND:DSP  SUBCOMMAND:  SEARCH TYPE:ORD  BROWSE KEY: ORD  DIRECTION:+ AMT:001
SEARCH STRING:  9100013973
ORD. #   :  91-00013973      TYPE    :  REP      \  PBK           ORD  :  12-03-91
REQ. #   :  91-0008910       VENDOR :  WILL       EST DEL  :  00-00-00   REQ  :  12-03-91
ISN      :  0391007734       CLASS   :  398.45    ACTION   :  00-00-00   RVW  :  00-00-00
STATUS   :  *on order*ready for ord*Acq Priority 2
             *vendor delay notice
AUTHOR   :  WENTZ, W. Y. EVANS
TITLE    :  THE FAIRY-FAITH IN CELTIC COUNTRIES

                    ORDERED         RECEIVED
#   LOCATION   VOL   CPY      VOL   CPY    LST.DATE
1   A           0     1        0     1     12-03-91
2   P           0     1        0     1     12-03-91
```

Figure 10.10   Order display in Acquisitions purchase order maintenance

This function allows for receipt of all copies for multiple locations by the command REC ALL, or for receipt line by line for each location, and for receipt of part orders. The system can be compiled to produce routing slips for the received items.

Invoicing at time of receipt builds up the invoice, by entering the invoice number and amending the default unit price, if necessary, on the receiving lines (see Figure 10.11). This saves duplication of input in the Invoicing function, where the invoice can also be compiled by inputting order number, copies and price as a separate process from receipt.

Vendor reports can be added to the system using ADD REP (see Figure 10.12), although these do not at present link to the exception reports by altering the action date; Geac are developing this to allow vendor reports to over-ride preset action dates. For outstanding orders, claims (or reminders) can be produced. Claims are controlled by the action dates and estimated delivery date, and can be generated automatically, or added to individual orders after the order exception report is produced. The Claim exception report identifies those claims which have not been responded to by the claim action date.

```
1 ONLINE ACQUISITION SYSTEM 12-03-91   DISPLAY: part/all   ACCESS LEVEL: 6
FUNCTION: PURCHASE ORDER (RECEIVING)    TIME: 15:02   SHERIDAN, MARGARET

COMMAND:REC  SUBCOMMAND:ALL  SEARCH TYPE:ORD  BROWSE KEY: ORD  DIRECTION:+  AMT:001
SEARCH STRING:  9100014121
ORD. #   : 91-00014121    TYPE    : ORG      \ HBK           ORD  : 12-03-91
REQ. #   : 91-0008916     VENDOR  : JMLS     EST DEL : 10-06-91  REQ  : 12-03-91
ISN      : 0904568040     CLASS   :          ACTION  : 00-00-00  RVW  : 00-00-00
STATUS   : *on order*ready for ord*Acq Priority 2

AUTHOR   : PRESSLAND, DAVID
TITLE    : THE ART OF THE TIN TOY

ORDERED       RECEIVED        :   RECEIVING
VOL  CPY      VOL  CPY        :   VOL  CPY
000  001      000  001        :   000  001

COMPLETED :  Y      PROCESSING INFO :  N    SHELF OR TRUCK # :
NXT DEL   : 10-06-91    DAMAGED :  N      ACTION DATE : 00-00-00   CATALOGUE:  N

INV : 681339           LNE: 0000    TYP: CMP    UN.COST: 0,000,010.95    D%:  00
ADJ : 0,000,000.00
DSC : Y REG:Y TAX:Y
```

Figure 10.11   Acquisitions purchase order receiving

```
1 ONLINE ACQUISITION SYSTEM 12-03-91   DISPLAY: part/all   ACCESS LEVEL: 6
FUNCTION: PURCHASE ORDER (ADD REPORT)    TIME: 15:08   SHERIDAN, MARGARET

COMMAND:ADD  SUBCOMMAND:REP  SEARCH TYPE:  BROWSE KEY:  DIRECTION:+  AMT:001
SEARCH STRING:
ORD. #   : 91-00014131    TYPE    : APP      \ HBK           ORD  : 12-03-91
REQ. #   : 91-0009097     VENDOR  : WILL     EST DEL : 11-04-91  REQ  : 12-03-91
ISN      : 0391007734     CLASS   : 398.45   ACTION  : 00-00-00  RVW  : 00-00-00
STATUS   : *on order*ready for ord

AUTHOR   : WENTZ, W. Y. EVANS
TITLE    : THE FAIRY-FAITH IN CELTIC COUNTRIES

REPORT # : 000000000   DATE   : 12-03-91    TIME : 15:08    TERM # : 001
LOCATION : A           REPORT : REPRINTING
BY : SHERIDAN, MARGARET
ACT : 12-05-91         CLAIM  : N
```

Figure 10.12   Adding Acquisitions vendor reports

Geac are developing the claims routines to allow claim cycles to be stored at order level, updating the cycle derived from the vendor record.

Returns of damaged items can be recorded on the system. Cancellation of orders does not remove the order record from the file, but only marks it as HISTORICAL, and items may still be received against cancelled orders. When an order is cancelled on line, all outstanding claims are also deleted automatically.

Two useful commands in Purchase Order Maintenance are DSP OTH (see Figure 10.13) and DSP HIS. These display information relating to the order including receipt, invoice and completion dates.

```
1 ONLINE ACQUISITION SYSTEM 12-03-91   DISPLAY: part/all   ACCESS LEVEL: 6
FUNCTION: PURCHASE ORDER MAINT         TIME: 15:10   SHERIDAN, MARGARET

COMMAND:DSP SUBCOMMAND: SEARCH TYPE:ORD BROWSE KEY: ORD DIRECTION:+ AMT:001
SEARCH STRING:  9100000973
ORD. #   : 91-00000973    TYPE    : REP       \ CAS            ORD  : 10-01-91
REQ. #   : 90-0023335     VENDOR  : ULV2      EST DEL : 00-00-00   REQ  : 28-12-90
ISN      : SOUND 42       CLASS   : RS        ACTION  : 00-00-00   RVW  : 00-00-00
STATUS   : *on order*printed*Rcpts COMPLETE

AUTHOR   : STREET, Pamela $B JERMYN, Jane
TITLE    : The way of the river. (C)

                        OTHER INFORMATION
ENTRY DATE : 28-12-90              ENTRY BY :  SOUTH RIBBLE ACQ 1
EDIT DATE  : 09-01-91              EDIT BY  :  HOLDING, FRANK
LAST RECEIPT DATE : 22-01-91       CANCELLED DATE :  00-00-00
LAST INVOICE DATE : 22-01-91       RENEWAL DATE   : 00-00-00
COPIES PAID      : 0               YEAR END DATE  : 00-00-00
AMOUNT COMMITTED : 7.00            YEAR END AMOUNT :      0.00
CURRENCY RATE    : 1.0000          AGENCY : SL
OUTSTANDING ORDERS : 01
```

Figure 10.13 Acquisitions purchase order information

To complete an order, and remove any outstanding commitment, the AUT CMP command can be used. If the vendor can only supply part of a multiple copy order this command will decommit the outstanding amounts. Currently the decommitment and expenditure on part orders are pro-rated against all locations, however, Geac are developing a more equitable system linking commitment and spent amounts to the actual number of copies allocated.

Archiving of completed orders enables removal of old records from the online and storage of the information on tape, allowing data to be retained for the required audit period. The data relating to the order, that is invoices and cheque requests, is linked and removed in the archiving processes.

Serials control subsystem

The serials subsystem is used to create order records for serials (including annuals or standing orders), to receive issues or parts, and to create claims for missing issues.

A serial record is created by adding to the order record information about the terminology and frequency of the issues or parts. The system makes predictions about the receipt of items, which are confirmed as issues are received, or can be used to claim missing issues or return incorrectly supplied items. An important feature of the serial record is the review date. This is used for review and renewal of subscriptions, which can be renewed individually or as a block, and the funds recommitted.

The Level Screen is used to describe the terms applied to the serial, for example volume, issue, part; the numbers of these are also defined, for example one volume, with twelve issues, each in two parts (see Figure 10.14). Prediction of the receipts is entered on the Frequency Screen to set the date of arrival and interval between receipts (see Figure 10.15).

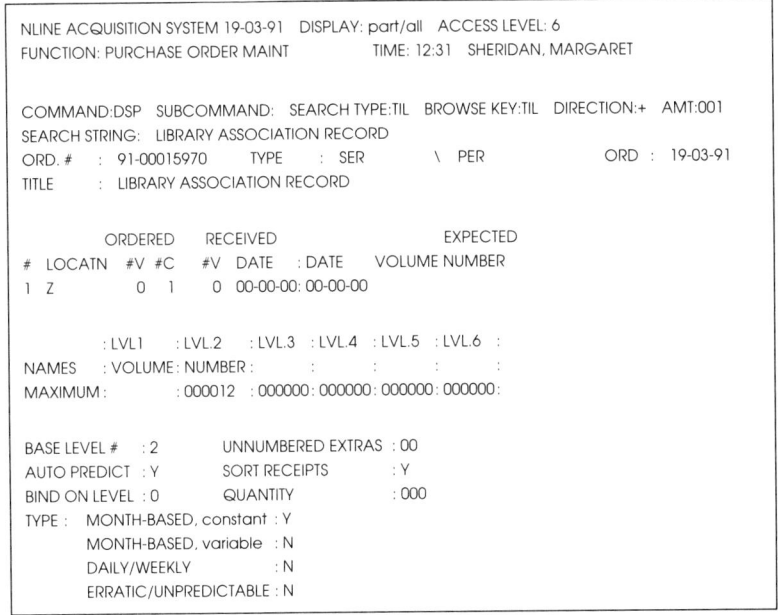

Figure 10.14 Acquisitions serials subsystem levels screen

```
NLINE ACQUISITION SYSTEM 19-03-91   DISPLAY: part/all   ACCESS LEVEL: 6
FUNCTION: PURCHASE ORDER MAINT              TIME: 12:31   SHERIDAN, MARGARET

COMMAND:DSP   SUBCOMMAND:   SEARCH TYPE:TIL   BROWSE KEY:TIL   DIRECTION:+   AMT:001
SEARCH STRING:   LIBRARY ASSOCIATION RECORD
ORD. #     : 91-00015970      TYPE    : SER        \ PER              ORD  :  19-03-91
TITLE      : LIBRARY ASSOCIATION RECORD


            ORDERED      RECEIVED                EXPECTED
#  LOCATN   #V  #C    #V  DATE     : DATE     VOLUME NUMBER
1   Z        0   1     0  00-00-00: 00-00-00


# of NUMBER                 : 01
DATE OF FIRST ARRIVAL       : 01
ARRIVAL INCREMENT (DAYS)    : 00
MONTHS BETWEEN RECEIPTS     : 01

ARRIVAL DELAY (DAYS)        : 020
NOTES  :
```

Figure 10.15   Acquisitions frequency screen

For predictable regular serials the system information should be correct, and the receipt is straightforward. If the prediction is incorrect because of variations in supply, the item can be received or returned and the predictions reset. The command REC ALL can be used when each location receives at least one copy of the serial; currently invoice information cannot be entered at receipt. Duplicate issues, back issues and extras can be receipted, and claims entered for missing issues. Frequency changes and changes of title can be accommodated. There is a binding control function available for use with serials.

The serials subsystem is used by some of the libraries using Acquisitions in the UK; its application is more widespread among European Libraries. Some aspects of the subsystem are complex and involved; Geac are reviewing these to simplify and improve this function.

Vendor query

This function holds information on all suppliers used by the library. The vendor record contains details of addresses, contacts, the type of material supplied, and payment methods (see Figure 10.16).

```
1 ONLINE ACQUISITION SYSTEM 12-03-91   DISPLAY: full/all   ACCESS LEVEL: 6
FUNCTION: VENDOR QUERY/UPDATE          TIME: 15:11   SHERIDAN, MARGARET

COMMAND:DSP  SUBCOMMAND:  SEARCH TYPE:  BROWSE KEY:COD  DIRECTION:+  AMT:001
SEARCH STRING:  JMLS

NAME  : JMLS LIMITED                   CODE  :  JMLS         F.S.:
ADDRESS FUNCTION: BOK*                 CLAIM MODE: 1FOR*
ADDRESS: P.O. BOX 17                   ALT NAME: N
         GAMBLE STREET
         NOTTINGHAM                    S.A.N.:
         NG7 4FJ                       MAIL CODE:
PHONE: (0602) 708021    EXT: 0000      CONTACT: STUART LUNN   TELEX: 000037577
STATUS : *Send auto claims             USAGE  :
TYPE   : DIST                          AGENCY : Z
CLAIM RULES:                           CLAIM CYCLE: 0030
CREDIT RULES:                          DELIVERY CYCLE: 0090
CREATION DATE: 26-05-87                BY: FOWLER, DAVID
EDIT     DATE: 12-03-91                BY: SHERIDAN, MARGARET
NOTE:

OUTSTD:       4  COMMIT:     201.09  SPENT YTD:     0.00  MIN BALANCE: 000,000.00
COMPLT:       1                      SPENT NET:     0.00
```

Figure 10.16 Acquisitions vendor record

In compiling the vendor record the details entered include:

Name	– the usual business form of name
Code	– site defined, up to eight characters
Address	
Function	– this is used if the vendor has more than one address for different functions, for example Subscription, Book Approval
Claim mode	– up to three methods of claiming can be specified, including forms and letters
Address	– the main address of the supplier; additional addresses can be entered here
Alternative name	– if the payment is different from the main vendor name
Type	– such as publisher, distributor, exchange partner
Claim cycle	– the number of days between the date a reminder is issued and the date a response is expected
Delivery cycle	– the estimated delivery time for the vendor; if materials with differing delivery cycles

are supplied by the vendor separate vendor records will be required. For example, a library supplier providing approvals, replacements and items from abroad could have three records, with estimated delivery dates consistent with the type of material.

The vendor record also displays the number of outstanding and completed orders, the outstanding commitment and the year to date spent amount.

On the status screen various descriptors can be applied, for example:

Deposit vendor
Prepayment required
Automatic claims

Setting the status flag for automatic claims, if so compiled, produces the printed claims for that vendor without reporting initially on an exception report.

Account/budget query

This is used to create accounts for each department or cost centre within the library. It is important to consider when implementing the system, that the fund structures, order types and categories can be combined to provide reports as required on overall spending patterns, and for spending by types of material, type of order, format, location and category. The fund structure can contain up to six levels to reflect these aspects. Reports are then produced by grouping the levels in the accounts together. Many of these elements are input at the time of making the request, so some sites have now defined an account mapping system, building up the account number automatically when the request is created.

The system uses four-part accounting to audit level, with budget accounts for library spending control. An equity account corresponding to the overall funding available is set up for Financial Services, with corresponding equity accounts for each library agency. Asset accounts are created for Financial Services and Library Budgets to reflect budget allocations. Financial Services budget asset accounts can be used to give global totals by different primary factors; for example, a Financial Services Non Book Media Fund will show online commitment and spending on Non Book Media, which may also be set as a level within the library budget asset accounts.

In practice there are generally fewer Financial Services budget asset accounts than library budget accounts. Financial Services asset accounts can be applied at the time of ordering or of invoicing. New money can be entered and money can be moved between accounts using the Journal Entry sub-system, and journal records are maintained (see Figure 10.17). On line the commitment, spent amounts and balances are displayed (see Figure 10.18). More detail on spending, with breakdown by account levels and order types is provided by the reports.

Year end procedures will transfer uncommitted balances and commitments into new accounts. Accounts are usually annualized, and the financial year to which they relate is displayed in the account record.

```
NLINE ACQUISITION SYSTEM 19-03-91   DISPLAY: full/all   ACCESS LEVEL: 6
FUNCTION: ACCOUNT/BUDGET QUERY       TIME: 12:33   SHERIDAN, MARGARET

COMMAND:DSP  SUBCOMMAND:DTL  SEARCH TYPE:  BROWSE KEY:COD  DIRECTION:+  AMT:001
SEARCH STRING:  AA21

ACCOUNT NUMBER  :  A000-A2000-10000        AGENCY  :  Z
NAME  :  BLACKBURN ANF LENDING             CODE    :  AA21
STATUS  :  *active*ASSET ACCOUNT*BUDGET ONLY
                                                                  CURRENT
                         TRANSACTION INFORMATION
  JRNL #      TYPE    ACCT DATE    AMOUNT +/-    ENTRY DATE    BY
  00002790    TRN     12-03-91        177.00     12-03-91     PITCHER, MARGERY
  00002789    TRN     12-03-91        177.00-    12-03-91     PITCHER, MARGERY
  00002723    TRN     30-01-91      1,000.00     30-01-91     WILLIAMS BRIAN
  00002709    TRN     03-01-91      3,500.00     03-01-91     WILLIAMS BRIAN
  00002686    TRN     14-11-90        300.00     14-11-90     WILLIAMS BRIAN
  00002681    TRN     06-11-90      4,300.00-    06-11-90     WILLIAMS BRIAN
  00002680    TRN     01-11-90        300.00-    01-11-90     BLACKETT, DAVID
  00002649    TRN     22-08-90     34,150.00     22-08-90     WILLIAMS BRIAN
  00002643    TRN     15-08-90     14,000.00     15-08-90     BOUSFIELD, SUSAN
  00002618    TRN     18-07-90      5,000.00     18-07-90     WILLIAMS BRIAN

                                 MORE ?Y
```

Figure 10.17 Acquisitions account transaction information

```
NLINE ACQUISITION SYSTEM 19-03-91   DISPLAY: full / all   ACCESS LEVEL: 6
FUNCTION: ACCOUNT / BUDGET QUERY        TIME: 12:35   SHERIDAN, MARGARET


COMMAND:DSP   SUBCOMMAND:   SEARCH TYPE:   BROWSE KEY:COD   DIRECTION:+   AMT:001
SEARCH STRING:   ZA2CT1

ACCOUNT NUMBER  :  Z000-A2000-CT100              AGENCY  :  Z
NAME  :  CENTRAL SERVICES SYSTEM COPY LENDING    CODE    :  ZA2CT1
STATUS  :  *active*ASSET ACCOUNT*BUDGET ONLY
                                                            CURRENT
ACTIVATION     DATE :  01-04-86      OPENING BALANCE   :   31,000.00
DEACTIVATION   DATE :  31-03-99      AMOUNT COMMITTED  :   24,856.72
LAST CLOSING   DATE :  07-04-90      SPENT/ACTUALS     :        0.00
ALLOWED COMMIT % :  105              ESTIMATED BALANCE :    6,143.28
                                     EDIT DATE  :  06-04-88
                                     BY  :  WILLIAMS BRIAN
```

Figure 10.18   Acquisitions account display

Invoicing

The invoicing function is used to create and maintain invoice records, and to prepare invoices for payment. Essentially, a copy of the invoice is held in the system, and any combination of discounts and surcharges itemized by the vendor can be replicated.

The main elements of the invoice record are the header, which contains such details as invoice number, vendor, total amounts, and the invoice lines, which can be individually identified by line number (see Figure 10.19)

Invoices can be entered into the system in two ways, by creation of an invoice header and addition of individual lines using the invoicing function, or by building up the line information at receipt in Purchase Order Maintenance and then verifying the invoice in the invoicing function. Creation of an invoice record in full in invoicing can seem time-consuming, as some of the information is already held in other parts of the system, for example order number, copies, unit price. However, for serials, standing orders and some pseudo orders this procedure is necessary.

An invoice header record is created, using the main invoice template. The invoice number, invoice type, gross totals, vendor, surcharges and discounts are entered The invoice type is usually for information, for example:

    INV   –   Regular invoice

PRO – Pro forma (no receipts)
PAR – Partial payment

Three of the invoice types must be used correctly for the system to operate properly:

CRE – Credit note: enables automatic accounting reversal
REN – Renewal: signals renewal of payment (for serials)
CMP – Complete: signals completing of payment (for archiving)

Discount can be entered as a total value for the invoice, which will pro-rate to each line, or as an overall percentage for the invoice in the discount percentage field. If several discounts are present on an invoice, each item line may have specific discount entered.

There is a default setting for foreign currency payments. Regular charges are entered in the header from the invoice document, and are pro-rated to each line item. This field can be used to record servicing and other handling charges. Special charges apply only to specific lines and are not pro-rated.

```
NLINE ACQUISITION SYSTEM 19-03-91   DISPLAY: part / all   ACCESS LEVEL: 6
FUNCTION: INVOICING QUERY / UPDATE        TIME: 12:36   SHERIDAN, MARGARET

COMMAND:DSP  SUBCOMMAND:   SEARCH TYPE:   BROWSE KEY:INV   DIRECTION:+   AMT:001
SEARCH STRING:   A683767
                                                                        TOTAL:
INVOICE NO :  A683767              INVOICE TYPE :  INV      GRSS :      314.72
STAT  :  *verified*authorized*report*                       DISC  :      31.47
NAME:  JAMES ASKEW & SON LTD (APPROVALS)                    RCHG:         0.90
       218-222 NORTH ROAD                ENTRY : 21-01-91   SCHG :        0.00
       PRESTON                           STTMT : 00-00-00   TAX  :        0.00
       PR1 1SY                           AUTHN : 24-01-91   NET  :      284.15
VEND : ASK1     FUNC :  BAP*             DUE   : 00-00-00   BAL  :      284.15
AGENCY : Z    VOLS :   0   CPYS :  28    INV CUR :  UK

              ORDERED                              INVOICED
LINE  TYP   ORDER NUMBER   CPY   UNIT PRICE    CPY   UNIT PRICE   D%    NET AMOUNT
0001  CMP   90-00042682      5      4.99        5       4.99                22.53
0002  CMP   90-00042690     18     14.99       18      14.99               243.61
0003  CMP   90-00042715      5      3.99        5       3.99                18.01
```

Figure 10.19 Acquisitions invoice record

When the header record has been created, invoice lines are added by entering order number, copies, unit price, and adjustments (usually special charges for individual items). The system automatically assigns line numbers, although these can be changed if the invoice document is numbered differently.

Action dates can be set for the whole invoice, or individual lines; the invoice or specific line will appear on an exception report if not paid by the action date.

Once an invoice is complete, it must be validated to check for discrepancies, and allow final verification of the amount due for payment. Invoices can be validated overnight or online using the validation commands:

'VLD TOT'	to transfer gross total, copies, volumes charges and discount to the header if these fields have not been filled in when creating header record
'VLD BAL'	to compare the totals of the lines with the fields in the header
'VLD PRO'	to pro-rate regular charges, discounts and taxes
'VLD CMP'	to ensure the invoice is complete and all copies invoiced have been receipted.
Using VLD	without a sub-command has the effect of entering VLD BAL VLD PRO and VLD CMP in turn

There may be a small difference in the net amount online, and on the invoice document, because of differing conventions of rounding. To correct this, an adjustment can be entered on one of the lines and the invoice revalidated. If the invoice does not validate initially, messages in the bottom line of the screen will show errors, for example:

'Missing receipts Line 003'

'Price discrepancy Line 005'

These examples are especially useful from an audit veiwpoint, as discrepancies between the order and the invoice are highlighted and can be checked before the invoice is passed for payment.

Invoices can be compiled at receipt by addition of invoice number, unit price, discount and adjustments to the receiving lines. The invoice function can then be accessed, the invoice number found and any regular charges, overall discount percentage and invoice date entered. Amount fields can be filled in using VLD TOT to calculate the totals. The invoice is then ready for verification.

Invoices can be updated, provided no cheque has been issued or payment already made. Single lines or whole invoices can be deleted, and marked as HISTORICAL, although they will not be removed from the system and can still be displayed. Credit notes can be entered, either attached to an invoice, or separately. When a credit is entered, the accounts are adjusted accordingly. DSP DTL is useful for showing information about an invoice line including number of copies ordered, received and invoiced, last invoice and receipt date, and pro-rated charges and discount.

When the invoice is validated it will appear as verified in the status field, and is ready for payment.

Cheque query

Verified invoices must be authorized for payment for the overnight to generate a cheque request, and this stage can be carried out by a different staff member so that both invoice and payment request are not created by the same person. At this point, money will transfer into the spent category of the accounts.

The system prepares the cheque voucher, which has all the information required for producing the payment. This can be entered online if necessary, rather than generating overnight (see Figure 10.20).

Currency Exchange Query

Academic and national libraries in particular pay invoices in different currencies. The Currency Exchange Query function is used to set and maintain rates of exchange (see Figure 10.21). Changes in rate are usually effected by the overnight currency exchange report, which amends the currency record, and recalculates committed amounts. Updating the rate online does not however change the existing committed amounts. Discrepancies in accounting can occur when there is a delay between the library's creation of a cheque request, and the actual payment by the Finance Section, which may then be at a different exchange rate, and currently this can only be dealt with by creating an offsetting invoice.

```
NLINE ACQUISITION SYSTEM 19-03-91   DISPLAY: part / all   ACCESS LEVEL: 6
FUNCTION: CHEQUE QUERY                TIME: 12:44   SHERIDAN, MARGARET

COMMAND:DSP  SUBCOMMAND:   SEARCH TYPE:   BROWSE KEY:CHQ  DIRECTION:+  AMT:001
SEARCH STRING:   00023867

CHEQUE # :   00023868            CHEQUE DATE   :  29-03-91         TOTAL :      284.15
INV CURR :   UK                  CHQ CURRENCY :  UK                INV RATE :   1.0000
VENDOR CODE :  ASK1              FUNCT :  BAP*                     BASE :       284.15
NAME    :  JAMES ASKEW & SON LTD (APPROVALS)                       PAY RATE :   1.0000
ADDRESS :  218-222 NORTH ROAD                                      PAY :        284.15
           PRESTON
AGENCY CODE :  Z                 AUTH'D BY :   SHERIDAN, MARGARET
DISPOSITION    :  *mail*         STATUS :   *outstanding*

INVOICE NUMBER           ITEM     TYP    STATUS          AMOUNT  NOTE              OK
A683767                  000      INV    *verified*>     284.15
```

Figure 10.20   Acquisitions cheque request display

```
NLINE ACQUISITION SYSTEM 19-03-91   DISPLAY: part / all   ACCESS LEVEL: 6
FUNCTION: CURRENCY EXCHANGE QUERY     TIME: 12:38   SHERIDAN, MARGARET

COMMAND:FND  SUBCOMMAND:   SEARCH TYPE:   BROWSE KEY:COD  DIRECTION:+  AMT:001
SEARCH STRING:  FR

COUNTRY NAME  :  FRANCE
COUNTRY CODE  :  FR
CURRENCY NAME :  FRANC
STATUS        :  ACTIVE

EXCHANGE RATE :  009.9502         PENDING RATE :  0009.9550
DATE LAST EDITED :  19-03-91      BY :  SHERIDAN, MARGARET
```

Figure 10.21   Acquisitions currency record

Staff Privileges

Each member of staff using Acquisitions is assigned in Staff Privileges the functions they are entitled to use, the funds they can control and the security level at which they can operate. Security levels range from one to seven, although in practice three is generally assigned to operators, and five to supervisors. At the higher levels staff can over-ride online warnings, for instance, to be able to order more than the maximum number of copies, or to exceed the maximum amount for an invoice.

In addition, privilege bits are set defining the functions each staff member can use. These can be set so that, for example, staff creating invoices are not able to authorize them (see Figure 10.22). A list of funds which a staff member can authorize is also attached to the staff record. Security levels and privileges combined ensure staff operation of the system meets audit requirements.

Every user signs on to the system with their name and password (or by wanding a bar code). The password is unique and cannot be accessed by other users.

```
NLINE ACQUISITION SYSTEM 19-03-91   DISPLAY: full / all   ACCESS LEVEL: 6
FUNCTION: STAFF QUERY / UPDATE         TIME: 12:38   SHERIDAN, MARGARET

COMMAND:DSP   SUBCOMMAND:   SEARCH TYPE:   BROWSE KEY:NAM   DIRECTION:+   AMT:001
SEARCH STRING:   WILLIAMS BRIAN

NAME :   WILLIAMS BRIAN                    IDNO :   000 000 394
STATUS       :  ACTIVE                     AGENCY :  Z
DEPARTMENT :  unknwn                       SECURITY LEVEL :  6
ACTIVATION DATE :  23-09-85                EXPIRY DATE :   01-04-97
                         STAFF PRIVILEGES
Pre-search              : Y    Journal entry       : Y    Invoice display        : Y
Request display         : Y    Order display       : Y    Invoice add/update     : Y
Request entry           : Y    Order add           : Y    Invoice authorize      : Y
Request add/update:     Y     Order update        : Y    Cheque display         : Y
Budget display          : Y    Fund assignment    : Y    Cheque create          : Y
Budget add/update :    Y      Order print         : Y    Cheque print           : Y
Vendor display          : Y    Staff display       : Y    Currency display       : Y
Vendor add/update :    Y      Staff add/update   : Y    Currency add/update :  Y
Staff privs update      : Y    Receiving           : Y    Claiming               : Y
Authorize all funds     : Y
```

Figure 10.22   Acquisitions staff record

Offline functions

Overnight the offline software is run; this is self-supervising, controlled by commands entered during the day. There are several routines which can be designated for offline processing, such as verifying invoices, changing currency rates and cancelling orders. Orders, claims and search requests are generated and produced overnight. In addition, the Acquisitions reports are printed.

Reports

Offline programs read through the databases, extract information and produce reports, for monitoring the acquisitions processes and providing management information. Over 60 reports can be run; those supporting acquisitions operations are usually run daily or weekly, while the information reports can be run monthly or as required. Reports can be modified through CCPs and some can be selective, for example vendors can be specified for the vendor reports. However, more flexibility in producing reports is required, using a system such as the Report Generator.

There are several types of reports:

1. Listings, for example the List of Vendors and Addresses;
2. Summaries, such as the Budget Account Summary;
3. Analyses, for example the Vendor Performance Statistics;
4. Utilities, for use with the system, such as Exception Reports.

Financial information: budget reports

These facilitate the monitoring and planning of commitment and expenditure for the accounts. The structure of these reports is determined by the account number format, and by the categories chosen for primary and secondary order types.

Account Purchase Order Summary

This lists all active accounts and the purchase orders assigned to these accounts.

Budget Statement by Order Type

Within each budget the figures for the commitment and expenditure for the current month and year to date are shown, for each order type.

Budget Account Summary

This summary lists all funds in four sections: Budget Asset, Budget Equity, Financial Services Asset and Financial Services Equity. The report shows the budget, the amounts committed and spent, and the remaining balance for all accounts.

Purchase Order Account Summary

All orders created within a specified period are listed, and fund information is shown.

Account statement by vendor/order type

This shows the total value placed with each supplier subdivided by order types.

Vendor reports

There are several reports providing listings of vendors' names and addresses, vendor type and code, Financial Services code, contact person, phone and telex numbers. Blacklisted vendors, exchange and recipient vendors are similarly listed. Vendor performance can be monitored, for all vendors or for selected suppliers by the following analytical reports:

Vendor Peformance by Elapsed Time

This is used to show the number of orders supplied within given date ranges, and an average supply time for each order type is calculated. For example, the number and percentage of orders supplied in less than 30 days can be shown, based on the difference between the date of the order and the date of the receipt.

Vendor Performance Statistics

The number of orders by order type and percentages of completed orders, of cancelled orders and claims are listed.

Exception reports

The Action Date is entered on line for requests, orders invoices and claims. This date controls the Exception Reports, so that outstanding records can be listed for staff to amend or process further. For example if an invoice is not verified or authorized by the action date it will be listed on the exception report.

Purchase order reports – monographs

These are used to monitor the order file, for example to review outstanding orders.

Order Type Report

This report lists order selected primary or secondary types within a specified range of dates by budget account and vendor.

Outstanding Order Report

Outstanding orders and associated commitments are listed

by primary or secondary order type, to enable the state of the outstanding commitment to be assessed.

Report of Orders for Cancellation
This report lists orders outstanding after a specified number of days to allow review before running a batch cancellation. A report of orders cancelled, sorted by account, can be run after the batch cancellation for information.

Purchase order reports – serials

Review Report
The review date is part of the serial order record, and is used by the system to produce the review report, which lists the invoice history and projected price for each item.

List Renewed Serials
This report lists all serial items renewed between selected dates, with an estimated price.

Receipt reports

There are several reports listing receipts and claims for specific periods. These are sorted by agency, monograph or serial, vendor, and order number.

Invoice reports

Invoice Ageing Report
This lists invoices which have not been paid, comparing a given date against the invoice due date.

Invoice Verification Report
Invoices can be marked online for verification overnight. This program goes through the invoice file for these invoices, marking them as verified and listing them in the report. If an error is found, the invoice is not verified, but is listed along with an error message giving the reason for the failure to verify.

Percentage Invoice Price Increase
This report shows the difference between the order price and the invoice price, over a minimum difference specified as a percentage.

Year end reports

Carry Forward Order Reports
This provides a report on orders with committed amounts which carry forward at the year end. For each account current commitment, year end committed figure and any expenditure since the year end as shown.

Carry Forward Order Report by Vendor
The report provides details for each vendor of current commitment, the year end committed figure and spent amounts since year end.

Year End Account Report
This is a summary for each account of commitment and unspent balances carried forward, and any unspent amount not carried forward at the year end.

System options

Conditional Compile Options or CCPs are used to provide each library with detailed definition of its individual acquisitions system. The answers to the CCPs are compiled into the software for each site. Broadly CCPs are used to select operating methods, to set defaults, to build in restrictions, and to customize some screen displays.

Operational choices include:

005 To add FS accounts at the time of ordering. Financial Services accounts can be added at the order stage instead of at the time of invoicing.

R03 Do funds apply as a percentage? Academic libraries generally like to use percentage of total costs for accounts, whereas public libraries usually apply cost of copies to each account.

U01 Create invoice details at time of receipt. This is an alternative method to building the invoice detail in the Invoicing function.

U31 Brief Screen entry. This allows compilation of the order on one screen, instead of several.

System defaults include:

R05 Default request action date setting. This sets the number of days a request remains on the system before appearing on an exception report.

R43 Default location code. This location will appear as a default on the location line.

R44 Default Budget account record number. This number will appear as a default on the fund line.

Examples of restrictions are:

N03 Price discrepancy per cent to prevent invoice verification. This sets the allowable percentage difference between the price on the order and the price on the invoice, which can only be over-riden by supervisory staff on a security level of five and above.

N04 Invoice total value to stop verification. This prevents the verification of invoices exceeding a total specified value by operators on a security level of less than five.

002 Total allowable cost for orders. This sets a maximum cost for orders, which can only be over-riden by a supervisor.

008 Threshold for 'copies per location' warning on ordering. This gives a warning level for the number of copies permitted for each location.

Development

New features and enhancements are incorporated in each release of Acquisitions software. These developments usually consist of changes made by Geac and requirements from users. The current Geac development list includes modifications to the Brief Screen, revisions to the Serials Subsystem, and downloading of external data, such as CD-Rom databases. User requirements to be incorporated in the current list include further development of online ordering, flexible reporting systems and enhancement of statistical information.

11 Community Information module and news services

Local Information

The Community Information module was originally developed with the name 'Local Information' in the UK as a result of contracts being signed with several public libraries which had each independently indicated the need for a local information database. The first such contract was with Somerset County Libraries and the module was developed in consultation with them. In March 1984 the software was released to a second client, who took over development and debugging trials, while Somerset staff concentrated on other developments. Though this resulted in several improvements to the software, the module was seen to require considerable revision in order to make the fullest use of its potential. Accordingly, a working party, comprising representatives from most of the public libraries in the UK then using Geac, was set up in late 1984 to provide a mutually agreed specification for the future development of the module. This working party, chaired by Alison Hunter of Hillingdon, included representatives from Bexley, Islington, Redbridge, Sutton and Westminster, while Camden, Somerset and the few academic sites who were interested were also invited to comment. The result was a draft specification which was forwarded to Geac in March 1985. Based on the existing software module, this draft specification suggested a number of major enhancements for future development, including greater storage capacity, improved keyword searching facilities, bulk updating facilities, word processing and the introduction of a degree of Boolean searching.

By September 1985, Geac had provided Hillingdon with three further versions of the software; the latest one including some amendments from amongst those recommended in the specification. Though still far from perfect and well-short of the ultimate goal, the module was deemed to have reached a state of development sufficient for its launch to the public. As a consequence, the first limited database was made available during October, although initial publicity was kept to a minimum. Publicity was not actually encouraged until January 1986, by which time the database had grown to some 3000 entries.

The Local Information software was based upon the existing Circulation software, but it was felt by several people, including staff at Hillingdon, that the OPC had more user-friendly features, and this thinking eventually caused Geac to rewrite the software encompassing many of the searching and index display features of the OPC. The first version of the new software, renamed 'Community Information' to underline the fundamental changes it had undergone, was installed at the London Borough of Sutton in late 1989. Enhancements in the Community Information module over the Local Information system include the extension of the keyword search to the subject as well as the name field, the introduction of a field for contacts, the ability to use the contact field for automatic mailing of communications, and the integration of the news system into the package. Included in the Sutton package was remote spooling of print-outs to designated polled printers, and most significantly, the ability for remote users to dial-in.

Geac were by now being faced with many requests from existing and potential customers for facilities in the package, and at their request the working party was reconvened in January 1990 to attempt to arrive at a consensus on the kind of facilities most wanted. Many of the suggestions were welcomed by Geac, and it is to be hoped that some at least will find their way into future releases of the product.

The latest version of the software was installed in the London Borough of Hillingdon in January 1991. The database has the capacity for some 20,000 entries. Criteria for inclusion in the Hillingdon database are that the information should be both local and useful. Details included cover council information, local services, local organizations, business information, sources of help and advice, accommodation, recreation, local events, and the current condition of sports pitches. The system has also been used successfully to disseminate election results boroughwide (Hunter, 1986).

The database

Each entry in the Community Information database comprises four fields:

1. SUBJECT: 60 characters maximum
2. NAME: 150 characters maximum
3. CONTACT: name/address, telephone and postcode fields
4. DETAILS: 710 characters maximum on 1st page (can be extended to additional pages)

The subject field can be set up to include a subheading and/or a 'see' reference. The subheading is identified by the use of a $b delimiter (which can be altered to something more user friendly, such as &, using LPLANG) and allows one or more additional subject terms to be entered for any entry. Each subheading is indexed and the entry listed and retrieved by that term as well as by the main subject heading.

'See' references are added by means of a $s delimiter, in the form 'HANDICAPPED $s DISABLED' (= HANDICAPPED see DISABLED). Searches for 'handicapped' will automatically retrieve and display the entries under 'disabled'. The non-preferred subject term with its 'see' reference is included and displayed in the alphabetical list of subject headings, which thus acts as a thesaurus for the system.

There is also a facility to create 'Reference' entries: these are information/ 'see also' entries which appear at the beginning of a sequence of entries filed under a particular subject. These can be used to direct the searcher to several related subject headings (see Figure 11.1), or to highlight important explanatory information.

In addition to the four main fields, status details of individual entries are held and may be displayed by the use of the 'D' key, or function key 7. This is essentially for staff reference and gives details of date, time, terminal number and initials of the operator who created the entries. The same details are also shown for updates to the entry. It also gives a count of the total number of times the entry has been updated; any expiry and automail dates which have been set; and (most importantly) the number of times that the entry has been displayed (see Figure 11.2). This last statistic enables staff to respond more directly to public demand.

Statistics of use, including the number of times records covered by each subject heading have been displayed, can be obtained by running the batch program LBSUSE. The field containing the count of the number of times displayed can be reset to zero at intervals to produce statistics relating to a given

```
SUBJECT SEARCH

Your Search :  ACCOMMODATION              Matches   14 entries
Subject   :  ACCOMMODATION
Name      :  Information entry

Contact :
                                                Tel :
                                                Post code :
Details   :  see  ACCOMMODATION AGENCIES
                  BED and BREAKFAST ACCOMMODATION
                  ESTATE AGENTS
                  GUEST HOUSES
                  HOTELS
                  HOUSING ADVICE
                  MOTELS
                  RENTED ACCOMMODATION

                                        Amended on :   11-08-89
     H  -  For Help                N  -  Show next entry
     L  -  Show preceding entry    S  -  Find a new subject
     E  -  Begin a new search      C  -  Show Additional Commands
Enter your choice here :                         Then press SEND
```

Figure 11.1 Community Information System information entry

```
STATUS DETAILS FOR PAGE

Your Search :  SWIMMING                   Matches   17 entries
Subject   :  SWIMMING POOLS
Name      :  Hayes Swimming Pool

Contact :  Winchcombe, Mr                      Tel :
           (manager)
                                               Post code :
Details  :  Central Avenue
            Hayes              Tel :   081 573 2785
OPEN     :  Mon   12.30 - 9.30pm              Sat  10am - 4.30pm
            Tue   7 - 8am, 12.30 - 7.40pm     Sun  8am - 1.45pm
            Wed   12.30 - 9pm
            Thur  7 - 8am, 12.30 - 7.40pm
            Fri   12.30 - 6.40pm
Created :  06-12-85 at 17 : 32 on term  15   Inits :  amh     Displayed :  46
Amended:  09-01-91 at 12 : 21 on term 109    Inits :  jf      Updated :    17
Expiry date :  00-00-00                      Automail date : 00-00-00
     H  -  For Help               M  -  Show next entry
     N  -  Show next entry        L  -  Show preceding entry
     S  -  Find a new subject     C  -  Show Additional Commands
Enter your choice here :  M                       Then press SEND
                                     CONTINUED ON NEXT SCREEN>>>
```

Figure 11.2 Community Information System status details

time period, for instance on an annual basis. This is achieved, with caution, by the use of a program called MODIFY. Limited analysis of the package's **TCP1 file, detailing the number of Sends, and the number of characters sent can be obtained for each terminal and port, on an hourly basis, from the program LPTCPA.

The date the entry was created or last amended appears in the bottom righthand corner of each entry to give the user an indication of the currency of the information.

Creating and amending records

ADD and UPDATE functions are available by password only. As with Circulation, the password can be in the form of a bar code, which has to be physically wanded. Status details are automatically displayed at the foot of the screen in these functions so that the operator's initials can be added on completion. Data is entered almost entirely in free format. Pressing the SEND key then results in the immediate adding or updating of the indexes and of the 'created on' or 'amended on' information at the bottom right of the screen.

A further command 'AM' allows further details to be added if there is insufficient space within the first screen to display all the information desired. When this option is used the subject, name and contact fields are retained on the screen and the details field is cleared for completion as required. When such a record is displayed, the message 'Continued on the next screen >>>' appears at the foot of the screen, and the option 'M' is offered to the user, with the cursor positioned appropriately. Choosing 'M' will cause the next page to display, from where the option 'O' will return the user to the first page of the entry. The command 'UM' allows the added pages to be updated.

An expiry date can be set for any entry if required, and separate expiry dates can be set for any added page. An early warning period of entries due to expire can be defined in an overnight program called LPEXWN, which produces a report on entries due to expire after the relevant time. Another program, LPEXPG automatically removes entries which actually have expired, listing them for checking purposes.

An automail date can also be set if required. Letters addressed to the 'contact' can be generated at a specified date by running the program LPAUTM, in order to request the checking of the accuracy of the information currently on file.

The delete function is also password-protected, and a check mechanism 'Delete this entry?' requires the operator to confirm that deletion is desired. An added page can be deleted separately from the main entry. The online deletion function actually only sets a flag for the entry to be deleted: the entry is then completely removed by an overnight run of the garbage collection program LPLIGB.

Searching the files

Access to the module can be made available via the inter-online communications module, or as another choice from the Public Query facility of the Circulation package. Using the terminal configuration program SPCNFG access can be allowed or denied to each individual terminal.

Once chosen, the module displays one or more introductory pages, giving explanations and help, which lead in turn to the main menu (see Figure 11.3). The menu offers three search types: Subject, Name, and Keyword, and access to the Local News and Events file.

Selection of any of these choices presents an appropriate screen template and requests the input of the search term. As with the OPC, some degree of control of the appearance of these screens is available to individual sites. Use of the '/' key allows command chaining from the CIS main menu, avoiding

```
HILLINGDON LOCAL INFORMATION

                    Your choices are :

          1.  SUBJECT you are interested in

          2.  NAME of an organisation

          3.  Single KEYWORD

          4.  LOCAL NEWS AND EVENTS

          5.  EXIT from Community Information

Type the number which matches your choice or
type H for help here :                          The press SEND
```

Figure 11.3 Community Information System main menu

the need to display these intermediate screens. Contextual help can be obtained by using the f1 function key, or keying 'H' at any point in the system. A significant advance with the CIS is the facility whereby sites can easily decide the text to be displayed in these help screens.

At all times the user is presented with a menu at the foot of the screen indicating the options available. One of these options allows the searcher to remain in the chosen search type and undertakes another search without the need to return to the main menu. Other options make it possible to stop the search and return to the Community Information menu (E) or to go back to the original TCP or Public Query menu (X). Commands in the Community Information module are, in the main, effected by a single character followed by the SEND key. Staff commands (A: AM: U & D) are represented by function keys, but 'H' (for help) is at present the only option in the public part of the module which is also available via a function key.

Searching by name

A 'name' in the Community Information database is the name of an organization/society, premises, or of an individual. It is possible to add alternative forms of the name or initials by which an organization is commonly known (e.g. CAB) by means of a $b delimiter. Both forms of name are indexed and retrievable from a name search. The name search is phrase-indexed and retrieves on the full form of the name, though there is implicit righthand truncation.

In a name search, the system displays the search term in the top left of the screen and the number of matches found on the right. The nearest 12 names on file are displayed with their corresponding subject heading (see Figure 11.4). The closest match to the search term will be displayed first. The list can be browsed forwards and backwards, and the number of a particular entry chosen, to display full details. The commands 'N' and 'L' enable browsing record by record. If no matches are found for the search term, this information will be displayed in the top righthand corner of the screen, and the nearest 12 names listed. If only one match is found, the full entry will be displayed.

Searching by keyword

All words in the subject and name fields are indexed individually, as well as by phrase, and keyword search covers both

```
NAME SEARCH

Your Search :  THAMES                          Matches  7 entries

     Matches on the following :
     NAME                                      SUBJECT
  1  Thames Regional Rowing Council            ROWING
  2  Thames Valley Hospice, Windsor            HOSPICES
  3  Thames Valley Housing Society Limite>     HOUSING ASSOCIATIONS
  4  Thames Valley Orchid Society              HORTICULTURAL ORGANISATIONS
  5  Thames Water Authority                    WATER
  6  Thames Water Authority : Customer Se>     WATER
  7  Thames Water Authority (Rivers Divi>      WATERWAYS
  8  Theatre Booking Agents in the Borough>    THEATRES
  9  Theatregoers Club of Great Britain        THEATRES
 10  Theatre Royal Windsor                     THEATRES
 11  Theatre Studies   GCSE                    UXBRIDGE COLLEGE
 12  Theatre 7 (Drama Groups)                  DRAMA GROUPS

         H  -  For Help                    F  -  Browse forwards in index
         B  -  Browse backwards in index   E  -  Begin a new search
         S  -  Find a new name             X  -  Exit Community Information
Enter number or choice here :                                Then press SEND
```

Figure 11.4 Community Information System name index

fields together. As yet, the keyword search only operates on single terms, with no facility for combining terms or redefining searches.

Searching by keyword has a similar result to name searching, in that the search term is displayed at the top left of the screen and the number of matches found on the top right. The first 12 entries containing the keyword are displayed by subject heading with their corresponding name (see Figure 11.5).

The list can be browsed forwards and backwards, or full details of a particular entry displayed by choosing the relevant number. If no matches are found for the search term, this is indicated in the top righthand corner and the nearest 12 matches are listed. If only one entry containing the required keyword is on file, the full entry will be displayed.

Keyword searching is the most effective means of retrieving information from the Community Information database, providing care is taken at the inputting stage to include all the necessary synonyms and acronyms. For example, local events can be retrieved by date, type, location, or organizing agency, and details of councillors retrieved by name, ward name, or

```
KEYWORD SEARCH

Your Search :  WINE                                    Matches   16 entries
       Matches on the following :

       SUBJECT                        NAME
   1   WINE CLUBS                     Greenhill Wine Guild Eastcote
   2   WINE CLUBS                     Harefield Amateur Wine and Beermakin>
   3   WINE CLUBS                     Hayes and Harlington Wine Circle
   4   WINE CLUBS                     Hesa Winemakers Club
   5   WINE CLUBS                     Ickenham Winemakers
   6   WINE CLUBS                     Northwood Guild of Winemakers
   7   WINE CLUBS                     Uxbridge Guild of Winemakers
   8   WINE CLUBS                     Uxbridge Wine Society
   9   WINE CLUBS                     West Drayton Winemaking Club
  10   ADULT EDUCATION (EVENING)      WINE APPRECIATION                    >
  11   ADULT EDUCATION (EVENING)      WINE APPRECIATION An introduction >
  12   WINE CLUBS                     Hesa Winemakers Club

          H  -  For Help              F  -  Browse forwards in index
          B  -  Browse backwards in index    E  -  Begin a new search
          S  -  Find a new keyword    X  -  Exit Community Information
       Enter number or choice here :                Then press SEND
```

Figure 11.5 Community Information System keyword index

party affiliation. The limited research into public use undertaken in Hillingdon, however, indicates that members of the public seldom opt for keyword searching unless they are already computer literate.

The ending of all words in the subject and name fields are also indexed individually, and it is possible to keyword search for 'ology', for example. Unfortunately, Hillingdon has yet to find a use for this facility, other than as a 'party trick' during demonstrations.

Searching by subject

A subject, as used in the Community Information system, is a general classification for the entries, as determined by the library itself. A list of subject headings used in the database can be displayed in alphabetical order by keying '*' from the subject search screen. To start the alphabetical list from a particular point, * is keyed, followed by the required letter or subject heading.

Twelve subject headings will be displayed, including subheadings denoted by the $b delimiter and 'see' references denoted by the $s delimiter. The number of entries on file under each subject heading is given on the righthand side (see Figure 11.6).

```
SUBJECT SEARCH

Your Search :                                          Matches   0 entries

    List of available subjects :                       Entries

      1   CAR CLUBS                                       4
      2   CARD CLUBS                                      3
      3   CAREERS CENTRES                                 1
      4   ELDERLY $b CARERS                               4
      5   CAR PARKS                                       5
      6   CATHOLIC CHURCHES $s CHURCHES - CATHOLIC        1
      7   CAVING                                          1
      8   CEMETERIES                                      7
      9   POPULATION $b CENSUS                            1
     10   CEREBRAL PALSY                                  4
     11   CEYLON $b ELDERLY - GROUPS                      1
     12   CHAMBER OF TRADE                                5

    H  -  For Help                    F  -  Browse forwards in index
    B  -  Browse backwards in index   E  -  Begin a new search
    S  -  Find a new subject          X  -  Exit Community Information
Enter number or choice here : F                         Then press SEND
```

Figure 11.6   Community Information System list of available subjects

The list can be browsed forwards and backwards, or a particular entry can be selected for display by choosing the relevant number in the listing. Brief entries will then be displayed, and full details of entries displayed by selecting the relevant number.

If the required subject is known to be on file, the term can be typed at the initial search screen or from the main menu using command chaining. The search term will be displayed in the top left corner, the number of matches found indicated on the right, and the first 12 entries under the required subject term are listed (see Figure 11.7).

The list can be browsed backwards and forwards, and the number of a particular entry selected in order to display complete details.

If no matches are found, this will be indicated in the top righthand corner and the closest 12 matches listed. If only one entry is on file under the required subject term, the complete entry will be displayed.

```
SUBJECT SEARCH

Your Search :   RECYCLING                                    Matches   7 entries
      Matches on the following :

        SUBJECT                         NAME
     1  RECYCLING                       Bottle Banks in the Borough
     2  REFUSE SITES $b RECYCLING       Civic Amenity Sites / Refuse Transfe>
     3  REFUSE SITES $b RECYCLING       Civic Amenity Sites / Refuse Transfe>
     4  REFUSE SITES $b RECYCLING       Civic Amenity Sites / Refuse Transfe>
     5  REFUSE SITES $b RECYCLING       Civic Amenity Sites / Refuse Transfe>
     6  RECYCLING                       Paper skip (recycling of mixed paper>
     7  RECYCLING                       Recycling Officer
     8  REFLEXOLOGY                     Mary Martin School of Reflexology
     9  REFLEXOLOGY                     Reflexologists in the Borough
    10  REFUSE                          Fly tipping - action line
    11  REFUSE                          Furniture - unwanted
    12  REFUSE                          Hazardous waste disposal

           H  -  For Help                F  -  Browse forwards in index
           B  -  Browse backwards in index   E  -  Begin a new search
           S  -  Find a new subject      X  -  Exit Community Information
     Enter number or choice here :                          Then press SEND
```

Figure 11.7 Community Information System added entries

Searching by contact

This means of searching the Community Information database is available only after a valid password has been accepted. The contact index is accessible as choice 7 from the main menu (see Figure 11.3). A contact search will indicate the number of matches found, and list contacts alphabetically close to the search term with the corresponding name of the entry (see Figure 11.8).

Full details of an entry can be displayed by selecting the appropriate number.

If an automail date is set for a particular entry, a letter will be generated at the appropriate date addressed to whoever is detailed in the contact field. The contact can thus be asked to check details of his/her organization and the entry updated as necessary.

The introduction of a contacts field has been necessary in order to comply with the UK Data Protection Act. Accommodating the additional field, however, has meant the reduction of the details field on the first page of an entry from 1200 characters to 710 characters. Entries where a 'contact' is not appropriate now have a rather bare appearance. An improvement would see the introduction of two alternative display formats, with the contact field suppressed when blank.

Time-out facility

The module has a time-out facility which allows the system to return the terminal to the main menu screen whenever searching appears to have been concluded. The entry of a valid password or access level prevents the time-out from working, as this is only of use in the public side of the package, and would in fact be irritating in staff mode.

Response to the package

Other departments of the Council within Hillingdon have reacted enthusiastically to demonstrations of the system in use, and the successful election results service undertaken in 1986 (Hunter, 1986) established the system as an effective means of disseminating council information boroughwide.

Figure 11.8 Community Information System contact index

Several departments have been sufficiently impressed to order their own terminals for connection to the library service, in order to input and extract local information. Other departments have arranged to input details of their services from terminals located in the library. A terminal for public use has been located in the Civic Centre foyer.

Some applications are perhaps worth recording. One is the Leisure Department's use of the system to record the state of play of sports pitches during inclement weather. Previously, it had always been impossible to advise sports teams of the condition of pitches during bad weather and it was left to the teams to turn up only to discover that the ground staff had declared the pitch unplayable. Now the teams are advised to visit or telephone their local libraries, where the Community Information system gives the latest state. This has the added advantage of being operational throughout Saturdays in 17 libraries.

The Adult Education Office has been inputting details of day and evening classes in the Borough, and during enrolment week updates entries in order to indicate whether classes are full or have vacancies for late enrolments.

Youth Services have opened up access to the Community Information database to new groups of users. PCs have been installed at a number of youth centres in the borough for dial-in to the library system as described in Chapter 13.

Outside the Council, several agencies such as Citizen's Advice Bureaux, voluntary agencies and Job Centres have also seen the advantages of disseminating their information via the library system and the value of the database to them in answering enquiries. The invention of the dial-in interface has opened up access to many, providing they can afford the necessary PC and modem.

As detailed elsewhere in this book, developments in the Netherlands where library data is disseminated to the population via the local cable TV network are being watched closely in Hillingdon, with the hope that a similar project may be undertaken in the near future.

News systems

In addition to the mainstream Community Information module there is another mechanism for disseminating local information; this is by setting up a News system. The mechanism for doing so is a little crude, but nevertheless it offers yet another facility.

The Geac system can support a whole range of different News systems through individual packages. They use editor files and can thus be created only on control consoles, or on a PC using a word processing package and then downloaded to the c.p.u.

The News service in the Community Information module is an improvement on those provided with other modules, in that the user is not obliged to see it. Local News and Events (or some such form of words) is the fourth choice from the Community Information system main menu. It can consist of as many pages as the library chooses, although it is rarely necessary to extend this beyond half a dozen or so. Each page gives the user the option of continuing on to the next screen, or returning to the CIS main menu (see Figure 11.9).

Another way of presenting a News service is by the installation of another package, called ZQNEWS. This consists only of an editor file, which can be browsed from start to finish, or the user may quit at any point, being returned to the main system TCP menu. It is possible to create different News systems for different sites within a network; for staff teminals only; or for different purposes.

Figure 11.9 Community Information System news screen

Reference

Hunter, Alison (1986), 'Hillingdon Election Results Online,' *Assistant Librarian*; **79**(9), September, pp.123–5.

12   Other GEAC products

There are many products produced by Geac of interest to libraries, some of which are described here. In particular, this chapter is concerned with Electronic Mail (GEM), the transfer of files to and from micros (GTALK), and the image processing system Picture Power.

Electronic Mail

Geac Electronic Mail (known as GEM) is a true Electronic Mail system and should not be confused with the message transmission functions in use in the Circulation and BPS modules. Sites that have taken up the option to use GEM usually find that it is of considerable value to them, enabling better communication between far-flung staff. Particularly where library staff working patterns are such that the staff are never all at work at the same time, nor indeed all libraries open at the same time, the ability to post a message to all or some of them in one operation is greatly appreciated. It has been used for several years in the London Borough of Hillingdon, where managers are convinced that considerable savings of stationery, and particularly telephone calls are made.

GEM has most of the features one would expect from an Electronic Mail service. Users can send messages to individuals, or groups, or all other users. 'Public' groups are set up by the system's administrator, and users can be allocated to as many groups as needed. Any user may send a message to all the members of any group, regardless of whether he/she belongs to that group. The same message can be sent to all the members of several groups in one operation. By using the system's directory, it is an easy matter to identify who is in a particular group, or to which groups a particular user belongs. 'Private' groups are set up by the individual user, who is the only person able to send messages to that group.

Unlike many EM systems, GEM allows users to identify themselves by their 'real' names, rather than having to remember a complicated and meaningless ID. Each user can also have one or two 'aliases' to allow for easier signing on. Messages may be sent to the user by using the full name or either of the aliases. Signing onto the system is achieved by entering the name (or alias) in one field, followed by the password in another. Passwords are assigned by the user, who may change it at any stage.

In sending a message, copies can be sent to other users; these can be carbon copies that the main recipient is told about, or blind copies that the main recipient does not know have been sent. Mail can be sent 'registered', with the result that the system posts a message back to the sender when the recipient reads it, 'urgent' which put it at the top of the pile of messages for the recipient, or 'confidential', requiring the recipient to choose to read it having been warned of its nature beforehand. One drawback of the system is that there is no facility known to the author to extend a message beyond one screenful. This does at least impose the virtue of relative brevity!

Once a message has been sent, the recipient will be advised of the fact by a system generated message 'mail waiting' the next time GEM is accessed, or if already in use the next time Send is pressed. Users may check their index of waiting mail, either sequentially, or by applying criteria such as only those not yet read, or those from a particular user, or those satisfying a range of dates. The commands to check the index are also used to read the mail, so again the user may choose only to read urgent mail, for instance.

Having read a message, it can be deleted, kept, or replied to. If choosing the latter option, the reply is typed after the text of the message. Once the reply has been sent, the option to keep or delete the message is repeated. It is also possible to reply to a message that has been kept.

It is the author's experience that this is a reasonably user-friendly system. At Hillingdon all staff have a mailbox; this amounts to around 190 individuals, and the vast majority use the system with little difficulty. The main problem in its use is that library staff have long been conditioned that the 'Send' key is the one that makes things work, but in GEM they also have to use the Return and Tab keys to move between fields. Whilst this is also the case in other packages, for some reason GEM's appearance is such that they forget. In the early days of a person's use of this system this can cause some difficulty, usually manifested in the sending of replies to messages without actually managing to type a reply before sending it!

In North America GEM is used by Geac for communication between themselves and their customers. It is of particular use for the reporting of faults, but many other messages are also exchanged. Regrettably, to date UK users have not yet succeeded in persuading Geac of the value of such an arrangement in this country.

GTALK

GTALK is a product which enables IBM compatible PCs to communicate with a Geac host. Its purpose is to allow several PCs to share common files on the Geac system to process extracts of Geac generated information in such uses as statistics and bibliographies.

The software operates in two modes: Control Terminal Emulation and File Transfer. When acting in Control Terminal mode the user is able to perform all the operations possible from a normal control terminal, but usually with the advantage that this will be in a remote location from the c.p.u. It is not possible to wire the PC into a daisy-chain when running GTALK, as it requires a single line to a port on the Geac host. Should the PC be required to act as a library terminal running LTE emulation software in a normal daisy-chain, this can be achieved simply by plugging the correct cable into the PC's serial port(s) at the appropriate time.

File transfer mode permits ASCII files to be transferred either from the PC to the Geac host, or from the Geac to the PC. In the London Borough of Sutton this is used to manipulate the Community Information System news file on a commercial word processing package on the PC, which is an easier job than using the Geac editing facilities. Other uses of this mode are to download results from the various packages' report generators for word processing manipulation in order to produce bibliographies, or lists of local organizations. Once on the PC the data can of course be subjected to all the manipulation desired by the use of commercially available software, so statistics from the Geac could be fed into a spreadsheet, merged with other data also from the Geac in a word processor, and then perhaps produced as a report via a desktop publishing package.

ImagePower

ImagePower is a PC-based add-on product for the 8000,

9000 and Advance systems, or it can be linked to library systems provided by other suppliers. Using the Picture Power software package it claims to provide a complete multi-user solution to the problem of image storage, retrieval and indexing. Picture Power itself is a system for digitizing in considerably compressed format images captured by a video camera. The resulting data, compressed by a factor of 15 times, can be stored on floppy disk, hard disk or re-writeable optical disk. For security, it can be backed up to tape.

Once stored on disk, the image can be retrieved to a high resolution monitor, where it can be manipulated in many ways. For instance, it could be greatly enlarged, and because of its compression such enlargements are possible without noticeable lack of clarity. The image can be turned, or the colours changed, or amalgamated with another image. The resulting picture can in turn be saved to disk if required, or a hard copy photograph print can be produced. The system can be used stand-alone, or networked through a LAN. When combined with dBase III or Clipper, the potential of the system is further increased. Simply used in this fashion, Picture Power is a remarkable system, and is used for such diverse functions as maintaining a photo-file of employees for use by security guards, suspects for use by police, signature verification, etc.

The system has an obvious use for recording images of pictures and objects in the care of libraries or museums, and it is here that the link to a catalogue becomes valuable. The package of Picture Power linked to the Geac system is marketed as ImagePower. Using a normal Geac library terminal, the user can search the OPC using the normal indexes. On retrieving a record with an associated picture, the system will ask the user if he or she wants to see the picture. If the answer is 'yes' the picture will be displayed on a nearby high resolution monitor.

This is achieved by assigning a bar code number to the picture, which forms the link between the catalogue and the picture file. The catalogue search causes the Geac host to send the relevant picture index (and the workstation ID) to the Picture Power server, which is a PC with a LAN card and Picture Power compression and digitizing hardware added. The Picture Power server then sends the appropriate picture to the correct Picture Power workstation monitor. ImagePower is in use in the Institute of Social History (IISG) in Amsterdam, and the Miami-Dade County Public Library system in the United States.

CD-ROM interface

Geac, working in conjunction with the Massachusetts Institute of Technology (MIT) have begun to develop software to download bibliographic and static item status (e.g. location) data from the Geac 8000 (initially, but 9000 to follow) for output on CD-ROM to provide an offline catalogue. The second stage of this project will be to provide access to a distributed CD-ROM catalogue on a network, but linking back to the Geac machine to provide status details.

Book security systems

In another cooperative venture, Geac in conjunction with the Dutch company ID Systems have developed an integrated circulation/security system. ID Systems have for many years been selling book security systems, based on the activation/deactivation principle. This new venture combines the bar code reading requirement of the circulation system with the activation and deactivation requirements of the book security system at the same workstation. As the book is passed across a specially designed counter top the bar code is read, and at the same time the security strip is activated or deactivated.

At present each workstation has to be set up as issue and deactivation, or discharge and activation, with no ability to easily switch functions, but that shortcoming will be addressed shortly.

13 Management information

An important aspect of a computerized library system is its ability to produce information about how the system is being used, and whether it is performing as well as expected. That the information should actually be useful to management for the better running of the library is essential, but sadly, for too long, librarians have been happily producing vast quantities of data upon which they have often been unable to act, or even understand. Simply knowing how many books are issued in a year is of only limited value unless related to total stock, membership figures and so on. The computer is perfectly happy and able to produce reams of figures; it is the responsibility of the librarian to ask for the right data, and having been presented with it, to actually make use of it.

The Geac system produces management information under two broad headings; standard statistical packages, and *ad hoc* reports.

Standard packages

The original statistical package that Geac provided as part of the Circulation system is LPTSTM. This provides figures for circulation functions such as issues, discharges, holds, etc. by terminal group. They can be set to restart at the beginning of a new period (e.g. month or term), and will also give annually cumulating totals.

This statistical package is an efficient producer of data, but these data are only basic. Public librarians want to break down their issue figures by material type, at least. It is a major failing of the TSTM program that this is not possible. The figure it produces for holds relates to holds placed, but a figure for holds satisfied would be equally useful. There is little value in the former figure without the latter, for it only tells half the story.

Analysing libraries' busy times is possible as the figures are subdivided by hourly periods. This has implications for dynamic staffing of small branch libraries, when staff can be sent to branches to cope with anticipated peak periods. Management can be better informed as to what times it is appropriate for each library to be open, and when it is not.

TSTM can safely be left without being run for a couple of days, without invalidating the totals. The hourly and daily totals for those days when the program has not been run will be a cumulation of the intervening days' figures, but all the transactions will be recorded and included in the end of period totals. At both Hillingdon and Dundee these figures have been used when carrying out O and M studies and they have been found to be most useful.

The second standard statistical package is a combination of two programs, LPSMAG and LPSPAG. These sprang from criticisms that the TSTM statistics were inadequate – Geac was spurred into creating extra analytical programs which look at use by material types and by patron class. The figures are subdivided by agency and location but not by hourly periods. Of the two, LPSMAG is the more useful on a regular basis and it goes a long way towards satisfying many of the statistical requirements that have been identified by user libraries.

LPSMAG runs daily against the security file of the previous day's transactions, analysing activity by agency for all material types. The site can specify whether to count issues, discharges, renewals or holds. The program makes a separate sweep through the files for each activity to be counted so, to an extent, the number of counts depends on the amount of time at the library's disposal. Several sites have found that there is not enough time to run this program on top of all the other overnight procedures the system has to perform, so they run the program during the day. As with the copying of security tapes, it is possible to do this with the live circulation system running, as the separate security files are used. As with the security tape copying, there are also implications for response times at peak periods, so it is best timetabled for quieter periods. Because LPSMAG runs against the previous day's transactions, it is important that it is timetabled to run after the midnight of the day concerned, or the figures will be meaningless.

There are other pitfalls: if no disc-to-disc security copies are made at the end of the working day, the program will have no new data to run against, and the result will be a string of zeros. In the event of such a circumstance, the loss of security will probably be of more concern, but the statistics will be lost. Unlike LPTSTM, LPSMAG does not include 'missing days' data; that is, if they are not counted on one day they are lost forever, invalidating the figures for a month. The author's own experience in Hillingdon, with a complicated overnight procedure, was that losses occurred frequently. The program was eventually rescheduled to an early part of each evening whereafter losses were less common.

LPSPAG has been used by Camden, where it is reported to be very similar to LPSMAG, except that it presents figures according to patron privilege rather than material type.

As an improvement on the above two programs, Geac have developed a suite of programs to collect and accumulate loan and hold statistics and produce a series of reports. The suite basically consists of three parallel subsystems: one for every material type/agency (or terminal group if preferred) combination; another for every borrower type (statistical class)/agency (or terminal group) combination; and one for every material type borrower type combination. The data accumulation programs are called LPSTTA, which accumulates the material type by agency and the borrower type by agency figures, and LPSTTB, which deals with the material type by borrower type data. As with LPTSTM, the programs should be run before a garbage collection of the transaction file, or some transaction data will be lost.

Reports can be printed as often as required and for any combination of transaction type and period number. There are three more programs to do this: LPSTPA reports on material types by agencies; LPSTPB deals with borrower types by agencies; LPSTPC is used for material types by borrower types. It is possible to group together agencies (or terminal groups) and material types or borrower types. Such groupings are site-defined, and these categories can be grouped or ungrouped in any combination. Sites can choose the periods over which they accumulate data; the usual pattern is for sites to collect data on daily, weekly, monthly, quarterly and annually. After each of these, other programs are run to clear down the relevant fields so that the next period's data can be accumulated.

As can be seen from the above, the level of detail in issue and hold statistics now available makes for a powerful management information tool. It is from this raw data that trends can be observed, and informed decisions taken.

Overnight reports

Using a program called LPTRSH, which is already familiar to all who have struggled through a complete recovery procedure for the Circulation system, the user can see exactly how busy the system has been. LPTRSH analyses the day's TCP file, which is a record of every transaction as it took place. From this can be seen the total transactions, of all kinds, the totals for each port, and finally totals for each terminal.

LPTCPA does a similar job, but breaks the figures down by time slots, usually compiled to be hourly, for each port, and also presents the data in graphical form by way of a histogram. Data for each terminal for the day is also included. The program can be equally well run against the Community Information TCP file.

The Fines Journal gives a large amount of information on the use of the fines subsystem. All fines transactions for the day are listed by terminal group, giving ample detail for the identification of transactions. This enables considerable supervision of the fines operation, but few sites seem to use it. The reports from the Cash Management system would seem to make it redundant for those sites using Cash Management (see Chapter 7).

LPTSCN monitors the system in terms of how many transactions exist, what the longest transaction chain is, and how many items are on loan. It also makes available even more valuable information. Items on loan are analysed by material type within each terminal group. Similar figures are produced for renewed loans, number of holds placed, and items in transit, again divided by terminal group. Most significantly, items remaining on the shelves are subjected to similar analysis by material type. Although this type of statistic still falls short of the needs of those libraries which wish to use the book provision techniques advocated by A.W. McClellan (1978), it can serve as the basis for such an exercise, and should also prove invaluable for stock-taking purposes.

LPOVER, the program which produces the overdue notices, provides data on how many notices of each type are produced, divided by agency. It also provides a count of patrons who are subject to stops, whether these are system generated (e.g. for exceeding fines limits) or manually created by staff. This information is analysed by type of stop and by agency. Although less immediately exciting than some of the other statistics now available, this information may well be extremely interesting to managers as a reflection of what is actually happening within their library service.

Ad hoc reports

There are two standard extract programs used in the Circulation module; one for bibliographical data (LPEXTR), and one for patron oriented data (LPPXTR). They are used for *ad hoc* reports on questions posed by the librarian, and are flexible enough to be considered useful tools in providing meaningful information.

Employing Boolean logic, they are not immediately easy to use, and some time has to be spent experimenting with the questions posed in such a way as to get useful information out of the system, and indeed to appreciate to what the resulting figures refer. They can produce raw figures, or be made to list the entries that satisfy the criteria as specified by the operator. In the case of listing, further manipulations are sometimes necessary, using a program called GLUG, to get the listing output in a legible format. Sorting routines can also be employed to put the data into a useful order.

Although it requires practice, it is possible to extract considerable amounts of data, either by using the standard extract programs, or by writing GLUG programs, or a combination of both. David Hayes at Camden, and Andrew Cooper at Leeds University have both devoted considerable effort to the development of expertise in GLUG, with consequent benefits to their systems

The Report Generator software is used for the production of lists in an easier fashion than using the extract programs, which preceded it by several years. Developed by Steve Lee at Sussex University, it is an example of user expertise being used to develop software locally, which was then bought by Geac for sale as a product. Whereas the extract programs can only access the data through the file for individual items, the Report Generator allows the user to choose whether to approach via the item file, or the bibliographic record file, **CALL. It is also possible to approach data via the indexes, during which procedure records can be selected for printing if required. The Report Generator can be used to produce output on paper or microfiche. It is used extensively in Hillingdon, where it is considered an extremely valuable tool.

Another Sussex development, which has recently been made

available by Geac, is the Statistical Tabulator, which is intended to harness the power of micro computer spreadsheet packages to the large amount of data held on the Geac database. In essence, relevant data is downloaded to the PC, where it can be manipulated in all the ways familiar to spreadsheet users. This is a new product, of which the author has as yet no experience, but it has been purchased by Suffolk County Library System, amongst others.

Statistics are easier to produce than lists, and for once can be made completely relevant. An analysis of the number of items borrowed per reader can be tied up with the number of items which are overdue in order to aid decisions about loan periods and limits for the number of permitted items per reader. In Hillingdon, membership statistics have been broken down by age and sex for comparison with small area census figures, giving for the first time accurate figures for the percentages of the resident population registered as members. This can be further compared with the statistics of patrons who have items on loan at the time of the survey to give the more significant figures relating to active membership.

Camden use LPEXTR to count how many times particular material types have circulated within a given period. They also use it for a form of stock-taking, by taking a section of stock and wanding every item on the shelves. The extract program is then used to count all items where the reshelve or circulation count is less than one; this indicates how many items within that section are missing. This sort of information can then be listed.

More prosaic figures are also valuable, and easy to extract. During the period of data entry to the bibliographic database, Hillingdon monitored the number of items located at each library, week by week. When compared with the estimated stock of those libraries, targets for completion of the task could be set. Dates for 'going live' were then projected and, in practice most of these were met. The fact that this operation could be constantly monitored and targets redefined in order to achieve success attests to the value in having detailed and accurate information, thereby enabling management to know exactly what progress was being made.

Transaction log analysis

Since the introduction of the Geac OPAC in Hillingdon in 1983, it has been apparent to the author that it is an extremely important development in public access to library files. It has been evident from the beginning that this exciting catalogue was being heavily used by the general public, but for a long time there was no concrete evidence to support this.

The Geac Transaction Log Analysis program, called BBSTAT, works against the TCP file for the OPAC. Just as the circulation package has a TCP file consisting of the day's transactions, so too does the OPC. By looking at this file, various statistics can be compiled, but there are one or two caveats. Because the TCP file is in a state of constant amendment when the package is available, BBSTAT can only be run when the OPC is down. In practice, this means running it overnight. Fortunately it is a very quick program to run, in Hillingdon's case taking only five minutes.

The second caveat is that the TCP file is cleared out every time the package is brought up. Therefore, if, for some reason, the catalogue is taken down during the day and then brought up again, when BBSTAT is run overnight it will only be able to count the transactions that occurred after the package was brought up for the second time.

BBSTAT is a mechanism for counting various conditions in the TCP file. It works by terminal number within terminal group, so individual terminals are clearly identified. Because it counts only transactions, it does not show data for a period when a terminal has not been used. Statistics are subdivided by hourly periods and, within each hour, by type of search or activity. It is therefore possible to see how many searches, in a given hour, were performed on a particular terminal, and whether they were undertaken by author, or title, or subject and so on. The use of the function keys and the major typed functions is also analysed.

The transactions for all the terminals within each terminal group are summarized for each day. Needless to say, the results are extremely illuminating, and BBSTAT has formed an important part of an MA project undertaken at Hillingdon.

As BBSTAT is only a counting mechanism, it does not go so far as to print out the search terms themselves. It is, however, possible to 'replay' searches from the TCP file; and, if these are copied on to tape, this could be done whilst the live catalogue was running. Unfortunately, this is unlikely to be a frequent occurrence in a busy site, where there are likely to be other more pressing demands on the use of the control consoles.

As with the other management information which is available, BBSTAT is another example of the way in which an automated system can be made to produce genuinely relevant statistics, with the possibility that decision-making can be made more reliable in the light of better information.

The University of Sussex developed a transaction log that works against the Public Query module of the circulation package as they do not have the full OPC. Like BBSTAT it produces statistics of catalogue use, but it also prints search strategies, as a matter of routine. As a result, staff at the university can see what errors are being made by searchers. They can then tailor user education to the searchers; or, tailor the system to the searches. Using their logging method, it has been possible to confirm that new methods of catalogue searching are both popular and effective.

There is as yet no equivalent Geac product to BBSTAT for the OPC in other packages. With the increasing popularity of the Community Information module, pressure is growing for a form of transaction logging on that too. At present, all that can be done is to run the LPTCPA program against the TCP file, which only reveals how busy a terminal has been in the package, not what it was being used for. This basic information is not available at all to those 8000 users who provide their Circulation Public Query information through the package ZQPUBL, which employs the security files, and does not include a TCP file.

Public Lending Right software

One final element of management information is worthy of note as far as UK sites are concerned. The Registrar of Public Lending Right requires libraries to supply details of the loan records of authors in order to enable the calculation of payments under the scheme. Though the Registrar seeks volunteer authorities to provide this data, and payments are made to cover costs incurred, it would seem sensible for any newly automating site to ensure that it could provide the data if so requested. Several Geac clients therefore specified such a module within their contracts and the software is now available. A series of three programs are used to extract data from the transaction files prior to every garbage collect, accumulate the data, organize it in a suitable format, and finally produce a tape for forwarding to the Registrar. Data can be restricted to certain agencies, to certain material types, and to certain patron privileges, depending upon what information the Registrar requires.

Reference

McClellan, A.W (1978) *The logistics of a public library bookstock*, Association of Assistant Librarians.

14 External Communications

From the early days of their involvement with libraries, Geac have demonstrated a willingness to link their systems to the outside world. This linkage now takes place in both directions and can be achieved via tape, as is often the case with Acquisitions, or by direct links. This chapter attempts to outline the major links which are available to Geac users.

Community Access module

The Community Access module was first made available as early as 1979. It allows online access from external sources to the Circulation package, and is designed to permit the catalogue element of the Public Query module to be searched from the home or from other sites on a campus rather than by visit to a library to use a normal library terminal. It is also possible to use the Community Access module to gain access to an individual's own record as in the Public Query module providing that the system has been compiled to permit keyboarding of membership numbers. The module cannot be used in conjunction with Local Information, which requires a different approach, as detailed later.

To operate the community access module a site requires additional hardware in the form of a dial-in modem, a direct telecommunications line attaching this modem to the normal telephone system and at least one port on the c.p.u. It is more usual for sites operating the community access module to have a multiplicity of lines and ports available for external users. The module also requires approximately 17k to 20k of the c.p.u.'s capacity on which to run. Communication rates from 9600 baud to as low as 300 baud can be handled by the module.

An option is available which requires that a valid identification number be given as part of the logging on procedure, whilst another permits the application of a maximum connect time for any individual session.

VuCat

Whereas the Community Access module allows external access to the circulation database, VuCat performs the same function for the OPC. The displays are exactly as are available in the library on normal OPC terminals but the use of function keys is ineffective. A facility is also available to disconnect inactive terminals and make the modem and telephone link available to another user. In the UK VuCat has been used by several academic libraries with success. It is usually accessible over X.25 from the Joint Academic Network (JANET), and is often also made available campus-wide over the University network. It is able to be used by dumb terminals, or PCs emulating dumb terminals, and prompts for use of the Carriage Return key instead of SEND.

Dial-in access to the entire system

The Community Access module and VuCat were both ways of making the initial library database, its catalogue, available to remote users. Since their development many libraries, particularly public libraries, have created databases of Local or Community Information, which they wish to disseminate at least as much as the catalogue, but for which no dial-in package existed.

For many years it was the contention of this author, amongst many other users, that it should be possible for a remote caller to access all the public elements of the library system, and be presented with a system substantially the same as would be the case using a public terminal in a library. In essence, what is required is access to the main TCP menu.

The solution came with the development of the VT220 terminal strategy. It quickly became obvious that whereas emulation of a Geac terminal might present problems to remote users, emulation of VT100 and VT220 terminals are standard elements of many PC communications software packages.

The library requires an 8212 Communications controller, which is linked to an ordinary X3.28 or X.25 library port, to which are attached terminals in the usual way, through the configuration program SPCNFG. The controller has eight ports for external attachments, which can be either directly connected VT220 terminals, or telephone lines, via a modem each (see Figure 14.1). The usual arrangement is to have a number of telephone lines set up with a 'group hunting' arrangement, so that if the first line is engaged the second line is automatically used, and so on. Only one telephone number therefore needs to be advertised for access. Software on the Geac 8000 or 9000, called CATDNE, downloads details of poll-codes, baud rate, allowed onlines etc. to the 8212 controller, which then takes over the polling of the 'terminals'.

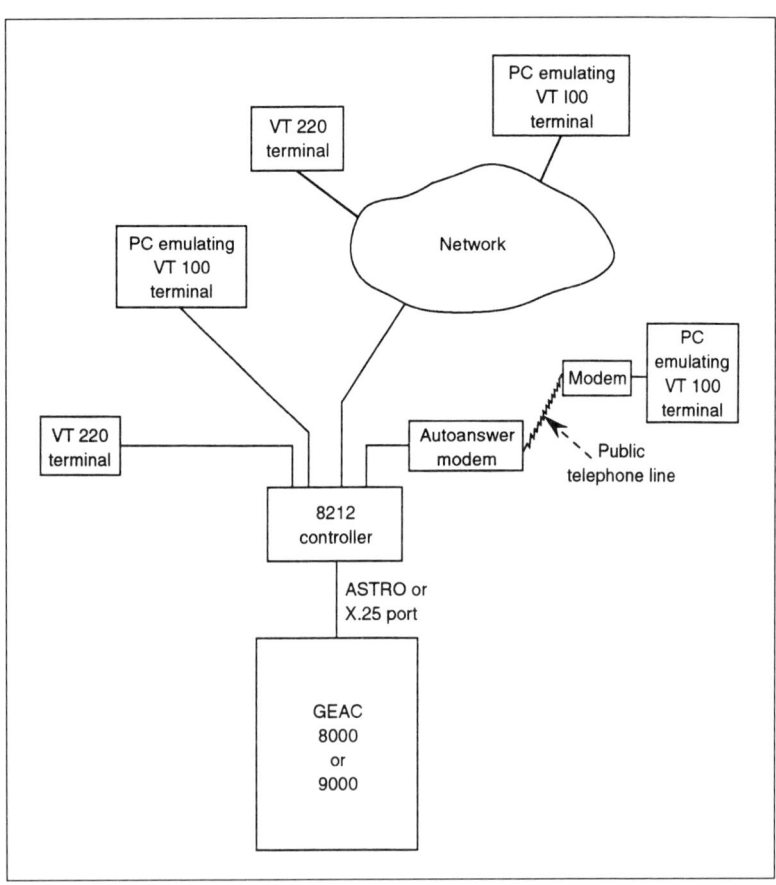

Figure 14.1 Diagram of 8212 controller and associated terminals

The first UK site to use this arrangement was the London Borough of Sutton, who connect their callers to an X.25 port, followed by Hillingdon, where the controller is connected to an ordinary X3.28 port. The author can report that after several months of use this system provides very few problems, and he has himself used it to good effect, demonstrating the Hillingdon system from Manchester.

Because the caller is actually emulating a Geac terminal, courtesy of the 8212 controller, it is necessary to assign a key as the SEND key, Carriage Return having no useful effect in this context. Some software needs to have that explicitly carried out, so on set-up the correct escape sequence must be known, but other software (e.g. DATATALK) appears to assign the + key on the keypad part of a PC keyboard as SEND without any need for further action.

Software known to work is KERMIT, which is in the public domain, DATATALK, and TERMITE, but the author sees no reason why any commercially available package capable of VT220 or VT100 emulation should not be satisfactory. Judicious use of the programmable function keys on a PC will even allow the function keys on the Geac system to be used. Access has so far only been achieved from IBM compatible PCs, but it does not seem unlikely that other types of micro could be used successfully, providing the VT emulation works properly.

Remote software support

In the years since the publication of the first edition of this book, software support has changed from being carried out predominantly by a programmer in person at the site, to the situation where the programmer usually dials into the site from the Bristol office. This can be achieved either via X.25, if appropriate access is provided, or as a direct telephone link. The site needs to provide a telephone line over which such calls can be made, and although it is easier if this line is not used for other purposes, it is not essential to provide a line dedicated to what one hopes is an infrequent requirement. Naturally, most use of this facility is made by sites during the implementation phase of their project, and in some of the larger and more complex systems it is not unknown for two or more Geac staff to be dialled into the system over the X.25 link at any one time.

Although it is regrettable to lose the personal contact with a programmer, it is undeniable that dial-in support is both efficient and cost-effective. Should an emergency arise, a telephone call to the Bristol Action Desk should result in a call back within half an hour, and the likelihood is that within that time an expert will be working on the problem. Because the programmer is working from the Geac offices, thorny problems can be dealt with by consultation with colleagues much more easily than if the programmer is on site.

Accessing external databases

Geac systems have a long and varied history of accessing external systems, with varying degrees of user satisfaction. An early attempt was made to provide software and an intelligent modem to access British Telecom's Prestel service, and although this worked, it was very limited in its capabilities, slow, and unable to handle the graphics and colour typical of Viewdata systems.

Access to other databases was also required, and Geac provided a package called Pass-Thru. This allowed a daisy-chained Geac terminals to access, via the Geac host, external databases using the normal seven-bit ASCII character set. Connection was possible via an autodialler modem, X.25 from control consoles, or direct wire to another local computer.

A directory of a number of external services could be maintained, each of which required a port on the Geac host. Although several services could be accessed, only one terminal could use the package at any one time.

A useful facility of this software was the ability to allow any library terminal to behave as a KQ terminal, allowing the operator to issue KQ console commands, with some limitations. This has been used in the London Borough of Hillingdon for many years with success, proving very beneficial as the computer and its control consoles are several hundred yards away from the Central Library, where the system manager is based.

Pass-Thru was a step forward, but its limitations made it far from ideal. It has been superseded by a product called TRAX (known as DataWay in North America). Using X.25 at present, TRAX enables any library terminal to connect to any other system. Once connected, the Geac terminal operates in the same way as would any terminal directly connected to the host system.

As with Pass-Thru, a directory of accessible hosts is maintained, which is displayed to the user in menu form. Associated with each entry is a set of up to 24 function keys (the menu for which can be brought up in a window at any time) and also a script which may be used to auto-logon or perform some other initial set-up before the user has to key in anything. Password protection is possible, on a per host basis.

Supported terminal emulations include Dumb TTY, ICL 75xx workstation, DEC VT100 and DEC VT52 (with restrictions), VUCOM IV, and IBM 3270, which will be used in conjunction with GeoGate (described in Chapter 5). TRAX does not at present allow Viewdata emulation, but development for this is understood to be well-advanced.

Navigation around the package itself is achieved via function keys. Administrative features such as call logging, length of session and the machine called will all enable some control to be kept of users, an important point when it is now possible to have up to 16 simultaneous remote sessions. Prices for this product vary according to how many simultaneous sessions are specified. Since it operates over X.25, it must be remembered that the appropriate hardware and software is required on the Geac host, as is suitable access to X.25 networks.

TRAX would appear to be a product with considerable potential, and it is hoped to make use of it in Hillingdon to provide public access to other council systems from library public terminals, as well as the obvious staff applications. The author has seen it in use in Suffolk County Library, where it is routinely used to access the Libtel system provided by booksellers John Menzies. There too the intention is to access other council systems, primarily for the financial systems running on the council mainframe.

Section 4　Support services

15 Customer support

The whole area of customer support is a very difficult one about which to write with any authority. Not only can it change considerably over a relatively short time but it is quite likely that there will be regional, let alone national, variations. The author therefore advises readers to treat the contents of this section with considerable caution, relying only on those elements which are obviously factual and merely noting the more subjective opinions.

Hardware support

The first concern of customers and potential customers who have discussed Geac with the author is support for hardware failures. This is perhaps because those with experience of other systems wish to compare, and those without experience do at least know that things mechanical and electrical are prone to failure. It is, of course, of considerable importance – though the author would place it on a lower plane than software support.

In Geac's case, the general consensus amongst UK clients is that the level of support is reasonably good. It would also appear that the situation in North America is somewhat similar, to judge by references in *The Informer*, the North American users' newsletter.

The situation does vary over time and there are different responses in relation to major and minor failures. In terms of time, it was certainly apparent that in 1984 Geac's organization was extremely stretched in the UK following the award of several contracts, some of them extremely large. The time taken to recruit and train the calibre of engineering staff needed for such support is such that expansion of the rate experienced is bound to lead to difficulties. That difficult period was overcome without clients finding that major repairs were left untended but minor failures were often outstanding for long periods. This is a situation which will still arise from time to time should there be any shortage of manpower or a sequence of simultaneous failures but both the company and its clients appear to have learned how to handle this.

The attitude of many clients has matured in this respect. Whereas, in 1983 and 1984, it was common to hear disgruntled comments from colleagues, there is now a recognition that minor repairs can wait. Conversely major repairs cannot wait and it is recognized that Geac's response to such occurrences is well within any contractual obligations.

Sites also report more than normal business relationships with the actual engineering staff who attend to their problems. The author knows of several sites, including his own, where engineers have attended to faults, arriving well after their normal end of duty and staying for many more hours in order to resolve a problem. Minor repairs do not often come into this category but it is not unknown where engineers have built up a friendly relationship with counter staff.

Normal Geac hardware maintenance contracts specify a maximum call-out of four hours for c.p.u. failures and eight hours for terminal faults. There are variations on this, some sites (including most UK public libraries) having a standard four hour call-out on all faults. It is also usual for cover to exist only between the hours of 9 am and 5 pm on Mondays to Fridays inclusive, though for an additional sum extended hours or Saturday cover can be provided for problems which lead to a library being out of action. Geac now offer, for a price, engineering cover on a 12 hour, 16 hour or 24 hour a day basis. Whatever the case, it is assumed that calls must be logged to Geac's area engineering office or via a call-out service within sufficient time to arrange for an engineer to attend that day.

An alternative arrangement is to have a stock of on-site spares, often obsolete terminals, that can be plugged in when a terminal fails. The failed terminal is repaired, or removed for repair, with a commitment to have it back in operation within a specified period, usually a week. At this time of course, the spare is returned to storage. This arrangement seems to work fairly well with several customers, who benefit from lower maintenance charges as a result.

Engineers are highly mobile and are issued with paging systems and car telephones so that they can be kept in constant contact with their office. Normal procedure is to try to arrange calls within an area to eliminate lost time through travel but at the same time priorities are applied so that, on occasions, an engineer will be called off one job to attend a more urgent job elsewhere. Geac is quite happy for sites to specify the priorities to engineers if there is more than one problem within the one site, but all jobs must first be logged with the office.

The company is very experienced in the needs of libraries, and office staff and engineers alike are willing to work towards satisfying the customers' needs. Now that clients have also gained experience with the complex task of running large online installations the system works extremely well and few sites can find significant fault with their cover.

Hardware maintenance is expensive if it is good. Geac generally charge a figure which approximates to somewhere between 10 per cent and 15 per cent of original capital cost of equipment. This can only be a guideline as maintenance costs for the c.p.u. are much cheaper than this and terminal costs are higher. The final price is therefore dependent on the ratio of the two. It is also dependent on the negotiating skills of those who arrange the contract: over the years there have been several special deals struck which either reduce the maintenance charge or even increase it while reducing capital costs. The charge is generally subject to an annual inflation element (in the UK this is derived from the BEAMA index, a nationally published figure).

The other element of hardware support which is of general concern is the availability of spare parts. Geac maintain good collections of the most commonly required or important parts and these are frequently transported to engineers working on site by motorcycle couriers to save time. In the event of c.p.u. failures it is common practice for the office to arrange transport of replacement memory boards as a routine so that should the engineer discover the need the part is already on its way. In earlier years when the engineering organization was stretched it was not uncommon to find a delay whilst a spare part was transported from some considerable distance but this has not been the case in recent years. Despite these comments, it is still a common complaint that engineers turn up on site without suitable spares and then have to return to base. When a spare part needs to be ordered, it usually arrives first thing the following day, having been dispatched by overnight courier.

Machinery will always break down when it is most inconvenient but this tendency is greater in the absence of regular maintenance. Geac carry out regular 'preventative maintenance' (PM), at quarterly intervals, in the hope that problems can be anticipated before they arise and turn into full-blown crises. For such maintenance they require the system to be taken out of use for a matter of a few hours, and sites must timetable them for the least inconvenient periods. Although responsibility for ensuring that the PM is carried out rests with Geac, they sometimes need reminding, as more pressing problems may sometimes divert engineers. Personal experience has shown that allowing a PM to slip too far past its scheduled date is courting trouble, and is best avoided.

Preventative maintenance can be scheduled to take place on Sundays should the library be working to a six-day week. In these circumstances there are additional cost factors, not only for the employment of library staff; Geac naturally make an additional charge for engineering cover on Sundays. Despite this, there are advantages in carrying out such work without recourse to back-up procedures, which are both a reduction in service to public and staff and which absorb an additional amount of staff time. Hillingdon is a site which has chosen this option, and can report complete satisfaction with the arrangement, experiencing no difficulty with Geac's ability to supply an engineer when required.

Software support

Software maintenance, as such, often involves the improvement and enhancement of the various packages through new releases as described in earlier chapters. Of greater importance, though, is the support that is occasionally needed in time of crisis because some fault has occurred which has led to a system failure. Those sites which operate a complicated suite of software and therefore have need for a complicated program to manage overnight procedures can find that their system is subject to overnight failure as a result of errors within their batch programs. In these circumstances the level of software support is just as, if not more, important than hardware support. Fortunately it is not needed nearly so often, and it costs considerably less.

As with hardware support there were periods in the early 1980s when the UK branch of the company found itself stretched too thinly to cover its clients adequately. In those years the number of programmers employed was increased dramatically but the lead time was such that it was some considerable time before the company provided what its library clients considered sufficient cover. That is not to say that complete failures were not attended to with urgency and diligence but there was so little time left over from 'fire-fighting' activities that contractual obligations to tailor software to local requirements were often given a low priority. The situation has been mostly resolved by two means. The first was the simple addition of more staff, though numbers vary. The second was the adoption of a policy of greater standardization of the software.

This is not to say that clients cannot have the freedom to have local variations, which is, after all one of the great strengths of the Geac system. What Geac decided to do was to include all the variations within the software but to allow each client to choose to activate each compile option or not, according to their wishes. This leads to the software packages being both large and complicated, but each site will ultimately be working on a standard package and programmers will be able to find their way around it without having to be intimately familiar with the individual site.

As remote software support has become more common (see Chapter 13), personal visits from programmers are needed less frequently than used to be the case, though the author believes there is much to be gained and learned from the direct contact of programmer and client, which still takes place early in an implementation at least. The usual routine in the UK when a software problem arises, if it is serious, is to telephone the 'hotline' which is usually answered automatically by an answering machine. During office hours the machine is constantly monitored, as it is located in an office given over to the 'action desk', and often the programmer on support duty will cut in to answer the call. In any case, Geac commit themselves to answer the call within half an hour, and this is usually achieved. Once they have called back, they will often dial-in to rectify the problem, perhaps having consulted with colleagues first.

Less urgent problems are communicated to Geac by means of an Incident Report Form, which is acknowledged fairly quickly. Customers have mixed levels of satisfaction to the level at which these faults are actually rectified, which can probably be put down to the fact that programmers are already very fully occupied.

Training

Geac offer training in two distinct categories. Firstly, they offer detailed training courses for a fee at their offices, and secondly they offer basic training in the use of the system on site.

The detailed training is generally of a highly technical nature and the courses can last up to several days. Such courses are not for the beginner, and in some respects are not for the librarian but for computer operators or data managers. They are not essential if it has been decided that such a detailed knowledge is unnecessary, but the author would encourage librarians to undertake such courses once they have spent some time operating a c.p.u. With the knowledge gained it is possible to get even more value from the system than before. Geac also offer a course designed specifically for library staff who do not possess a strong computer background but who will be operating a system. Though these courses usually attract a fee, most contracts include a certain number of training credits which would allow several free days to be taken.

The second form of training is designed to instruct those staff who will be operating the issue terminals and is usually given prior to a site commencing live operations. Many of the Geac staff now have a long experience with the equipment, though this was not always the case, and they have the knowledge, patience and understanding required to ease nervous staff through a difficult period. Even more importantly, some of the training staff have been directly recruited from Geac's own client libraries and therefore have a good working knowledge of libraries.

The volume of training given by Geac varies according to the customers' needs. In some sites only a handful of staff have been trained by Geac and these have then trained their colleagues. In others, Geac staff have returned to the site as each new library has been added to the network and internal training has been minimal. The author can only comment that local circumstances must dictate training needs, but that training must take a high priority whenever a change of the magnitude involved in the installation of a Geac system is undertaken.

The subject of training has achieved a higher profile amongst customers than was the case earlier, largely due to the signing of contracts with large county library systems, with a need for high quality training of large numbers of staff in fairly short timescales. A Working Party was formed to present priorities for training to Geac, and many of its recommendations were adopted in the formation of the System Manager's course.

Documentation

In earlier chapters Geac's documentation of their software has been criticized. This criticism is even stronger when one considers the lack of documentation for training purposes. The company does produce product descriptions, which are naturally more akin to sales material. It also produces technical manuals covering the c.p.u. and its central configuration peripherals. It does not produce much which is of relevance to the assistant in a library, faced with a lack of knowledge of the less frequently used elements of the software. To some extent this reflects the fact that the number of local options is such that a true staff manual would be impossibly complicated. As mentioned in Chapter 9, the cataloguing system BCS is an honourable exception to this criticism, with a very useful manual.

Geac do provide Terminal Operator's manuals but these are not suitable for counter staff, though they can be helpful to more knowledgeable system management staff. To overcome the problem several sites have produced their own manuals and are prepared to release copies to others to form the basis of local manuals.

In addition to printed documentation, the system itself contains documentation areas for each of the various elements.

User groups

Geac supports a user group for libraries in the UK which meets twice a year in differing geographical locations. One of these meetings (i.e. once a year) is held jointly with the European group, with the venue alternating between Europe and the UK. A similar group meets twice each year in North America. Meetings usually last for two days and comprise a combination of company announcements and customer soundings. Apart from clients having an opportunity to put points of complaint or praise as a single body, they also permit considerable interchange of news and ideas.

In addition to the main users' group, there are subsidiary groups which meet at regular intervals to discuss common problems in relation to the Circulation, Cataloguing and Acquisitions packages, etc. These groups are generally open only to sites with an obvious interest but they also include those existing or potential sites where the package concerned is receiving consideration for purchase. These groups have an obvious advantage to potential customers in that their members can give a view of the effective operations of the package concerned. However, attendance of non-purchasers of the package is only by invitation and is usually restricted to very serious potential members.

One further group holds meetings on a bi-annual basis; this is PLUG, Public Libraries Using Geac. Unlike the other groups, it was formed without Geac's assistance and is not supported by the company in any way. Geac personnel do attend on occasions to assist with discussions on particular points, and serious potential customers are also invited if appropriate. PLUG has been responsible for providing common specifications such as that on Local Information and another on statistical outputs. As more 9000 public library users came on the scene, it was found that it was more fruitful for the group to split into two subgroups, one for 8000 users, and one for 9000 users, meeting four times a year. These meetings concentrated on technical matters, and all members benefited from the interchange of knowledge. As the number of public libraries using 8000 machines has dwindled even further, the two groups have now remerged as a single technical subgroup of PLUG attended by system managers.

All of these groups provide Geac with useful feedback on problems and requirements. They also provide sites with a forum within which ideas can be exchanged and new approaches identified.

The role of library consultants

Customer support could not be discussed without reference to the role of the Library Consultants employed by Geac. Consultants are usually experienced professional librarians who have a thorough grounding in library automation. Quite often they have been recruited from customer libraries and have therefore gained an experience of Geac from the other side of the fence. As with all poachers turned gamekeeper, they can greatly assist the company in carrying out its task and in so doing help the clients. Their role is occasionally that of trouble shooter, often that of salesman but is most properly considered as that of translator. By being able to talk the same language as customers and being able to translate the expressed needs into terms understandable by non-librarian systems analysts and programmers they serve a very useful purpose.

Each site is allocated to one of these consultants long before any contracts are written and it is they who put together a proposal. On agreement of a contract, the consultant retains an interest in and contact with the site and helps them over their initial and any continuing difficulties. Though many other Geac personnel have contact with each site for specific matters, it is the consultant who keeps an overall watching brief.

16 Response times

When considering the effectiveness of an online system, it is generally on the area of response times that discussions eventually centre. It does not matter how sophisticated the software is, if response times are not satisfactory then operators lose faith in the system. Throughout this book there have been references to response times and the various elements within the system configuration which can affect them. These will act to some degree to guide the user of a Geac system through some of the options at their disposal. However, it is not possible within the confines of a book to examine the needs of any individual system or of systems as a whole. It is a matter for local determination.

It is important for every systems manager to recognize that response times are all important, and it is their responsibility to obtain the best from the system within the confines imposed by local requirements for speed of response. Some librarians have gone into print in describing their system and declared that response times are not of major concern and have therefore not featured within the contract. It is the author's experience that among Geac clients there is a healthy regard for the need to specify responses within a contract and it is to Geac's credit that they are willing to do so. The author believes that no company will give a commitment that 100 per cent of responses will be within any given limit, unless that limit is so generous as to be worthless. Geac have undertaken contracts where the guarantee is for 90 per cent of responses within a limit; for example the current Hillingdon 8000 contract is for 90 per cent of circulation responses within two seconds and 90 per cent of OPAC transactions within four seconds.

As has been repeatedly stated throughout this book, the 9000 series, particularly using the newest processors, is very considerably more powerful than the 8000. When used in conjunction with multi-threaded circulation software, the throughput of transactions is most impressive. It is impossible to generalize on this point, as there is no such thing as a 'standard

9000'; the capabilities of the machine depend on how many FFPs are employed, and whether multi-threading is in use. By way of illustration however, at Suffolk County Library Service their four FFP multi-threaded machine has accommodated 60,000 GODOs in an hour with no degredation of response times. (20,000 on an 8000 will cause the responses to begin to degrade.) A benchmark test run for Essex County Library before they bought their 9000 system achieved response times of 99.1 per cent in under two seconds, and 94.5 per cent in under one second. In the test 36,000 book loan transactions, 1,600 catalogue searches and 250 holds were simulated in an hour. Geac's calculation was that in a real situation this would equate to 67,000 interactions in an hour.

Customers will clearly need to be precise in specifying their requirements and the expected load so that the system can be configured appropriately. Having done so, benchmarking tests can be run to establish that the configuration is correct, and adjustments made as necessary. An important factor of the 9000 series would appear to be that should a site's requirements grow to the point that the current configuration can no longer perform adequately, expansion can be done to rectify the problem.

In addition to the increased power of the hardware, and the ability of multi-threading to spread the load, there are other methods of maintaining fast response times. Clearly, a major reason for response time degradation is if there is a bottleneck of transactions at the c.p.u. One technique for easing problems at this level is to reduce the amount of processing required of the c.p.u. This can be achieved by removing much of the routine screen display and manipulation work from the c.p.u. to the terminal, with the effect that this kind of processing is done locally by dedicated intelligence, and there are no telecommunications overheads slowing matters down. Only when data needs to be sent to, or retrieved from the c.p.u. is communication with it necessary. Whilst this will still be needed for every transaction, the amount of backwards and forwards transmission is considerably reduced, freeing the c.p.u. to process the data it does have to deal with much more quickly. The Screen Manager project, which is due for completion in the very near future, is expected to have addressed this technique.

One of the tasks performed by the c.p.u. is the constant 'polling' of devices; in effect sending frequent messages to each terminal and polled printer to maintain contact. This takes up some of the c.p.u.'s processing resources, and if it is already working very hard will inevitably reduce its ability to process transactions as quickly as it should. Polling can be handled remotely, however, by the 8212 and 8215 controllers described in the chapter on networking. The relevant poll-codes are downloaded to the controller from the c.p.u., which is then relieved of the need to send the poll-codes again, as the controllers take over that job. The new Terminal Control Server is also expected to take this responsibility from the c.p.u. Such an approach will not be required in all cases, but may have a beneficial effect on very large networks with several hundred terminals.

Support in times of trouble

The author presumes that all online library systems have experienced periods when responses were less than desired. If this were not the case then it is likely that the system installed was effectively too powerful, and consequently cost more than necessary. Having experienced occasional problems himself, the author can only state that, in his experience, Geac are willing to go to great lengths to achieve the contracted limits. On occasions this has led to direct hardware costs to the company, and always involves them in manpower costs. Despite this they are willing to provide support at the highest level and to expend considerable time in resolving problems.

Resolutions can only be achieved by both sides collecting considerable volumes of data on what the activity levels of the system are in each of its many parts. Obviously some activities are more destructive of responses than others, and as a knowledge of the different effects of each transaction become more fully understood it is possible to present the options to the client. On occasions it will be discovered that the system is being asked to undertake a type of work or a level of work for which it was not configured. It may be necessary to vary working practices or improve the power of the system to enable it to cope.

No system should be planned without expecting, from the start, that it will change within a matter of only a few years. Such changes in policy are bound to occur and the Geac system is flexible enough to accommodate them. Geac have a long history in high transaction online systems and their staff will be able to assist clients to squeeze the best out of their equipment. The power of the 9000 series is such that very large systems can be accommodated, by the provision of extra FFPs if necessary. As outlined in earlier chapters, Essex County Library is one such system; it is believed to be the largest automated system in the UK at the very least. Despite its size, Circulation response times remain very fast, and yet the full possible power of the machine has not been called upon; it has seven out of a possible eight FFPs, and these are of the older variety. It is this that gives this author confidence in suggesting that the system is expandable to cope with the requirements of most, if not all library services.

Section 5   Conclusion

17 Concluding remarks

Computerized library systems are immensely complicated, and the Geac system is a particularly sophisticated and ambitious one. When one buys a Geac system, one is buying a remarkably complicated device, and this has to be realized by all concerned from the start otherwise major difficulties will be experienced.

'Turnkey' systems can theoretically be simply switched on and they will work. This is true to a large extent, as the hardware and software has already been developed. The elements that are untested are how the policies of individual libraries will affect matters. Because of their complicated nature, library systems cannot simply be plugged in and expected to interpret those policies perfectly; a great effort must be made by those responsible for running the system to understand the principles by which they work.

This is not to say that a Geac system requires computer specialists to run it. As has been stated, it can be run equally well by library staff as by a data processing department. The author does believe strongly, however, that those library staff should have as their main responsibility the supervision of the system, so that the full advantages of librarians being in total control of their system can be attained.

The sophistication and wide range of facilities available from Geac make it inevitable that some facilities have been entirely overlooked, and others only dealt with briefly. It is most likely that no one individual (whether librarian or Geac employee) is aware of the total range of software. The central core of the system, for most users, is the Circulation package, and it is this that has been described in greatest detail.

The world of library automation has moved on considerably in the years since the first edition of this book was published. In particular, systems employing relational databases have made considerable inroads into the market. Whilst relational databases undoubtedly have many advantages for accessing and manipulating data, it still seems that high performance is only possible by significantly adding to special coding, reducing the 'standardness' of the product, which is seen as one of the main attractions. Geac are able to demonstrate that their product, non-standard though it might be, is very definitely capable of very high performance on very large systems at reasonable cost. Some of the recent developments, and plans for further development, as outlined in this edition, enhance the attraction of the Geac GLIS, despite the fact that it does not 'conform' to fashionable standards. In particular, the new approach to the holds subsystem, and the integration of data under the holdings and pieces management project, should bring many of the advantages of relational database system to a system already proven as able to provide high performance under formidable loads. The Screen Manager project should further improve performance, whilst at the same time greatly enhancing the power of the customer to decide on the appearance of the system to suit the library's clients.

The latest threat to Geac's current GLIS system is likely to be the growing insistence by many local authorities and academic institutions that their computer systems use the UNIX operating system. The argument for this is again the level of standardization providing value for money, but at present it also seems that to achieve high performance of online transaction processing, the operating system needs to be enhanced with extra code. Geac do of course have a UNIX product for smaller systems in ADVANCE, but it is this author's expectation that the market will force Geac to adopt UNIX for the larger systems too before another edition of this book is required.

One final point, made in the preface to this book, needs repeating. A book is not the best medium for conveying the details of a complex and rapidly developing automation system. By the time that this text is published it will already be out of date. Serious researchers, especially those who must make recommendations on the purchase of a system, should seek more recent information from practitioners in the field, particularly those in sites with some operational similarites to their own.

Section 6 Appendices

Appendix A Geac users – worldwide

Information supplied by Geac, March 1991

	SITE	CPUs	APPLICATIONS IN OPERATION	NO. OF TERMINALS
1.	UNITED KINGDOM			
GLIS sites				
1.1	University of Aston	3FFP 9000	CIRC BCS VUCAT ACQ	50 + 100 network channels
1.2	University College of North Wales, Bangor	8000	CIRC ACQ CIS MRMS/OPC GTALK RSS	40
1.3	British Library Document Supply Centre	2 × 8000	ACQ MRMS/OPC TRAX	88
1.4	Metropolitan Borough of Doncaster	8000	CIRC ACQ	50+
1.5	University of Durham	3FFP 9000	CIRC BCS VUCAT	30+
1.6	University of Edinburgh	5FFP 9000	CIRC BCS ACQ	80+
1.7	Essex County Council	7FFP 9000	CIRC ACQ BCS	450+
1.8	District of Falkirk	8000	CIRC LOC	30+
1.9	University of Glasgow	3FFP 9000	CIRC BCS ACQ	100+

	SITE	CPUs	APPLICATIONS IN OPERATION	NO. OF TERMINALS
1.10	University of Hull	3FFP 9000	CIRC ACQ	40+
			(Has own software enhancements)	
1.11	Lancashire County Library	4FFP 9000	CIRC ACQ LOC	233
1.12	Lancashire Polytechnic	8000	CIRC ACQ MRMS/OPC VUCAT	25+
1.13	University of Leeds	9300	CIRC BCS ACQ	100+
1.14	London Borough of Bexley	8000	CIRC PUBLIC QUERY SOFT	100+
1.15	London Borough of Bromley	3FFP 9000	CIRC ACQ	165+
1.16	London Borough of Camden	2 × 8000	CIRC ACQ CIS GEM GTALK RSS ZQPUBL	140+
1.17	London Borough of Enfield	2 × 8000	CIRC ACQ CIS RSS PRESTEL LINK	70+
1.18	London Borough of Hillingdon	8000	CIRC CIS OPC GEM SOFT DIAL-IN	150
1.19	London Borough of Islington	8000	CIRC ACQ PUBLIC QUERY	80+
1.20	London Borough of Redbridge	8000	CIRC ZQPUBL SOFT	100+
1.21	London Borough of Sutton	8000	CIRC ZQPUBL CIS SOFT RSS DIAL-IN	79
1.22	Norfolk County Council	4FFP 9000	CIRC ACQ	110+
1.23	North Staffs Polytechnic	8000	CIRC ACQ MRMS/OPC	56
1.24	Somerset County Council	3FFP 9000	CIRC ACQ SOFT	130+
1.25	Strathclyde University	3FFP 9000	CIRC BCS	70+
1.26	Suffolk County Council	4FFP 9000	CIRC ACQ PUBLIC QUERY TRAX GEM	310
1.27	Sussex University	3FFP 9000	CIRC PUBLIC QUERY	110+
			(Has own software enhancements)	
1.28	Westminster City Libraries	8000	CIRC ACQ LOC SOFT	112+

ADVANCE SITES				
1.29	Polytechnic of the South Bank		Geac 3000 Advance UNIX processor CIRC ACQ CATALOGUING OPC	100+
1.30	House of Lords		ICON 2000 CATALOGUING OPC	12
2.	CONTINENTAL EUROPE			
2.1	*The Netherlands*			
2.1.1	Alkmaar Openbare Bibliotheek	6000	CIRC	66
2.1.2	Almere Openbare Bibliotheek	8000	CIRC	50
2.1.3	Amstelveen Openbare Bibliotheek	6000	CIRC	50
2.1.4	Amsterdam Openbare Bibliotheek	9000	CIRC CATALOGUING/OPC	255
2.1.5	Breda Openbare Bibliotheek	8000	CIRC	80
2.1.6	Doetinchem Openbare Bibliotheek	6000	CIRC	40
2.1.7	Flevoland Openbare Bibliotheek	9303	CIRC	175
2.1.8	CBD Friesland	8000	CATALOGUING/OPC	20
2.1.9	IISG	8000	CATALOGUING/OPC ACQ	25
2.1.10	Stichting Informatievoorziening en Bibliotheekwerk Limburg	9000	CIRC	255
2.1.11	Dienst KCO/Afdeling Media Stadsbibliotheek Maastricht	8000	CIRC	30
2.1.12	Tiel Openbare Bibliotheek	6000	CIRC	25
2.1.13	Utrecht Openbare Bibliotheek	2 × 8000	CIRC	100
2.1.14	PBC Utrecht	9000	CIRC	300

	SITE	CPUs	APPLICATIONS IN OPERATION	NO. OF TERMINALS
2.1.15	University of Utrecht	2 × 8000 1 × 9000	CIRC CATALOGUING/OPC ACQ	250
2.2	*Sweden*			
2.2.1	Linkoeping	8000	CIRC CATALOGUING/OPC ACQ	30
2.2.2	University of Stockholm	2 × 8000	CIRC CATALOGUING/OPC ACQ	63
2.3	*France*			
	GLIS SYSTEMS			
2.3.1	Bibliothèque Nationale	2 × 9000	BCS/OPC	294
2.3.2	Bibliothèque municipale de Chartres	8000	CIRC CATALOGUING/OPC ACQ	34
2.3.3	Bibliothèque de l'Université de Technologie de Compeigne	9000	CIRC BCS/OPC	23
2.3.4	Bibliothèque municipale de Dijon	9000	CIRC BCS/OPC ACQ	57
2.3.5	Bibliothèque municipale de Lyons	9000	CIRC BCS/OPC ACQ	136
2.3.6	Bibliothèque municipale de Montreuil	8000	CIRC CATALOGUING/OPC ACQ	52
2.3.7	Bibliothèque municipale d'Orleans	9000	CIRC BCS/OPC ACQ	46

2.3.8	Bibliothèque Publique d'Information (The Pompidou Centre)	9000	CIRC BPS/OPC ACQ	70
2.3.9	Consortium des bibliotiques de Saint-Etienne (municipale, universitaire, musée, école de commerce	9000	CIRC BCS/OPC ACQ	201
2.3.10	INIST du CNRS	9000	CIRC BPS/OPC ACQ	76
2.3.11	Mediatheque de la Cité des Sciences et de L'industrie de La Villette	9000	CIRC BCS/OPC ACQ	201
2.3.12	Rennes	9000	CIRC BCS/OPC ACQ	65

ADVANCE SYSTEMS

2.3.13	Bibliothèque Regionale de la Vallee d'Aoste	Multi-user mini system	CATALOGUING/OPC ACQ	9
2.3.14	Bibliothèque de la Direction du Livre et de la Lecture		Micros. All Advance functions	?
2.3.15	Bibliothèque du Centre national de Cooperation des Bibliothèques Publiques		Micros. All Advance functions	3

Remainder of Advance sites use all Advance functions on Mini-computers. (Details not known.)

2.3.16	Bibliothèque de l'Ecole Normale Superieure de l'Enseignement Technique de Cachan			8

273

SITE		CPUs	APPLICATIONS IN OPERATION	NO. OF TERMINALS
2.3.17	Bibliothèque de l'Université de Nice			32
2.3.18	Bibliothèque municipale de Brive			20
2.3.19	Bibliothèque municipale de Limoges			57
2.3.20	Bibliothèque municipale de Bagneux			16
2.3.21	Bibliothèque municipale de Nevers			17
2.3.22	Bibliothèque municipale d'Auxerre			23
2.3.23	Bibliothèque municipale d'Alfortville			23
2.3.24	Bibliothèque municipale de Sevres			14
2.3.25	Bibliothèque municipale de Villebon sur Yvette			14
2.3.26	Bibliothèque municipale de Melun			20
2.3.27	Bibliothèque municipale de Rodez			12
2.3.28	Bibliothèque municipale de Montauban			21

2.3.29	Bibliothèque municipale de Saint-Herblain		4
2.3.30	Bibliothèque municipale de Montbrison		6
2.3.31	Bibliothèque du Conservatoire National Superieur de Musique de Lyon		11
2.3.32	Bibliothèque du Conservatoire National Superieur de Musique de Paris		20
2.3.33	Bibliothèque du Musée National d'Art Moderne		22
2.3.34	Bibliothèque Centrale de Prêt des Yvelines		17
2.3.35	Bibliothèque Centrale de Prêt de l'Allier		?
2.3.36	Bibliothèque Centrale de Prêt du Cher		?
2.3.37	Bibliothèque Centrale de Prêt de la Mayenne		?
2.4	*Italy*		
2.4.1	Biblioteca Apostolica Vaticana	8000	CATALOGUING/OPC ACQ
2.4.2	European University Institute, Florence	8000	CIRC CATALOGUING/OPC ACQ
2.4.3	Aosta Regional Library	ADVANCE site	58
			32
			?

	SITE	CPUs	APPLICATIONS IN OPERATION	NO. OF TERMINALS
2.5	*Switzerland*			
2.5.1	Neuchatel Public and University Library	9000	CIRC BCS/OPC	29
2.5.2	Pestalozzi Bibliothek, Zurich	6000	CIRC PUBLIC QUERY	46
2.5.3	ZentralBiblithek, Zurich	8000	CATALOGUING/OPC ACQ	91
2.6	*West Germany*			
2.6.1	United States Army in Europe (System based at Heidelburg with 46 military establishments linked into it)	2 × 8000	CIRC CATALOGUING/OPC	250
2.6.2	Canadian Armed Forces Library, Lahr	ADVANCE site		?
2.7	*Portugal*			
2.7.1	National Library of Portugal	9000	CATALOGUING/OPC ACQ	90
2.8	*USSR*			
2.8.1	Library of Academic Sciences, Leningrad	8000	CATALOGUING/OPC ACQ	15
3.	UNITED STATES			
GLIS sites				
3.1	AIR University Library, Maxwell Air Force Base	2 × 8000	CIRC MRMS/OPC ACQ	69

3.2	Albuquerque Public Library	8000	CIRC MRMS/OPC ACQ	80
3.3	Alexandria Public Library	6000	CIRC MRMS/OPC ACQ	20
3.4	Anchorage Municipal Library	2 × 8000	CIRC MRMS/OPC ACQ	136
3.5	University of Arizona	8000	CIRC MRMS/OPC ACQ	65
3.6	Bibliomation Inc. (Operates consortium of public and academic libraries in Connecticut)	4FFP 9000	CIRC	240
3.7	Brandeis University	8000	CIRC MRMS/OPC ACQ	40
3.8	California State University	2 × 8000	CIRC MRMS/OPC ACQ	86
3.9	Case Western Reserve University	8000	CIRC MRMS/OPC ACQ	67
3.10	CircCess (Capitol Region Library Council) contains 29 public + 9 academic libraries	9000	CIRC	210
3.11	Clarion University of Pennsylvania	8000	CIRC MRMS/OPC ACQ	30
3.12	Georgetown University	2 × 8000	CIRC MRMS/OPC ACQ	79
3.13	University of Houston	2 × 8000	CIRC MRMS/OPC ACQ	112
3.14	Indiana Cooperative Library Services Authority	2 × 8000	CIRC MRMS/OPC	152
3.15	Joint Computer Program for Libraries, The Skokie Public Library	2 × 8000	CIRC MRMS/OPC	117
3.16	Kitsap Regional Library	8000	CIRC MRMS/OPC	69
3.17	Lehigh University	8000	CIRC MRMS/OPC ACQ	67
3.18	Los Alamos National Laboratory Library	8000	CIRC MRMS/OPC ACQ	27

	SITE	CPUs	APPLICATIONS IN OPERATION	NO. OF TERMINALS
3.19	University of Maryland	2 × 8000 1 × 6000	CIRC MRMS/OPC ACQ	232 16 WP
3.20	Massachusetts Institute of Technology	8000	CIRC MRMS/OPC	40
3.21	McMillan Memorial Public Library	6000	CIRC MRMS/OPC ACQ	?
3.22	Miami-Dade County Public Library	9000	CIRC MRMS/OPC ACQ	150
3.23	University of Michigan, Dearborn	6000	CIRC MRMS/OPC ACQ	15
3.24	Minneapolis Public Library	9500	CIRC MRMS/OPC ACQ	112
3.25	Monroe County Library. Consortium of public libraries using 8000 and 3FFP 9000		CIRC MRMS/OPC	104
3.26	New York University, Elmer Holmes Bobst Library	1 × 8000, 1 × 4FFP 9000, 1 × 6000	CIRC BCS/OPC ACQ	270
3.27	Oberlin College Library – with Oberlin Public Library	3FFP 9000	CIRC BPS/OPC	122
3.28	Old Dominion University	8000	CIRC MRMS/OPC	52
3.29	Palos Verdes Library District	8000	CIRC MRMS/OPC ACQ	46
3.30	Pasadena/Glendale Public Libraries	1 × 8000, 1 × 9000	CIRC BPS/OPC	95

3.31	Peninsula Libraries Automated Network (PLAN)	4FFP 9000	CIRC	210
3.32	Princeton University	8000	CIRC ACQ	109
3.33	Rio Hondo Community College	8000	CIRC MRMS/OPC ACQ	25
3.34	Rochester University	1 × 8000, 1 × 9000	CIRC MRMS/OPC BPS ACQ	87
3.35	Rutgers University	1 × 8000, 1 × 4FFP 9000	CIRC MRMS/OPC BPS ACQ	237
3.36	St. Joseph's University	8000	CIRC MRMS/OPC ACQ	46
3.37	Scranton University	8000	CIRC MRMS/OPC ACQ	56
3.38	Smithsonian Institution	2 × 8000, 1 × 9000	CIRC MRMS/OPC BPS ACQ	169
3.39	South Central Library System, Wisconsin (11 libraries in the network)	8000	CIRC MRMS/OPC	74
3.40	University of Southern California	2 × 8000	CIRC MRMS/OPC ACQ	182
3.41	State University of New York (Albany)	2 × 8000	CIRC MRMS/OPC ACQ	84
3.42	State University of New York (Buffalo)	8000	CIRC MRMS/OPC ACQ	40
3.43	Temple University	1 × 8000, 1 × 9000	CIRC MRMS/OPC ACQ	109
3.44	University of Tennessee	1 × 8000, 1 × 9000	CIRC MRMS/OPC ACQ	144
3.45	University of Southern Texas	6000	CIRC BPS/OPC ACQ	25
3.46	Texas Women's University	8000	CIRC MRMS/OPC (With Boolean) ACQ	58
3.47	Union County College	8000	CIRC MRMS/OPC ACQ	13
3.48	United States Air Force Academy, Colorado Springs	2 × 8000	CIRC MRMS/OPC ACQ	58
3.49	United States Military Academy, Westpoint	1 × 6000, 1 × 8000	CIRC MRMS/OPC ACQ	48

	SITE	CPUs	APPLICATIONS IN OPERATION	NO. OF TERMINALS
3.50	United States Naval Academy, Annapolis	8000	CIRC MRMS/OPC ACQ	34
3.51	Utah State University	2 × 8000	CIRC MRMS/OPC ACQ	51
3.52	Villanova University	8000	CIRC MRMS/OPC	38
3.53	University of Washington (Seattle)	2 × 8000, 7FFP 9000	CIRCMRMS/OPC ACQ	245
3.54	Wayne Oakland Library Federation	2 × 8000	CIRC MRMS/OPC ACQ	113
3.55	Wyoming State-wide Circulation System	1 × 8000, 1 × 9000	CIRC MRMS/OPC ACQ	97
3.56	Yale University	8000	CIRC MRMS/OPC ACQ	35

ADVANCE sites

	SITE	CPUs	APPLICATIONS IN OPERATION	NO. OF TERMINALS
3.57	Baker & Taylor			?
3.58	Boise State University			?
3.59	CSU			?
3.60	Coastal Plain Regional Library			?
3.61	East West Center, Honolulu			?
3.62	El Camino College	CIE 680/200	CIRC OPC	18
3.63	Federal Trade Commission	Prime 9955, Prime 6550	CIRC OPC	11
3.64	Fort Bragg			?
3.65	Gettysburg College	Prime 450	CIRC OPC	21

3.66	Honolulu Community College			?
3.67	Kapiolani Community College			?
3.68	Kauai Community College			?
3.69	Kenosha Public Library			?
3.70	Leeward Community College			?
3.71	Maui Community College			?
3.72	Metropolitan Community College, Omaha	Prime 9750	CIRC OPC	16
3.73	Morningside College	2 × Prime 9955	CIRC OPC	15
3.74	Oregon State University	C.ITOH 550	CIRC OPC ACQ	64
3.75	San Francisco State University			?
3.76	Sayville, Long Island			?
3.77	Seton Hall University			?
3.78	Southern Union State Junior College			?
3.79	University of Hawaii	2 × Ultimate 7200	OPC	185
3.80	USAF/Pacific Air Forces			?
3.81	West Ohahu College			?
3.82	Windward Community College	CIE 680/210-0117	CIRC OPC	10
4.	*CANADA*			
4.1	Agriculture Canada Library	8000	CIRC MRMS/OPC ACQ	34
4.2	Ajax/Whitby Public Library Network	8000	CIRC MRMS/OPC ACQ	40
4.3	Brantford Public Library	6000	CIRC MRMS/OPC ACQ	30
4.4	Brock University	8000	CIRC MRMS/OPC ACQ	64
4.5	Burlington Public Library	8000	CIRC MRMS/OPC ACQ	79

	SITE	CPUs	APPLICATIONS IN OPERATION	NO. OF TERMINALS
4.6	Calgary Public Library	2 × 8000, 3FFP 9000	CIRC MRMS/OPC ACQ	158
4.7	École Polytechnic de Montreal	8000	CIRC MRMS/OPC ACQ	33
4.8	Etobicoke Public Library	2 × 8000, 1 × 9000	CIRC MRMS/OPC ACQ	127
4.9	Fraser Valley Regional Library	8000	CIRC MRMS/OPC ACQ	67
4.10	Greater Victoria Public Library	2 × 8000	CIRC MRMS/OPC ACQ	97
4.11	Kitchener Public Library	8000	CIRC MRMS/OPC ACQ	60
4.12	London Public Library	8000	CIRC MRMS/OPC ACQ	67
4.13	Mississauga Public Library	1 × 8000, 1 × 9000	CIRC MRMS/OPC ACQ	351
4.14	University of Moncton	9000	CIRC MRMS/OPC ACQ	33
4.15	Novanet Division (Academic consortium of five institutions)	1 × 8000 2FFP 9000	CIRC MRMS/OPC ACQ	152
4.16	Ontario Legislative Library	6000	CIRC MRMS/OPC ACQ	38
4.17	University of Ottawa	1 × 8000, 3FFP 9000, 6000	CIRC BPS/OPC ACQ	140
4.18	Regina Public Library	9000	CIRC BPS/OPC	176
4.19	University of Saskatchewan	2 × 8000	CIRC MRMS/OPC ACQ	117
4.20	Scarborough Public Library	5FFP 9000	CIRC BPS/OPC ACQ	93
4.21	Simon Fraser University	2 × 8000, 4FFP 9000	CIRC MRMS/OPC ACQ	74
4.22	District of Surrey Public Library	8000	CIRC MRMS/OPC ACQ	59
4.23	Thunder Bay Public Library	8000	CIRC MRMS/OPC ACQ	48
4.24	Toronto Public Library	2 × 8000	CIRC MRMS/OPC ACQ	113
4.25	University of Waterloo	1 × 8000, 1 × 9000	CIRC MRMS/OPC ACQ	161

4.26	University of Western Ontario	$2 \times 8000, 1 \times 9000$	CIRC MRMS/OPC BPS ACQ	158
4.27	Yellowhead Regional Library	8000	CIRC MRMS/OPC ACQ	16
4.28	York Public Library Network	8000	CIRC MRMS/OPC	92

ADVANCE site

4.29	Oshawa Public Library, Ontario			?

5. *Australia*

5.1.	Clann (College Libraries Activity Network, New South Wales)	3×8000, 6FFP 9000	CIRC BPS/OPC ACQ	380

Appendix B Glossary

ACCESS LEVEL — Security level required to perform a function. Implies control of action levels through use of passwords.

AGENCY — A collection of at least one terminal group sharing the same loan periods and fine rules. Often synonymous with a library or branch.

APPLICATION — Term used to refer to the modules that use the computer as a tool, as opposed to those necessary to run it. For example, the Circulation module applies the computer to circulation control.

ASTRO — Geac's internal name for the Communications Processor.

ATTACH — As a verb, to indicate connecting a job or terminal to the computer in such a way that they can communicate. As a noun, to indicate the current level of such connections.

BCS — Bibliographic Control System. Consists of two main elements: BPS, which is the MARC-based cataloguing system, and OPC, the Online Public Catalogue.

BACK-UP — Subsidiary system for maintaining circulation functions when contact with the live Circulation package is lost. Can be either 'soft' back-up, when a separate package is used on the c.p.u., or 'micro' back-up, when supporting hardware is used. Also used to refer to exact copies of software or databases, maintained to protect against the loss or corruption of the originals.

BAR CODE — A label containing a series of printed lines of varying width which constitute a coded number readable by light pens or laser scanners.

BATCH — Collection of programs processed as one unit automatically by a program written in more or less natural language, without requiring the presence of the operator.

BAUD — A measure of speed of data transmission, usually equal to one bit per second.

BIT — The smallest possible unit of information, it equates to 0 or 1.

BOOK LOCATION — Within a terminal group it is possible to have several book locations e.g. Adult, Junior, Reference, etc. Used for statistical purposes by LPEXTR.

BUG — An error in a program, hence DEBUGGING – the process of correction.

BYTE — A collection of bits, functioning as an addressable unit. Normally eight bits in a byte in Geac systems.

CCD SCANNER — Bar code reading device which scans the entire bar code instead of the fraction of it seen by a light pen.

C.P.U. — Central Processing Unit, the unit at the very core of the computer system, which carries out arithmetic, logical and control functions.

CURSOR — A small lighted square or line which indicates the position

	where the next character will be entered on the screen. In Geac systems it can be either static or blinking (pulsating).
DAISY-CHAIN	Terminals linked in a line so that if the cable is broken those terminals downline will lose communications with the c.p.u.
DATABASE	Information store of related files of records held on computer.
DISC	Medium used for storage of data requiring fast retrieval. Discs are either hard, those in the c.p.u., or floppy, those in the back-up micros.
DUMMY PORT	An executing job or program which does not have a physical port associated with it.
DYNAMIC FILE	A file made up of segments of disc that are widely scattered, used mainly for storing programs.
FIELD	A particular area of the data containing a defined element.
FIRMWARE	Microchips upon which are encoded software instructions to the computer.
FUNCTION KEY	A key on a terminal to which a specific function can be assigned by the software, thus reducing the number of key strokes needed to issue a command.
GLIS	Geac Library Information System.
HANGING	State where software 'freezes' and there is no response to any command. Can be caused by a bug or faults within the hardware or telecommunications links.
HARDWARE	Physical pieces of equipment used in a computer system, including magnetic media and memory boards as well as terminals.
INK-JET	Printer that creates the image by projecting a stream of electrically

	charged droplets through a magnetic field which deflects the stream to form the printed image.
JOB	Unit of work to be done using the computer, often accomplished through the use of a program or batch.
K	1,024 words of memory. Commonly used by Geac staff instead of referring to core.
LAN	Local Area Network – usually confined to a single building, or group of adjacent buildings.
LARGE FILE	Disc file made up of contiguous tracks, as opposed to dynamic files. Used mainly for the storage of data
LIBRARY TERMINAL or POLLED TERMINAL	Those terminals that are controlled by the online system.
LIGHT PEN	Input device used to read bar codes.
LINE DRIVER	Device for amplifying signals along telecommunications links.
LPEXTR	Report generator program to produce lists or statistics, running against the bibliographic item file.
LPPXTR	Report generator program to produce lists or statistics, running against the patron files.
LPSMAG	Statistical program giving daily figures of issues, discharges and renewals by terminal group, subdivided by material type.
LPSPAG	Statistical program to count activity by patron privilege class.
LPTSTM	Statistical program logging basic issue, discharge and renewal figures by terminal group, subdivided by hourly periods.
MARC	Machine readable cataloguing, usually applied to the internat-

MEMORY ional standard format of records to enable standardization.
Part of the computer consisting of electronic circuits, where data and program instructions are stored prior to processing by the c.p.u., which can therefore access them very quickly.

MENU Listing of the functions available online, and their mnemonics, to aid the user to choose and perform one of a variety of options.

MICRO-COMPUTER Small, easily portable computer worked by a micro-processor, which acts like a c.p.u but usually only able to support one user at a time.

MINI-COMPUTER A powerful computer, usually dedicated to a specific purpose, but capable of supporting a number of users at the same time. It is intermediate in size between a micro-computer and a mainframe.

MINI-PRINTER Small printer associated with a terminal or a collection of terminals used to produce issue slips, routing slips, fines receipts, etc.

MODEM Modulator-demodulator, which converts binary signals from computers into analogue signals and vice versa for transmission along and receipt from telephone lines.

MRMS Marc Record Management System. Cataloguing system based on 8000 machines, now virtually obsolete.

NIM Network Interface Machine. Device to control 'translation' of different communication protocols.

ONLINE In virtually instant communication with the c.p.u.

OPAC	Online public access catalogue. Also called OPC
OPERATING SYSTEM	Set of programs that control the computer and its processing, rather than applications programs.
OPTIONS	Features of the software which are not mandatory but site selectable.
PACKAGE	Suite of software related to a particular application.
PASSWORD LEVEL	Security level, by implication requiring the operator to key in a password.
PERIPHERALS	Input, output and storage devices under the control of the c.p.u. such as terminals, printers, disc and tape drives
POLICY PARAMETERS	Variable conditions which determine how systems work in individual sites.
POLL-CODE	Terminal address, which must be unique for each terminal or miniprinter sharing the same port.
POLLING	Action of the c.p.u. in examining each terminal or printer in turn to collect any data ready for transmission.
PORT	Means of entry to and exit from the computer.
PRESTEL	UK public viewdata service.
PROGRAM	Sequence of instructions to be executed by the computer. When the program is executed, it performs some function or operation. It requires a port or a dummy port in order to be run.
PROM	Programmable read-only memory. See FIRMWARE.
PROTECTED FIELD	Field which cannot be changed by the operator, they are not highlighted on the system and the cursor passes over them.

RELEASE	Particular version of a software package.
RESPONSE TIME	In the library context, the time taken by the system to act upon an instruction from a terminal, e.g. to complete an issue transaction.
SCREEN IMAGE PRINTER	Any printer which prints that which is currently being displayed on the screen of a terminal to which it is connected.
SOFTWARE	Program(s) upon which the computer works, including operating systems and applications programs.
SPCNFG	Special Configuration Program by which library terminals are attached to the system, and which determines which packages each terminal may access.
SPIKING	A peak, generally of electrical power but also used to describe erratically high response times.
TCP	Terminal Control Program. Most packages have a TCP file, which is a record of the day's transactions as they occurred.
TCS	Terminal Control Server. New, microcomputer based device to handle communications from terminals operating under different protocols. Likely to supersede NIMs and back-up micros.
TERMINAL GROUP	Library-defined group of terminals which form a logical unit within which items circulate, such as a branch library.
UNPROTECTED FIELD	One that can be changed or erased by an operator.
USER AREA	Type of large file containing a dynamic area of its own. Each package has several user areas to

	control data, software and documentation.
WAN	Wide Area Network. Can be across a single geographic area, or much wider. Often uses X.25 protocol.
WAND	As a noun, meaning light pen. As a verb, meaning to read a bar code with a light pen.
WINCHESTER	Disc drive technology where the discs are completely sealed from the surrounding atmosphere and the read/write heads ride on a cushion of air fractionally above the disc surface.
WORD	The number of bits that can be handled by the c.p.u. at one time. Geac employ 16-bit words.
X.25	A standard for communications between computers. Sends data in 'packets'. Particularly applicable over wide areas.

Appendix C Annotated Bibliography

Articles

1. Kruiniger, Hans (1979), 'Geac Library System,' *VINE* (27), March, pp. 11–29.
   Describes the circulation package, by a Geac systems analyst.
2. Barraclough, Elizabeth (1979), 'A brief evaluation of Geac,' *VINE* (31), November, pp. 26–8.
   Describes the first two Canadian installations, following visit from UK.
3. McSean, Tony (1980), 'News from Geac,' *VINE* (36), November, pp. 39–40.
   Notes on the early UK sites, by a Geac library consultant.
4. Geac (1980), LMG Report, 1(4), December, pp. 9–13.
   Gives brief description of system in issue devoted to online suppliers.
5. Graham, T. (1981), 'Geac in action at the University of Hull,' *VINE* (39), August, pp. 4–11.
   Describes the first UK site and the system in operation.
6. Bett, Carolynne E. (1981), 'Geac; a brief introduction,' *Ontario Library Review*, 65(3), September, pp. 180–2.
   Gives brief company history.
7. Leeves, Juliet (1981), 'University of London shared circulation system,' *VINE* (40), October, pp. 4–9.
   Describes the federal site of the university and the complications arising.
8. Clayton, Marlene and Leeves, Juliet (1980), 'Sharing an online circulation system; the planning, the practice and the potential [University of London system],' *in* Fifth International Online Information Meeting (8th–10th Dec. 1981), *Oxford and New Jersey Learned Information*, pp. 175–80.
   Further detail on the London University installation.
9. Young, R.C. and Stone, P. (1982), 'A Geac-based circulation control and stock management system at Sussex,' *VINE* (42), March, pp. 3–7.

Describes the local enhancements being developed in addition to the Geac system.
10. Botten, David A. (1982), 'Public access to online files at the Polytechnic of the South Bank,' *VINE* (42), March, pp. 26–30.
Discusses the implications and practical considerations of the Public Query module.
11. Botten, David A. (1982), 'The Geac 8000 system at the Polytechnic of the South Bank,' *Program*, 16(2), April, pp. 67–77.
Full description of the installation.
12. McSean, Tony (1982), 'Geac library systems: a survey of current installations,' *VINE* (43), May, pp. 25–30.
Notes on the UK scene up to the Somerset installation and a brief note on the University of Utrecht.
13. Morley, John and Lockyer, Dora (1982), 'Somerset County's integrated system,' *VINE* (44), August, pp. 15–21.
Description of the first UK public library installation and the retrospective task involved.
14. Leeves, Juliet (1982), 'University of London shared circulation system – progress report,' *VINE* (44), August, pp. 28–33.
Updates the earlier article on this site and covers in more detail the retrospective conversion task and live circulation operations in one of the libraries.
15. McSean, Tony (1983), 'Home or away,' in *Independent versus cooperative catalogue systems*; proceedings of a seminar held at the School of Librarianship and Information Studies, Newcastle upon Tyne Polytechnic, Sept. 22nd 1982; ed. by Watson, Margaret and others, Library Association University College and Research Section (Northern Group).
Discusses advantages of locally created database as opposed to cooperative systems and makes points about Geac system, by a Geac library consultant.
16. McSean, Tony (1982), 'Camden converting from Plessey to Geac for circulation,' *VINE* (46), December, pp. 14–16.
Describes the process of converting the machine readable database from one format to another and the installation in the first London borough library.
17. Graham, T.W., Lane, R. and Richards, K.M. (1983),

'Keyword and Boolean searching on Geac at Hull University,' *VINE* (48), May, pp. 3–7.
Describes the local enhancements to the Public Query module.
18. Clarke, John and Morris, Graham E. (1983), 'Hillingdon's implementation of an integrated library system,' *VINE* (48), May, pp. 17–20.
Describes the planning process and the implementation plans, including the adoption of the OPAC, Acquisitions and Local Information modules.
19. Law, Derek (1983), 'Recon via REMARC at Edinburgh University Library,' *VINE* (49), August, pp. 13–18.
Describes the massive retrospective conversion task.
20. Leeves, Juliet (1983), 'Survey of automated issue systems in public libraries,' *VINE* (52), December, pp. 1–41.
Complete issue devoted to the state of automation of UK public libraries, including tables showing each major supplier, makes generalized statements about trends.
21. Persky, Gail, Aquilla, Diane, Slonim, Jacob and MacRae, L.J. (1984), 'A Geac local area network for the Bobst Library [University of New York],' *Library Hi Tech*, 2(2), pp. 37–45.
Description of the Local Area Network installation.
22. Law, Derek (1984), 'Dutch and Belgian library systems: a compendium,' *VINE* (53), April, pp. 33–42.
Gives a brief description of the installation at the University of Utrecht.
23. 'Geac and users,' (1984), *VINE* (54), June, pp. 31–4.
Update of state of penetration of UK market including table of sites.
24. Lee, Stephen (1983), 'Online keyword catalogue at the University of Sussex' (based on a contribution made at the Seminar on Keyword Catalogues and the Free Language Approach, Imperial College, London, October 1983), University of Sussex Library, March 1984.
Describes the local keyword system enhancement to the Public Query module.
25. Dunbar, Graham (1985), 'Lancashire goes for Geac in a big way,' *VINE* (58), March, pp. 16–18.
Describes largest UK public library installation to date.
26. Clarke, John (1985), 'The Geac experience at Hillingdon', *VINE* (59), July, pp. 40–2.
Paper presented at Library Association Information Technology Group weekend conference at which sites using different suppliers were compared.

27. Kidd, Tony and Favret, Leo (1985), 'The Geac Acquisitions System: the product and its use at the University of Aston,' *VINE* (60), October, pp. 22–32.
Detailed description of the Acquisitions package and Aston's use of it.
28. Hunter, Alison (1985), 'Geac Local Information System at Hillingdon Borough Libraries,' *VINE*, (61), December, pp. 18–25.
Description of the first operational Local Information module.
29. Young, R.C., Stone, P.T., Pickles, J.S., Lee, S.R. and Lambert, P.J. (1986), 'Geac with local enhancements: the integrated real-time system at the University of Sussex Library,' *Program*, (20), 1, January, pp. 1–25.
Full description of the local software based on the Geac circulation package but with considerable local improvement, including a form of Boolean and transaction logging on the Public Query module.
30. Young, R.C. and Lee, S.R. (1986), 'The Geac-based OPAC at the University of Sussex Library,' *Program* (20), 2, April.
Describes the local version of the Public Query module, considerably enhanced.
31. Lambert, Peter (1986), 'Periodicals automation at the University of Sussex Library,' *UKSG Newsletter*.
Describes the local system for periodicals control based on the Geac Circulation software.
32. Clarke, John E. (1986), 'Guten tag, Pet!: Here's online public access,' *Public Library Journal* (1), 1, Mar/Apr, pp. 1–4.
Describes the public access to library files at Hillingdon – access is given to Circulation for personal records, OPAC, Local Information, and News via a locally modified TCP screen.
33. Hunter, Alison (1985), 'Geac Local Information system 'live' at Hillingdon,' *ITs News*, (9), May, pp. 6–11.
Describes Local Information package and early public response.
34. King, Peter (1986), 'Automation Co-operation – the Uxbridge Technical College link to a new public library system: How a small college library can benefit from information technology,' *CoFHE Bulletin* (Library Association Colleges of Further and Higher Education), (47), Summer, pp. 7–9.
Describes the value to Uxbridge Technical College in being linked to the public library system in Hillingdon.

35. Hunter, Alison (1986), 'Hillingdon Election results online,' *Assistant Librarian*, 79 (9), September, pp. 123-5.
Describes the use of the Local Information system to provide an election results service.
36. 'Hillingdon' (1987), *Computernews* (computer newsletter produced by Community Information project), (27), December 1986/January 1987, pp. 6-7.
Independent critical report of the use of the Local Information package.
37. Westlake, Duncan (1989), 'Designing a library for Information Technology,' *ITs News*, (18), February, pp. 39-43.
Describes Hillingdon's new Central Library, and Geac's place in it.
38. Pachent, Guenever (1989), 'Networking in the Community,' *ITs News* (20), October, pp. 30-4.
Written by a senior member of staff at Suffolk County Library, describes the Suffolk approach to problems posed by wide dissemination of information.
39. Pachent, Guenever and Reed, Doug (1989), 'The hitchhiker's guide to SCILSnet,' *VINE* (77), December, pp. 25-30.
Describes Suffolk's ambitious implementation of Geac systems.
40. Evans, P. (1989), 'Advance: Geac's new PICK-based system,' *VINE* (75), October, pp. 13-19.
Written by a Geac member of staff working on the Advance system.
41. Towler, B. (1990), 'An extended Public Enquiry system at the University of Hull,' *VINE*, (78), May, pp. 25-30.
Describes locally developed Public Enquiry system on Geac 8000, upgraded onto a 9000.
42. Leeves, Juliet (1989), *Library systems: a buyer's guide*, Gower.
Invaluable guide to available library systems, including Geac.
43. Batt, Chris (1990), *Information Technology in Public Libraries*, Public Libraries Research Group, 1990.
The third edition of a regular survey of the use of information technology in British public libraries, including the market shares of various system suppliers.

Index

access levels *see* security
account mapping 198
account query in Acquisitions 198–9
Acquisitions package 183–210
acronym searches (author-title) 174–6
added pages in Community Information 215
ADLC ports 22, 28
ADVANCE system 4, 14–15, 266
agencies 67
air conditioning 29
Alii 4
ALS, conversion from 9
anti-glare screens 40
APAK 32
Apple II micro
approval tapes 184
ARPANET 7
Aston University
ASTRO (Asynchronous-Synchronous Transmitter-Receiver) *see* communications operating system
ASTRO ports 22, 28
Australia 5, 9
audio-visual materials, booking system 131
auditing (*see also* Cash Management System) 194, 198–9
AUSMARC standard 9
authority controls 158, 164–5
automail dates in Community Information 215, 221
automatic running (*see also* overnight procedures) 73
AWA/URICA 9

backdated transactions 102
back-up systems (*see also* security) 37–9, 147–54
BAKPAK 32
banking systems 3

barcode reader 45–6
barcodes 43
BASIC, on ADVANCE system 15
BASIC, on System 6000 11
benchmarking 259
Bexley, London Borough of 7, 42, 211
bibliographic files 89–96
Bibliographic Control System (BCS) 155–82
    message broadcasting 126–7
Bibliographic Processing System (BPS) 156–165
Bibliothèque Nationale 8
bill for replacement 107–8
Bindery Management sub-system 135–7
BISAC (Book Industry System Advisory Committee) 184
bit map 24
book locations 68
bookplate printing in BPS 165
booksellers 184
book security systems, interface with 47, 230
booktrailers *see* mobile libraries
Boolean searching 12, 155
    in BPS 161–2
    in OPC 179–80
borrower files *see* patron records
'Boss' processor 27
brief screen in Acquisitions 191
British Library Document Supply Centre (BLDSC) 8
Bromley, London Borough of 9
budget query in Acquisitions 198–9
bulk updates using Portable Library Unit 151–2

C 11
cable television, interface with 47, 223
cache memory 24

297

calendar for materials booking 133
calendar of closed days 67, 106
Camden, London Borough of 7, 39, 61, 72, 79, 90, 95, 120, 130–1, 233, 235, 236
Canada Export award 6
cancellation of orders in Acquisitions 193
Case Communications Ltd. 51
Cash Management Sub-system 118, 137–41, 234
Cataloguing Module 155–182, CATDNE 242
categorization of stock 94, 178
CCD scanners 36, 46
CD-Roms 47, 154, 184, 230
cellular telephones 61
central configuration 19–33
charge *see* issue
cheque generation in Acquisitions 203
Circulation package 79–146
citation lists 180
claims in Acquisitions 192
CLANN (College Lib. Activity Network in N.S.W.) 9
clusters 27
codabar 43
colour, use of in terminals 46
command chaining 174, 216
committed funds in Acquisitions 199
Commodore microcomputers *see* back-up systems
communications operating system 11, 21–23
communications software packages 243
Community Access module 240–1
Community Information System 211–25, 234
Compaq PCs *see* back-up systems
compile options 69, 156, 209
configuration file (SPCNFG) 68, 76–7, 147, 216, 242
constant voltage transformers 30
contact in Community Information 221
control consoles 22
Cooper, Andrew 235
core files in BCS 158
corporate authors 179

Craig, Jim 156
creating records in Community Information 215
credit notes in Acquisitions 203
currency conversions 201, 203
current files in BPS 159

daisychaining 35, 147–8
data mailers 111
data partitions 22
Data Protection Act *see also* security 221
database structure 25–6
DATATALK 243
DataWay *see* TRAX
date stamping systems 44–5
DDN/ARPANET 8
deletion of item records 95
deletion of Community Information records 216
dial-in interfaces 212, 223, 240–4
directory of files 24
discs and disc drives (hard and floppy) 23–26,32
disc crashes 32
disc operating system 11,23–26
discharges 102–5
distributed processing 259
documentation 156, 255
Doncaster Metropolitan Borough 62
downloading 147, 149, 151, 153
drama collections 177
dummy port 20,21
Durham, University of 7
dust 29
DYNA (dynamic area) 24
dynamic files 24
dynamic stock 104

earnings of company 6
Easton, David 156
Edinburgh, University of 156, 160, 170
editing records
 in BPS 163–4
 in Circulation 94–6
elderly people's homes 131
electricity supplies 29–30, 35
electronic mail (*see also* GOAST) 60, 226–8
electronic ordering 184
Elites *see* terminals

Enfield, London Borough of 62
environmental conditions 29–31
Epson HX-20 portable microcomputer 39
erasure of item records 95
ergonomics 40
Essex County 7, 8, 51, 56, 82, 98, 131, 135, 149, 153, 259, 261
ethernet 55, 56
exception reports in Acquisitions 207
exchange tapes
expiry of Community Information records 215
external communications 240–5
external databases, accessing of 183–4, 244–5

Fact International 6
fast recovery 82
fees *see* Cash Management sub-system
financial services in Acquisitions 198
fines 104, 106–8
  in Cash Management system 138–9
fines journal 234
fire precautions 30
firmware 35, 42–3
France, developments in 46–7
Full Function Processors (FFPs) 13, 26
function keys 88, 169–70

Geac 3000 (ADVANCE) 14
Geac, possible meaning of name 3
GEM *see* Electronic Mail
Geogate 55, 245
German, R. Angus 3
gigadisc 47
Glasgow University 156
GLUG report writer 130, 235
GOAST (Geac Office Automation Support Tool) 12, 66
GODOs 7
Grantstown, City of (Australia) 9
Griffith University, Australia 9
Gruneau, Ted 3
GTALK 228
Guelph, University of 3, 7, 79

halogen gas 30
handling charges in Acquisitions 201

'hanging' 23
hardware maintenance 249–52
Hayes, David 235
H-bus 27
health and safety (*see also* ergonomics) 39–40
helical scan video tape drives 32
Helix Investments Limited 6
help pages and systems 142–4, 169, 185, 217
Hewlett Packard 3, 48
hierarchical databases 26
Highland Leasing plc 14
Hillingdon, London Borough of 7, 42, 65, 72, 120–1, 125, 128, 129–30, 134, 168, 211 *et seq.*, 226, 232, 233, 236, 243, 244, 252, 258
holdings 162, 165–8
Holdings and Pieces Management Project 159, 166–7, 266
holds 104, 113–23
  automatic messaging 126
  fees in Cash Management system 138, 140
  future plans 122–3
  in Public Query 98, 122
housebound readers 133–4
HUGO 11
Hull, University of 7, 69
humidity 29, 35
Hunter, Alison 211

IBM-PC 38, 243
IBM, SNA network protocols 55
IBM, supported emulations 48
ICL PC 39
ID Systems – book security system 230
Image Power image processing system 228–9
index sector 24
indexes and indexing 84, 89–91, 156, 160–2, 164–5, 213, 217–22
Informer terminals *see* terminals
Institute of Social History, Amsterdam 229
Integration project 159, 166
interloans 60, 134–5
Inter Online Communications module (IOC) 76–8, 168
invoices in Acquisitions 192, 200–3

299

Islington, London Borough of 32, 39, 211
ISO 57
Isserstedt, Robert K 3
issues 101–2
ISTEL 14

Jones and Erickson Software Technology Inc 7
journal entries in Acquisitions 199

KERMIT 243
Keyman 28–9
keywords 179, 217
Kilostream 62
KQ ports 22

Lancashire County Library 82, 135
Lancaster, University of – Interloan system 135
large files 24–5
laser readers 46
La Villette, France 46–7
'least recently used' logic 21
Lee, Steve 235
Leeds University 235
lettings system *see* Materials Booking
Library Consultants 256–7
Library directory (OSI products) 59–60
Library Maintenance sub-system 144–6,
Library of Academic Sciences, Leningrad 8
Libtel 245
light pens 36, 39, 45–6
Limburg, Netherlands 47
line drivers 61
Linkoping University, Sweden 56
loan fees 139
loan limits 102
loan periods 67, 145
loan transactions (*see also* issues; discharges; *and* renewals) 101–6
Local Area Networks (LANs) 38, 49, 53–6
Local Information Module *see* Community Information System
local memory 19
logical files 23–4
London, University of 7
LPEXTR extract program 68

LPLANG 79, 80, 88, 130, 170, 185, 213

mail code 113
maintenance *see* hardware; *and* software
management information 151, 231–9
Marc 155 et seq
Marc Records Management System (MRMS) 155
Massachusetts Institute of Technology (MIT) 43, 46, 230
Materials Booking sub-system 131–3,
material type 89
McClellan, A.W. 234
McDonnell Douglas Information Systems 9
Megastream 62
membership records *see* patron records
membership fees 138,139–40
memory 19–20
message transmission 123–6
Miami-Dade County Public Library, U.S.A. 229
Microdata *see* McDonnell Douglas Information Systems
microfiche catalogue production 153, 156
Minitel 47
Mississauga (U.S. site) 61
mobile libraries and bookbuses 150–1
modems 60–1
MRMS *see* Marc Record Management System
Multi-threaded circulation 81, 258

name searches in Community Information 217
National Radiological Protection Board 39
Netherlands, developments in 47
Network Interface Machine (NIM) 39, 49, 51–3
networks *see* telecommunications *and* local area networks
New York University 9, 12, 168
news pages and news systems 223–4, 228

9300 series 13
9500 series 13
Norfolk County 7, 135
Novell networks 56

office automation *see* GOAST
OKAPI 170
OPAC (OPC Module) 156, 168–82
   link to Image Power 229
operating languages 11, 14
operating systems 4, 14, 20–9
optional fields 83, 89
orders *see* purchase orders
OSI 57–60
overdue notices (*see also* datamailers) 109–13

parameters *see* policy parameters
PASCAL on 6000 11
Pass-Thru 244
passwords *see* security
patron privileges 67
patron records 83–88
PCs 37–9, 147–50
permanent files 24
Phantom processors – on ADVANCE system 15
PICK operating system 4, 14–15
Picture Power *see* Image Power
playsets *see* drama collections
Plessey barcode formats 43
policy parameters 66
poll-codes 23, 49, 69
polled block mode 22
Portable Library Unit 150–3
ports 21–23
Portugal, National Library of 8
potential requirements file in Acquisitions 184
power failures 28, 30
Prestel 244
preventive maintenance 251
Princeton University 7, 9
printers 40–2
printers, barcode label 43–4
printers, laser 41
printers, line 32
printers, mini 40–1
printers, screen image 41–2
priority 21
product file 157, 162
program operating system 11, 20–21

Professional services terminal 38
PROMs *see* firmware
proof lists 157
Psion organizer 39, 150
   see also Portable Library Unit
Public Lending Right (PLR) 106, 238
Public Libraries using Geac (PLUG) 256
Public Query Module 96–100, 117
public use, research into 219, 237
purchase orders in Acquisitions 191–4

Rank Xerox 13
'real' ports 21
recall notices 110–1
receipts in Acquisitions 191–2
recovery procedures 82
Redbridge, London Borough of 7, 31, 211
references in Community Information 213
re-issues *see* renewals
relational databases 15, 26, 265
Release 21 circulation software 81–2, 101, 103, 104, 114, 117, 147
reliability, central configuration 31–33
remote diagnostics 243–4
remote spooling 212
renewal fees 139
renewals 105–6
report generator 235
report writer – BCS 157
reports
   Acquisitions system 205–9
   Cash management system 140–1
   Circulation system 234–6
request query in Acquisitions 187–91
reservations *see* holds *and* Materials Booking
reserve room operations 127–31
response times 4, 91, 98, 103, 149, 162, 180, 232, 258–61
returns *see* discharges
RS232 interfaces 21
RS232-C daisychaining 35
rush processing in Acquisitions 188

sales *see* Cash Management
SAVE file in BPS 165

301

school project collections 129–31
Screen Manager 38, 46, 80, 99, 131, 169, 259, 266
search query in Acquisitions 186
search restricting
 in BCS 160
 in OPC 180
security 71–2, 74–6, 99, 144–5, 163, 204–5, 215
'see also' entries in Community Information 213
'see' references in Community Information 213, 219
self service issuing 47
serials 167, 195–6
Series 150 11
servicing charges in Acquisitions 201
SET search in BPS 160
Seton Hall University, U.S 4
shared memory 19
shelf check listings 120, 125
shelf location 94
shipping messages 67
shipping types (materials booking) 132
short loan collections 127
short-wave radio 61
slave processors 27
Smithsonian Institution 9
smoke detection 30
soft back-up 152–3
software maintenance 69–71, 252–3
Somerset County Library Service 7
South Bank, Polytechnic of 4, 7
spine label printing in BPS 165
spool files (*see also* remote spooling) 25
spreadsheets *see also* GOAST 228, 236
staff bulletins *see* news systems
staff manuals *see* documentation
staff privileges in Acquisitions 204–5
standing orders 195
static electricity precautions 31
statistical packages 231–3
Statistical Tabulator 236
status details in Community Information 213
stock taking 152, 236
Stockholm, University of 8
stop words 91, 171

subheadings in Community Information 213
subject headings 176, 219
subject searches in Community Information 219
Suffolk County 7–8, 52, 82, 98, 126, 135, 138, 236, 245, 259
Sussex, University of 7, 31, 69–70, 235, 238
Sutton, London Borough of 211, 212, 228, 243
Sweden, developments in 56
System 2000 13
System 4000 13
System 5000 14
System 6000 11–12, 29
System 8000 4, 10–11
System 9000 4, 12–13, 258
 system architecture 26–29

tables 67–9, 106, 142, 147
tape drives 32
tape processor 11
TCP/IP networks 55
telecommunications 48–62
Telepen, conversion from 153
temperature 29, 35
temporary files 24
terminal bit permissions 68
Terminal communications server (TCS) 37, 53, 55, 260
Terminal controller (8212) 37, 241–2, 260
Terminal Control Program (TCP) 20, 22
terminal emulation software 39
terminal emulations supported 245
terminal groups 67
terminal parameters 36, 41
terminals 34–40
 configuring on system 68
 8300 series 35
 Elite series 35–6
 environmental conditions 31, 35
 Informer series 35, 48
 internal software 36
TERMITE 243
time-outs 222
TinLend interloans system 135
Token Ring networks 56
Toronto Public Library 9

training 253–4
Training Circulation Module 70
transaction log analysis 236–8
transfers in BCS 159
transit records 103
transmission rates, backup recovery 149
TRAX 244–5
truncation of search terms 179, 217

uninterruptible power supplies (UPS) 28
United States Military worldwide network 8
UNIX 4, 14, 55, 59, 266
updating records in Community Information 215
URICA 9
usage statistics in Community Information 213
user areas 25
user groups 255–6
Utrecht, University of 8

validation in BPS 158
validation of invoices in Acquisitions 202
Vatican Library 8
vendors (in Acquisitions) 192, 196–8, 207
videotape backup systems 32
viewdata 47, 244, 245

Villette, La (French site) 47
volumes, addition of multi-volume works 167
VT protocols 35, 48, 53, 241
VT220 terminals 36–7
VuCat 241

waiting lists 115–6
waiving of fines 107, 138
Waterloo, University of 7, 79
weight 30
Westminster City Libraries 184, 211
Wide area networks 49–53
word processing (*see also* GOAST) 228
work files in BPS 158
working parties 254, 255
Wyoming Library Service
WYSE terminals and PCs 37

X.25 protocol 28, 48, 51–3, 241, 243, 244
X3.28 protocol 35, 48, 241

Yale University 5
year end reports in Acquisitions 209
Yvelines Bibliothèque Centrale de Prêt, France 4

ZOPL 11
ZQPUBL 98